A PROFESSOR AT THE END OF TIME

A PROFESSOR AT THE END OF TIME

The Work and Future of the Professoriate

JOHN BEST

RUTGERS UNIVERSITY PRESS

New Brunswick, Camden, and Newark, New Jersey, and London

Library of Congress Cataloging-in-Publication Data
Names: Best, John B., author.
Title: A professor at the end of time : the work and future of the professoriate / John Best.
Description: New Brunswick, New Jersey : Rutgers University Press, 2017. | Includes bibliographical references and index.
Identifiers: LCCN 2016024582| ISBN 9780813585932 (hardcover : alk. paper) | ISBN 9780813585925 (pbk. : alk. paper) | ISBN 9780813585949 (e-book (epub)) | ISBN 9780813585956 (e-book (web pdf))
Subjects: LCSH: College teachers—United States. | College teaching—United States. | Education, Higher—Effect of technological innovations on—United States. | Education, Higher—Aims and objectives—United States. | Learning and scholarship—United States.
Classification: LCC LB1778.2 .B474 2017 | DDC 378.1/2—dc23
LC record available at https://lccn.loc.gov/2016024582

A British Cataloging-in-Publication record for this book is available from the British Library.

This publication was supported in part by the Eleanor J. and Jason F. Dreibelbis Fund.

♾ The paper used in this publication meets the requirements of the American National Standard for Information Sciences—Permanence of Paper for Printed Library Materials, ANSI Z39.48–1992

www.rutgersuniversitypress.org

Manufactured in the United States of America

In memory of my beloved wife, Lorraine
Per avermi sempre creduto in me, grazie

CONTENTS

PREFACE

It may seem odd that I can no longer recover the moment in time when I decided to write this book. Somewhere in the febrile forges of my mind, in a place that I psychologically occupied a long time ago, an idea percolated up to me about writing a "reminiscence" of my work as a professor. And I see now that such a book, had I written it, would have been a conventional memoir—based on events, but detailing my responses, reactions, and experiences in the emotional domain as I reconstructed those happenings from a much later vantage point.

But as my career evolved and the events within it occurred, the concept of the book changed, not from the force of any single cataclysm, but rather from the accumulation of the mundane. It was events such as a conversation with a colleague in the Faculty Senate in the 2000s, in the course of which I surprised myself by saying that I no longer believed the current system of higher education in the United States was sustainable, that impelled me to set sail on a different course, away from that of a pure memoir. As I spoke with my colleague, I realized that it was not my responses and reactions that were all that important to anyone, but rather what had taken place during my time in the professoriate that was significant and worth noting. And it may be just as well that I rethought my original objective: when I began to apply the method that I will describe in the book to the events of my career, I discovered that many of the facts I unearthed, resting as they did on contemporaneous records, simply did not jibe with my memory, proving the latter to be often false.

Questions of the book's genesis lead to other questions: If the book is not a memoir, then what might I intend to accomplish? Saying that I have a story to tell about what I did, my work as a member of the professoriate, is a little too reductive. It is true that I have organized the book around what might be among the oldest still-existing cognitive structures in the world: the idea of a narrative having a beginning, a middle, and an end, in which a protagonist faces challenges, changes, suffers, possibly succeeds, and is transformed regardless of any difference in outward appearance. But while this book will tell such a story, there is more to it than that. The story of my work was part of a larger story—the story of an age cohort that shared many of those challenges during its time in the professoriate. Moreover, and creating some urgency in the telling, I believe that this larger story, despite its size, will become unrecognizable in the future.

Or perhaps it will simply sink out of sight forever. In thinking about the professoriate and its work during the twentieth century, I am reminded of some other famous narratives such as those of the *Titanic, Lusitania,* or *Empress of Ireland,* those mighty ships of the early twentieth century with their purported invincibility to any and all forces arrayed against them, natural or human-made. And the professoriate—with its lofty aims, its recognition of itself as a special and privileged workforce, its purposefulness and devotion to its mission, moving as it cut through intellectual and scientific problems as effortlessly as those liners sheared the ocean—has seemed to me as majestic as any mighty seagoing vessel. But, as we know in the case of the ships, any hubris resulting from their construction was misplaced. Whether from phenomena of nature, human intent, or human error, each of the vessels I named was wrecked and lost, along with the lives of over a thousand people. And if I am correct, one day the professoriate that we know could be similarly lost irretrievably in the waves of time, existing only as a spooky and remote wreck of what it had once been.

Although this book has been cast as a narrative, it is nevertheless an account of my behavior—my work—in the professoriate, constructed from a welter of records and other documents, rather than being built from my remembered experiences. And although the account is based on my behavior, as I suggested above, I do not intend it to be limited to that, and I have brought in supporting statistics about my generation whenever I needed to. Thus, I intend this work to be a prototype in recording how an entire generation of the professoriate made a difficult and sometimes ragged transition from a period of stability in higher education to the flux and uncertainty of a technological era in the midst of which we are firmly lodged. However, with regard to the book's scope, I do not want anyone to think that I am appropriating for myself any particular authority in speaking for that larger group. The professoriate contains a million stories, and each deserves to be heard. Mine is just one piece—as far as I can tell, the first—in a mosaic that awaits assembly.

A Professor at the End of Time is, therefore, not a book about how to be a college professor. There are numerous books written for prospective members of the professoriate who want to learn how to succeed, or at least survive, as a professor. But despite the lack of how-to advice in my book, I think it can be read with interest by those who are considering becoming professors, as well as by those who are or have been professors—if not as a prescription for success, then simply as an accounting of one professor's activities during the time he was given in the professoriate.

Once at a dinner I was asked, by someone who was not an academic, what it was like to write a book. Although *A Professor at the End of Time* is not my first book, I had recently gotten under way on it, and perhaps in my dawning appreciation of the magnitude of the task, I blurted out that it was like building a cathedral by oneself. Even though the early going may have felt that way, the analogy is neither accurate nor respectful of the efforts of all those who labored

Umberto Boccioni, *States of Mind II: Those Who Go* (1911). © The Museum of Modern Art/Licensed by SCALA / Art Resource, NY.

Working within the parameters of Futurism, a social and artistic movement of the early twentieth century emphasizing transition, technology, and speed, Boccioni use the angled shafts of light in *Those Who Go* to represent lines of force imposing themselves on the departing passengers of an express train, thus illustrating and accentuating their "loneliness, anguish, and dazed confusion." Like the passengers on a fast train, the professoriate currently finds itself beset with a number of forces they cannot control, as they hurtle toward some destination in the dark they do not know.

along with me. There are numerous people who helped me build this edifice, and without their help, it would not stand. Several of my former colleagues at Eastern Illinois University, including Bill Addison, Craig Eckert, Assege HaileMariam, Mike Havey, Bill Kirk, John Mace, and Jeff Stowell, read and criticized one or more chapters from the manuscript's first draft. Subsequent versions were much improved by the inclusion of their sage comments. The manuscript was similarly improved by the comments of one of my friends who has never been a member of the professoriate, Mike Carroll. I was also aided immeasurably by the comments of the anonymous readers who painstakingly and patiently made their way through every chapter of *A Professor at the End of Time*. Finally, the writers in the Writer's Café Study Group sponsored by the Osher Lifelong Learning Institute at the University of Illinois had a go at some selected pieces of the manuscript, and the beneficial effects of their cogent comments extended far beyond those sections they read.

At Rutgers University Press, I was expertly shepherded through the publication process by my gifted editor, Kimberly Guinta. Making a book requires the sustained and careful efforts of dozens of people; making the book good requires an even higher level of precision and dedication. I was aided by quite a few people at the press whose efforts were always in that category. Carrie Hudak served as the production editor, and her diligent oversight and expertise are apparent on every page of the book. Both Kristen Bonanno, who served as the editorial assistant, and Marilyn Campbell, director of the Prepress Department, did a wonderful job in their respective roles. Anne Hegeman, the production coordinator, likewise did a wonderful job bringing the book to fruition. Finally, Jeanne Ferris was the copy editor who gave the entire book a no-nonsense reading that nevertheless remained sympathetic to the book's overall concept and meaning.

At Eastern Illinois University, I was helped tremendously by the material support offered by John Mace, chairperson of the Psychology Department, and by Assege HaileMariam, interim chairperson of the same department, both of whom afforded me access to a number of the department's resources, including supplies and assistance from workers on their office staff. Ann Wolters and Debbie Kovacik, the office managers of the Psychology Department, were indefatigable in their help with printing drafts of the chapters and photocopying them. Outside the department, I appreciate the persistence and creativity of the librarians at Booth Library who helped me track down some of the references I used, at least a few of which were obscure and not very easily located.

In addition to all these forms of technical support, I also enjoyed tremendous support in other ways as well. After I retired, Jim Nees, a businessperson in my town, was very helpful in letting me rent office space in a building he owned at a price I could afford. And here I must mention also the contribution of two loyal workers, Michelle Steven and Bernadine Andrews, whose efforts not only freed me from housekeeping but also kept my household running smoothly, especially during some of the most trying times I endured while completing the book. My running partner, Darla Gardner, made sure that I stuck with my exercise program, and I am very grateful for her support as well.

It goes without saying that an author needs emotional support, and here I cannot thank my family enough. There is no longer any possible way I can ever return all the love and encouragement so generously offered by my wife, Lorraine, who passed away at a relatively young age during the writing of *A Professor at the End of Time*. My sons, Frank D. Tarantino and Matthew D. Best, were always inquisitive and attentive to the book's progress, and I thank both of them for their willingness to listen and their patience. My Italian mother-in-law, Tommie Davis, cooked dinner for me on many evenings and kept me company in the process, for which I am very grateful. She even appreciatively ate the dinners I cooked for the two of us, a fact that that might say even more about the depth of her support. I also enjoyed the companionship of my sister-in-law, Diane Davis Cuculich, and my nephew, Adam Cuculich, on any number of outings and occasions. To all of you, thank you for making such a difference in my life.

Throughout the writing of this book, I have thought of it book principally as another opportunity to be a teacher. And being a teacher means, at least, conveying an important message clearly. If it turns out in the judgment of its readers that my work is neither particularly important nor clear, despite everyone's best intentions to produce a quality work, then as an author I have singularly failed. But there is another less spectacular way to fail, for those who write a book without learning very much about their material, their connection to that material, or themselves have failed too, because they have missed an opportunity to grow, develop, and learn. It is in this second sense that I know I have already succeeded. I was hoping to have a modicum of fun discovering what I had actually done as a member of the professoriate, after I had the time to step back and look at my work objectively. But to my surprise and joy, I learned more about my career, life, and professorial self than I could possibly have imagined before beginning this writing. And I fervently hope that my enjoyment and delight in that learning imbues this book with those qualities that will encourage all its potential readers to join me on this strange and wondrous journey that we are about to begin together.

John Best
Tuscola, Illinois
Monday, May 30, 2016
Memorial Day

A PROFESSOR AT THE END OF TIME

1 · STANDING AT THE EDGE OF TIME

This introductory chapter sets, and then fills, the stage on which the action will occur in part 1. In this chapter, I give a brief history of the professoriate and its seemingly indispensable role in American higher education in the twentieth century. I also introduce the gathering forces that began to revolutionize the delivery model of higher education in the twenty-first century and that, by so doing, threatened the professoriate's existence as nothing before had done. I also describe the methodology that I will use in the remainder of the book to analyze the changing nature of my work and, by extension, the work of the professoriate from the closing decades of the twentieth century to the opening decades of the twenty-first.

When I told my friends the title of the work that I was proposing to write in my retirement, some of them thought it was science fiction. At the time, I quickly corrected them. But in a way, they were right: even though *A Professor at the End of Time* is not explicitly a book about a well-established science fiction theme like time travel, nevertheless time and time traveling (of a sort) are both definitely involved. This is a book about the ability of some things, be they institutions or concepts, to move through time, retaining at least some of their integrity and thus surviving whatever changes the passage of time may wreak on them. It is also a book about the perishability of other institutions or concepts that appear to be no less durable. Furthermore, it is a book that will invite its readers to examine some large, and seemingly permanent, institutions as they were in a not-too-distant past that now seems rather suddenly and irretrievably gone. And finally, this is a book that will invite its readers to imagine some of those surviving institutions and concepts in a bewildering and perhaps unwelcome future that I believe will nevertheless inexorably descend on us.

Bringing things down to earth somewhat: higher education is one of those seemingly constant and permanent concepts or institutions deeply embedded in the fabric of American life. For a number of reasons, I, along with many other people, believe it will continue to be part of the warp and woof of American culture. Even a figure like Daphne Koller, the cofounder of the online platform Coursera, has stated that a small seminar at an elite institution can produce "something magical," presumably not to be equaled in the online environment (Wolfe, 2015). Yet despite the factors contributing to continuity, the concept of higher education and the institutions that provide it seem destined to change dramatically—as in fact they already have.

And what of the fate of the faculty of those institutions who provide that higher education, sometimes known as the professoriate? Surely, one might think, they will remain with us as well. After all, it was not too long ago, relatively speaking, when many of the people involved in higher education, and not just the professors, would have endorsed the following equation:

Professors = University

That is, the professors *were* the university,[1] and vice versa. It was inconceivable to think of one without the other. And for some people, apparently, that is the way things remain. When I sometimes prankishly asked my faculty colleagues to identify the most important people at the university where we worked, they often replied, "We are." Actually, for a number of reasons that I hope to make clear in the rest of the book, I do not believe that the professors are currently the most important people at my university or perhaps any university, if they ever were. And although the equation I offered above no doubt provides reassurance and solace, as I try to demonstrate, it could hardly be less true of the present-day university. For my now-former colleagues who believe that their fate as professors is permanently intertwined with that of the concept of higher education, they may be nonplussed and chagrined to find that the academy can shed them (although not necessarily by tomorrow) and still move forward.

In the preface, I expressed a hope that my readers would accompany me on a journey, and in this chapter I provide the equipment that will be needed along the way. I delineate some terms that I use throughout the book, hoping to help readers navigate through time without getting disoriented. I also describe the highly contoured landscape of higher education as it operates in early twenty-first-century America. Along the way, I delineate the appearance and development of a particular set of circumstances or forces that appeared in the waning decades of the twentieth century. These forces coalesced during my career and created a markedly different work environment by the time my tenure concluded, one that persistently demanded changes in how I went about my role in the business of higher education. In chapter 6, I return to a more complete exposition of those forces.

Thus, in addition to being a book about time, this is also a book about work. Specifically, it is about the work that I, as a typical member of the professoriate, did as time changed, from a period that that has been called the golden age of higher education (Thelen, 2011) to the technological era in which we currently find ourselves.

In this chapter, I discuss the factors that framed that work, both the larger and more structural factors that were in play when I was a professor from a time near the end of the twentieth century to the beginning of the second decade of the twenty-first century, and the personal factors that seemed to be true of my cohort of Americans who became college professors during that time.

I use a particular form of investigation to examine those works and days, a form that might be somewhat unusual in that it relies on a set of voluminous and varied materials that I have at hand, some of which have been in my possession since I created them more than thirty-five years ago. I have included a description of my methodology in this chapter, and I hope I have provided enough information to distinguish what I intend to produce here from other more conventional forms of reflection, such as the memoir or autobiography.

In subsequent chapters, I show fully what my work as a professor entailed, and how I operated as simply one agent in a huge sector of an even larger segment of the vast domain of higher education. I show how that sector, and the professoriate that labored within it, were dramatically reworked not only by technological forces, but also by the economic and structural factors that came to be more prevalent as the twentieth century waned.

SOME TERMINOLOGY

I have asserted that that the concept of higher education will probably still be around in the future, but, shockingly, the concept of the professoriate may not make it. What is the warrant for that? Before I respond, I would like to offer some terminology to help pin down some of the concepts that I have been bruiting about in the first section.

At the Edge of Time

John Thelen's (2011) dubbing the period 1945-70 the golden age of higher education is well justified. It is very easy to trace the numerous signs of growth and development in higher education in the twenty-five-year period after World War II. For example, the number of students going to college in the United States increased from 10-15 percent of a typical high school graduating class in 1940 to 40–50 percent by 1970. The number of professors employed in colleges followed suit, increasing from perhaps 150,000 in 1940 to approximately 600,000 by 1970—meteoric growth that meant there was not necessarily a lot of competition for each academic job that became available. A portion of the student expansion was fueled by the development of a junior college or community college system that began to blossom in the 1960s, but there is no doubt that four-year colleges were experiencing dramatic growth on their own. The economic value of holding almost any sort of four-year college degree was unquestioned, and for legislators across the country who perceived this value, higher education was seen a tremendous investment. Consequently, the cost of an expanding public higher education system was largely subsidized by state governments eager to reap the income-tax benefits of a highly educated workforce. However, as the later decades of the twentieth century rolled by, things began to change. Beginning in the 1980s, the rate of growth began to slow, and the number of students enrolled began to plateau, leading some researchers (for example, Tuchman, 2009) to refer to this time period as a shift in higher education from a growth industry to a mature industry. Once higher education became a mature industry, the attraction of complete or near-complete subsidies for it was no longer so strong for legislators, and the levels of financial support heretofore enjoyed by public higher education began to recede.

Moving past this golden age to the point where the technological infrastructure of higher education, now so taken for granted, became more visible, insistent, and intrusive as the twentieth century began its closing decade, we come to that brief slice that I have labeled the edge of time. Standing at the edge of time means to put oneself at that point. Looking backward from the edge of time, one could see continuity with the past, promising stability and a continuation of a golden age. But looking forward from the edge of time was to peer into a gathering darkness, although few members of the professoriate could have foreseen how complete a change was forthcoming in that darkness.

The End of Time

As higher education sailed up to the edge of time, unforeseeable forces were unleashed that produced a crisis in the truest sense of that term: a turning point. There would continue to be change, but it would have less, and perhaps very little, continuity with the past. Moreover, the change that will continue to occur in the future will be even less linear, and therefore less predictable than change has been until now. So the narrative arc that was visible in higher education from the period after World War II to the edge of time will no longer be present. Here, and for the remainder of the book, I therefore use the expression "the end of time" to mean our time, which began when peering into a dark future required a step into what became the technologically advanced present. From the end of time backward into the past, one might see and trace a narrative of predictable change, even if at times those changes were somewhat unwelcome. But from the end of time forward into the future, as the forces impinging on higher education and the professoriate would converge with perhaps brutal impact, there would not be as much agreement about the way either of those concepts or institutions should continue to operate.

Establishing the Past, Present, and Future

When I use the expressions "now" or "the present," "the end of time," and "the technological era," I mean a relatively narrow window of time in the late twentieth or early twenty-first century. It might be possible to put a more specific, albeit symbolic, date on the end of time, but most of the changes that I have documented here occurred incrementally, beginning around 1990 or so, and at least a few of those changes had completed their trajectories by 2010. Thus the onset of the technological era does not exactly correspond to the millennium, nor to any of the beginning and ending dates of the various birth cohorts (they will be discussed a little later in this chapter) that occupied various roles in higher education during the time I was involved in it.

That takes care of the now. What about the past? Although I have not established a specific date for the end of time, I have nevertheless tried to identify specific dates in the past (that is, in the golden age or the period immediately following it). In most cases, the corpus of information from my career (summarized in the appendix) enabled me to determine those dates with good precision.

And what about the future? Like everybody else, I think of the future as a time period that is clearly out in front of us, perhaps far out, when the forces and pressures on the professoriate will have had their clear and definitive effects. But the future is now, too. The changes that are affecting the professoriate and higher education are already well under way, even if some or most of the members of the professoriate are not aware of them. Scholars and researchers (for example, Wildavsky, Kelly, & Carey, 2011) in the area of higher education are already fully alive to the changes that are taking place and have projected their visions of the future accordingly. How long will it take for the effects of that future, which has already begun to arrive, to be completed? I have seen references to a thirty-year period and to an eighty-year one. The future that I will envision (discussed in chapter 7) is much farther out that that, in part for symbolic reasons. However, I do not believe that there is too terribly much hinging on the specific number of years. If the changes that I and others foresee actually happen to the professoriate, their effects will be profound whether they occur in twenty, fifty, or a hundred years.[2]

Audiences and Stakeholders, Now and in the Future

To succeed, an author must visualize a potential audience of various constituents and stakeholders whose needs shape and mold the writing. I have written *A Professor at the End of Time* with several such groups in mind, including current and former members of the professoriate, those who aspire to join their ranks, theorists and researchers of higher education, policy makers with fiduciary responsibility for the higher education industry today, parents of college students, and even perhaps college students themselves—who could certainly be excused for wondering just what it is that their professors do all day.

But I have a confession to make here. When I discussed this book project with my friends, I told them that I had another audience in mind in addition to those mentioned: a future audience of researchers and scholars of higher education who would be looking back from their present to understand our particular present. In response, my friends suggested that I should not have corrected them so quickly about my book's not being science fiction. After all, meeting the needs of readers in the here and now is hard enough without the burden of trying to imagine the objectives and interests of those who have not yet arrived.

It is true that my main objective in writing *A Professor at the End of Time* is to create an empirically based account of my professional doings as a member of the professoriate from the end of the golden age through the beginning of the technological era—an account unlike any other, to the best of my knowledge. And I also believe that a documentation of those doings, and how they occurred at various points in the past and the present, will make a compelling story that needs to be told and to be read, now, by those who have a stake in that future and who have some power to make changes in the here and now.

But addressing this future audience, while the present audience listens in, accomplishes something else for me as well. It enables me to use the terms "past," "present," and "future" as more than simple tokens showing that some aspects of higher education change over time. As I have defined them here, these terms establish a trope that I intend to use as an authorial device: by looking at things as they might look in the future, I am asking my current readers to step back from their perhaps implicit assumptions about how those things look now. And when the reader does that—looks from the perspective of the futurist—he or she may better see how misaligned some of those institutions are from the needs of the people they were designed to serve. Going even further, the reader may see how frankly odd in their operations some of those institutions or things are.

Higher Education

I have used the terms "higher education" and "higher learning" throughout the book, and to a certain extent, I have relied on my various audiences' knowledge for comprehension. Still, there are a couple of terminological points that I need to deal with here to erect the conceptual scaffolding that I use to discuss higher education. The first point concerns the diversity of the forms of higher education in the United States. Within the approximately 4,140 degree-granting institutions of higher education that were in operation in the United States in 2005 (National Center for Educational Statistics, 2006), there are several clearly discernible forms or models in operation, marked by institutional differences in mission, size of enrollment, extent of physical plant, cost to students, and numerous other factors.

First, there are 1,070 public two-year institutions and 596 private two-year institutions in the United States (National Center for Educational Statistics, 2006). While this group of institutions will face its own unique set of challenges and opportunities in the decades to come, the role of the teacher on these campuses has been stable for a long time.

The same cannot be said for the 629 public four-year institutions (serving the needs of 6.8 million students) and the 1,845 private four-year institutions (serving 4.1 million students), (National Center for Educational Statistics, 2006), for which numerous categorical and organizational schemes (for example, Hermanowicz, 2011) have been applied in an effort to make sense of the churning and roiling world of the institutions that offer baccalaureate degrees.

For example, Mark Schneider and K. C. Deane (2015) acknowledge that there seems to be a sort of category of universities ranking below the name-brand private institutions and the flagship public campuses. This category might include the 400 or so state comprehensive universities (SCUs) that are responsible for educating over 70 percent of all undergraduates at four-year public institutions. But Schneider and Deane also acknowledge that there are substantial differences even among such schools, although they share certain aspects of their mission—for example, their focus on "diversity, equity, and inclusive excellence" (American Association of State Colleges and Universities, 2016). Bruce Henderson (2007) has also focused on the characteristics of the SCU as an organizing motif, recognizing that other approaches to categorizing universities, such as those carried out by the Carnegie Foundation for the Advancement of Teaching, have led to very complex schemes that may be accurate reflections of the often bewildering landscape of contemporary higher education in the United States (McCormick & Zhao, 2005). For example, Henderson (2007) noted that the SCUs were often in the middle range of selectivity among universities, but often somewhat lower in retaining those students whom they had admitted. This discrepancy was perhaps an inevitable consequence of the fact that the SCUs had always been intended as a democratizing force in American society, creating opportunities in higher education for those population segments that may not have always had them.

But at the possible risk of oversimplifying, I would like to suggest that, in terms of their effects on the professoriate, there might be only two broad categories—or, as I call them, systems—of higher education in operation (Heller, 2013). And this brings me to one of the important themes that will run like a leitmotif throughout the book, concerning the reality of these two systems and the differences between them. Following Nathan Heller and other commentators, we can name one of these the "elite system," although that name has some unwanted connotations. Despite that, the name is accurate in the sense that the proportion of schools sharing the distinguishing characteristics is small. These characteristics include the following: The institutions are well-known brands, in the sense that they have national name recognition among students and their families who might be in the market for an institution to attend. The institutions accept a small percentage of all the students who apply, and the students they accept are, in general, highly able intellectually. These institutions value research and scholarship, and the faculty members who work at them produce copious quantities of both, including the majority of the research and scholarship that is cited by the other leading figures in their fields. Depending on who is doing the counting, and what factors they are weighing more heavily, the institutions of the elite system might make up approximately 10 percent of all the four-year institutions of higher education in the United States (Leahey & Montgomery, 2011).

The other system—that is, the other 90 percent of the four-year schools—consists of institutions that do not share these crucial characteristics of the schools in the elite system. These institutions accept the majority of students who apply, and perhaps as many as 33 percent of their accepted students are seriously underprepared for higher education (Elliott, 2013; Otterman, 2011). As a consequence, many or most of them will not complete their academic program. These schools may or may not have a stated research or scholarship component in their mission, but teaching is always the primary mission, and sometimes it is the only one. The schools generally have much less national visibility or recognition than do the schools in the elite system. Some of the institutions may be striving for such recognition—there are some incentives to do so—but most of them are very comfortable not doing so and focusing on serving the needs of their existing clientele. This second system currently lacks a definitive name. Heller (2013) refers to it as the "populist" system, which is certainly accurate as these schools strive to serve the needs of many. Norton Grubb and Marvin Lazerson (2005) have referred to such schools even more simply as "second-tier" institutions.

The lack of a commonly agreed-on name is understandable. For one thing, the category of institutions is not really that systematic—the other 90 percent of the schools are very different from each other in a number of important ways, even though they may share some defining attributes. However, although it may be presumptuous of me to put a name to this group of institutions that really is not a category, it will nevertheless be helpful for me to do so throughout this book. Without any intention to offend anyone, but simply in recognition of the size, scope, and mass of the higher educational enterprise in the United States today—with its emphasis on seeing those students who complete the bachelor's degree as a kind of product, and with the resulting pressures to commodify the educational process—I have chosen to refer to this other 90 percent of schools as "the industrial system," although I know that many workers in higher education will bristle at the implications of this term.

But in focusing on size and scope, I'm also making a processing argument for the term "industrial-scale institutions." The overarching mission of these schools is to process, or convert, nonbaccalaureate people into people with bachelor's degrees. Thus, the term "industrial-scale institution" is (in part) a deliberate nod to what Schneider and Deane (2015) call the completion agenda, the shift in national policy that acknowledges that increasing access to higher education is insufficient, if by doing so completion rates are not also enhanced.

There are some provisos that need to be stated immediately. I am not trying to claim, or even to suggest, that there are not significant and substantial differences among the institutions that could be counted as industrial-scale schools. But I am going to argue that as far as the future vitality of the professoriate is concerned, those differences may not matter. Similarly, I do not want to be misunderstood as suggesting that a student cannot receive a meaningful and useful education anywhere but at an elite school. Many of the industrial-scale schools in the United States are fulfilling their educational mission with distinction. Finally, I am fully aware that there are many highly talented students who find themselves at an industrial-scale school; indeed, I taught many of them over the years I was in the profession. But despite all that, my analysis has led me to conclude that it is impossible to understand the fate of the professoriate as we know it now without a grounding in these basic facts about how higher education is organized, sold, and bought in the United States today.

The Professoriate

There are about 1.70 million providers of postsecondary education in the United States today (Quora.com, 2016). This number includes the 160,000 or so graduate teaching assistants who teach in college and universities in a regular basis. Subtracting their number (they are primarily students, after all) leaves about 1.54 million professionals who earn their living in whole or in large part by working in some sector of postsecondary education. That number includes all those who teach at the public and private two-year degree-granting institutions, technical and vocational schools, and other proprietary schools in the country. Excluding them gives us those people who are usually referred to as the professoriate, generally defined as that set of individuals who earn their living primarily by serving as faculty members who deliver educational services and products in an institution located somewhere on the spectrum of the four-year schools I identified above. There are perhaps 600,000 (Finkelstein, 1984) to 700,000 (Schuster, 2011) such people in the United States today. And all of them would probably squeeze the words "college professor" into the blank space of any loan application asking for one's occupation, as I did for the thirty-six years that I was in the business. But the fact that they can all be identified with a single name belies the considerable differences that exist among the members of the professoriate.

It is not news to anybody involved in higher education to read that the three traditional dimensions or roles of the professoriate (teaching, research, and service) are afforded different levels of resources, time, effort, and energy at different institutions depending in part on where the institution in question might find itself on the spectrum of higher education I outlined. Generally, the size and scope of an institution's research mission contributes disproportionately to its success in branding itself: many or most of the brand-name institutions are also research institutions. For reasons whose operation I clarify in chapter 4, the linkage between the size of the research mission and the impact or strength of the brand will, I believe, tend to buffer or protect those institutions from some of the economic forces that have beset the industrial-scale schools. And as those institutions have been buffered somewhat, so will the members of the professoriate who work for them. I need to be very clear: those institutions and their professors are facing their own set of possibly calamitous problems. But their story is not mine to tell. If I am correct about the forces that have currently been set in motion, then it is the hundreds of thousands of professors at the industrial-scale schools in the United States whose continued existence will be the most vulnerable to the economic and technological forces that are on the loose now.

WHAT MAKES NOW THE END OF TIME?

What is the warrant for asserting that now might be the end of time, rather than simply being a continuation of the changing times that have actually been the status quo of higher education and the professoriate throughout the twentieth century? A look back at the history of higher education in the United States throughout the second half of the twentieth century would reveal many other periods in which cultural forces, if not other forms of pressure, threatened to overwhelm the academy and the professoriate. What reason is there to think that now might be different from then? In chapter 6, I return to this topic with a more complete discussion of the panoply of forces that threaten the professoriate, and I am optimistic that I will be able to show that these forces, taken *in toto*, have not previously had the same effect that they currently have. In this section I offer a more limited discussion of two of the principal drivers of change in higher education: the completely enveloping spread of technology and the relentless, debilitating cost pressures.

Technology Changed Everything

The first and probably most obvious reason for referring to the present as the end of time has to do with a host of massive and all-encompassing technological changes in the way in which higher education services and products could be delivered to students as the twenty-first century dawned. The emergence of the Internet and its content portended another way to educate people, with implications for the role of the professoriate, and that was true whether the delivery model was the traditional face-to-face approach or a new-seeming online model.

The creation and development of the Internet spawned those now omnipresent online classes, which are offered remotely with either synchronous or asynchronous interactions between the student and the professor or other teacher. And the evolution and development of online courses changed the traditional face-to-face delivery model as well. One possible reason for this is that once online courses were commonly available, as they were by the end of the first decade of the twenty-first century, the face-to-face courses seldom stayed completely in their heretofore traditional mode—a process I document more fully in chapter 3. Essentially, even as professors adapted some of the characteristics of their face-to-face courses for use in the online world, a sort of cross-fertilization occurred in which some of the techniques and practices of the online courses worked their way into the structure and organization of the face-to-face courses, in turn creating something like a hybrid delivery model. As my career advanced into the new millennium, I began to conceptualize the face-to-face course as being on two channels. On the first channel, the physical one, there was the traditional presentation: mostly spoken by me, with segments involving exchanges with students, and augmented with a number of visual aids. This channel possessed all of the characteristics of the traditional college class: it was synchronous; we were all in the same place at the same time. The people involved had clearly separate and recognizable roles (teacher or student), and the professor was likewise clearly identifiable, both physically and behaviorally. Over on the other channel, the electronic one, there might be some additional communication, consisting of mass e-mail sent to the entire class on a daily basis that contained suggested readings, assignments, or comments on what had taken place in class that day. Like many professors, I refer to these kinds of materials as content: basic factual knowledge that I possessed and could share directly with students in a sentential declarative format. There might also be some information flowing over the electronic channel that was not content. For example, I also offered guidance, suggestions, or responses to individual students, again delivered via e-mail. To a much greater extent than the physical channel, the electronic channel promoted a two-way flow of information. By the end of time, students felt free to submit written assignments and homework, and to ask questions about that work, using this channel as well—all processes that had been more or less restricted to a face-to-face encounter previously. The electronic channel had some of the characteristics of the online courses: it was asynchronous and disembodied, without clear physical identifiers regarding the role being played by the actors. Now, there were never any requirements for me or any other professor to run this second channel; it simply became more commonplace for me and others to do so as the twenty-first century progressed.

There is a final question in this section: even allowing for the possibility that the reality of the online courses altered the content and delivery of the face-to-face courses, why should that outcome, which might be dismissed as merely a behavioral change or a change in practice, contain a threat to the integrity of the professoriate as a whole? As I show in chapters 2 through 5, the members of the professoriate play a number of roles, and each of those roles is multifaceted. That is, teaching involves a number of functions: to name just a few, sharing knowledge, building critical thinking, interpreting and commenting on factual information, and constructively criticizing the academic work of others.

For people who are not members of the professoriate, there probably is no direct way for them to know what I am about to write, but the reality is that the online courses tend to emphasize the sharing of the professor's factual knowledge over those numerous other functions of the professor. That is, in the short term, sharing the knowledge in a course came to be predominant over other functions such as the interpretation or contextualization of the material being shared. Although the transfer or transmission of information is crucial at all levels of education, many theorists or commentators (for example, Deresiewicz, 2015) believe the professor's work consists of much more than that. Yet when professors come to believe that content is king, or at least behave as if they believe it, they may wind up doing their students a profound disservice. On one occasion toward the end of my career—and therefore, at the end of time as I have defined it—I was leading a group of professors in a biweekly discussion of the role and function of the professor as a teacher. Our meetings were based on successive chapters from a well-known book, *The Courage to Teach* (Palmer, 1998). One of the exercises suggested by Parker Palmer involves asking professors to visualize themselves metaphorically in terms of what their ideal selves might be as teachers. One of the most highly regarded professors at my institution was participating in the discussion group, and her response to this exercise was to state that her best or ideal self as a teacher was a content provider, and the more content the better. Her metaphor for her ideal self was that of an immense soybean combine of the type that could be seen at harvest time in the fields around our university, relentlessly spewing from its capacious output chute a never-ending torrent of harvested beans into a passively receiving dump truck for haulage to the grain elevator.

What were the factors that led to this phenomenon? It may not be possible to produce a complete list. As the twenty-first century unfolded, many institutions updated their learning spaces with the creation of "smart classrooms," an expression referring to the inclusion in the room of a sophisticated projection system and a computer capable of connecting to the Internet. Professors working in that environment began to use presentation software as a teaching aid, with PowerPoint becoming probably the most frequently used program. By the end of the first decade of the twenty-first century, virtually every professor in my department used it at least to some extent in virtually every course, whether face to face or online. The students tended to like this practice, perhaps even more so when the content was presented in the face-to-face classes in an accessible way that mimicked the online courses. But there may have been a hidden cost in doing this.

Over fifty years ago the prescient communication theorist Marshall McLuhan (1964) asserted that message equaled the medium. During his time, he did not specify the mechanism by which the message was reduced to its medium, but we know now: the message is folded up, convoluted, and contorted to meet the demands of the channel across which the information in the message must flow. And that is how the linear and sequential arguments that were built and stated by the professor in the form of sentential logic, and perhaps written on a blackboard, became disembodied single words—decontextualized and ephemeral—on an overhead screen whose appearance and vanishing was without any significance to those viewing them. Thus, as Michael Bastedo (2012) has noted, "information technology is treated as a broad spectrum of rapidly evolving environmental demands rather than a cognitive structure that changes the nature of tasks, roles, and rewards" (p. 9).

Economic and Structural Factors Changed Things, Too

But technology is not the only factor that makes now the end of time: there are also economic factors and other factors that I am going to label "structural" that have converged to make many more people's dreams of higher education excessively costly, and perhaps financially unattainable. And this phenomenon has deep and durable implications for the professoriate.

The economic factors have to do with the well-known fact that the cost of attending a four-year college or university has increased much more steeply than has the consumer price index, and this has been true for several decades. In the period 2001–10 alone, after adjusting for the effects of inflation, the cost of tuition rose 42 percent at public universities and 31 percent at private ones (National Center for Education Statistics, 2015b).

Several factors have contributed to this greater-than-inflationary increase, and in chapter 6 I provide a more complete description of them. However, part of the increase is the result of a retrenchment by state governments in their financial support of public higher education. This cutback has produced a shift from the state-supported public institutions of the 1960s and 1970s, when much or even most of the cost of tuition and fees was subsidized by the state, to the state-assisted public universities of today. Students at the public universities are still not paying the true cost of their education, but with each passing year, they pay a larger and larger proportion of it. To meet that cost, students and their families have several options, but none of them is particularly appealing. The student may choose to work a greater number of hours during the school year to contribute a significant amount to his or her education. While many students can handle an academic workload along with long hours at a physically demanding, relatively low-paying job, for many other students, combining an academic load with a job means that they sign up for, and complete, fewer courses during the academic year, thus prolonging their time to graduation. As the research literature on this topic shows, the longer students have to attend school to complete their degree, the less likely they are to do so (Bound, Lovenheim, & Turner, 2010). In this regard, I think it is significant that there is a tendency among many professors and administrators in higher education to downplay their institutions' four-year graduation rate, and if they do report it to recognize that not very many of their students will attain it. As it stands now, at the four-year state-assisted institution where I spent the bulk of my career, 32 percent of the students complete their four-year program in four years. Even the six-year rate (which is now considered the final, or total, rate) is only 59 percent, and this is actually enviable in comparison to many of my institution's peers.

As unpalatable as the work option may be, at least if and when the student completes the degree, he or she may owe only a relatively small amount, and perhaps nothing. An alternative course of action might consist of borrowing more money in the short term, and thus meeting the cost of going to school full time in the here and now.

At my institution, in the last year that I was professor (2012–13), the total estimated cost of attendance was $23,528 for a student who was paying the in-state tuition rate. The vast majority of the students (83 percent) received some form of financial aid (this figure, and the ones following, are for the academic year 2010–11). There were many students (79 percent) who received a grant of some type, and the average amount of this grant was $5,244. Essentially, such grants are a reduction in what amounts to the sticker price of the education, so neither the student nor the institution incurs any real costs there. But for an almost equally high percentage of students (71 percent), the financial aid was in the form of a loan. And the average loan amount ($9,965) was far larger than the average grant. Paying off a loan of nearly $40,000 could have a crushing effect on the individual's actual purchasing power for years following the completion of the degree, even if the degree itself pays off in terms of a higher-paying job.

In addition to these purely economic factors are what I have labeled structural factors. These factors have to do with changes in income distribution in the United States during the time that the cost of attending college was increasing faster than the consumer price index. Based on statistics compiled by the Pew Research Center (Cohn, 2012) the proportion of middle-class households (defined as those in which the household income was 67-200 percent of the national median) declined from 54 percent of all households in metropolitan areas in the United States in 1980 to 48 percent in 2010. This falloff has been accompanied by increasing income polarization—the proportion of households in each of the upper and lower tails of the income distribution is growing as the percentage of households in the middle lessens. The percentage of high-income households (those with greater than 200 percent of the median income) increased from 15 percent of all households in 1980 to 20 percent in 2010, and the percentage of low-income households increased slightly, from 31 percent in 1980 to 32 percent in 2010. But the overwhelming number of college students came from the pool of middle-class households during the closing years of the twentieth century and the early ones of the twenty-first.

When these students request financial aid to go to college, they and their families fill out an extensive series of forms that eventually yields the expected family contribution (EFC), or the dollar amount that the parents or other caregivers are expected to contribute to pay for the student's education. But as a result of the structural disparity in income that has occurred, there are fewer and fewer families who can meet this financial obligation. At my institution, going back to the most recent academic year for which I was able to locate the statistics (2010–11), 27 percent of all students had an EFC of $0. This figure had increased from 18 percent in 2007–8 (Donna, 2011). Looking at the next year (2011–12), in those cases when the EFC was $0, the accepted student received a federal Pell Grant of $5,550 and a state Monetary Assistance Program (MAP) grant of $4,720. The total of this amount ($10,270) went toward the direct cost (full-time tuition, fees, room, and board) of attending my institution that year, which was $19,075. What about the balance of the direct costs, which was $8,805? Some of that balance might be subsidized by institutional grants or scholarships. But it was far more likely that this balance was paid from the student's work-study program or federal loans. So, as these figures demonstrate, when his or her family is not able to financially support a student, then he or she is more likely to be forced to take the work or loan options we saw above, with their attendant negative consequences. For example, at my institution, fully 69 percent of the 2011 graduating class had an average cumulative principal borrowed of $21,049 for federal loans and $26,500 when private education loans were factored in (Donna, 2011).

As the cost of higher education continues to accelerate, and more and more families become unable to meet those costs, it has become common in the early part of the twenty-first century for commentators (for example, Alexander, 2006) to raise persistent and troubling questions about the sustainability of the entire higher educational apparatus as it is currently configured. And those facts are the basis for another area of threat to the professoriate as it exists today.

THE CHANGING WORK OF THE PROFESSORIATE

The proportions of time devoted to the core tasks of the professor's work—teaching, research, and service—have been known for some time. For example, Martin Finkelstein (1984, pp. 87-96), reports the results of several studies done during the golden age, or shortly thereafter, to show that 60 percent of the professoriate spent nine or more hours per week in teaching, and an equal or greater amount of time in preparation for that teaching. As expected, though, there was a lot of variability in those percentages, depending on the nature of the professor's institution. Thus, while Everett Ladd (1979) reported that 34 percent of the professoriate at research institutions spent nine or more hours per week in teaching, this was true of 78 percent of the faculty members at comprehensive colleges and universities. The professors at research universities were still heavily involved in preparing for their teaching, though: 50 percent reported spending nine or more hours per week in teaching preparation, compared to 61 percent of the professors at the comprehensive schools. Naturally enough, the emphasis on research at the research institutions was reflected in the allocation of the professoriate's time. Ladd (1979) reported that 60 percent of the professors at research institutions spent nine or more hours per week on research, in contrast to only 21 percent of the professors at comprehensive colleges and universities. And these time values are correlated with the publication productivity of the faculty member. For example, at research institutions, only 18 percent of faculty members reported not having published in the previous two years, compared to 46 percent at comprehensive colleges and universities (Ladd, 1979).

We can learn quite a bit from these figures. But there is an unsatisfying aspect to them nevertheless. Aggregated as they are across a number of different institutions in different states, I do not think they are sufficiently detailed to answer many of the important questions we might have about the professoriate during either the golden age or the technological era. The reason is because it is not just the time allocations that we need to know about, although they are important. But more important are the details of what professors did, and these are missing from the purely numerical tabulations. What does teaching really mean on a day-by-day basis, now and before the technological era? Is there an accurate understanding of what the members of the professoriate actually do (and did) to accomplish that teaching? And, adopting the trope about the future audience that I laid out above, if the professoriate is truly as threatened as I believe it might be, will it still be possible to learn what professors did when there are no longer any such people who could supply a report?

Understanding the Professoriate Today: A New Methodology

To answer such questions, a different approach is required. In 1976, the noted military historian John Keegan published the book that many consider his masterwork, *The Face of Battle*. There, Keegan closely analyzed the events on three epic battlefields, including Waterloo, to answer the question, What happened? But not, as it had always been answered, from the perspective of a commanding general—rather, from the perspective of the individual soldier's actions and behaviors. For example, a general might order an attack of a certain size, in a particular direction, and at a specified time. All those dimensions would then become part of the history of the battle or campaign. But the problem with this approach, as Keegan recognized, was that the general's history squeezed out all the other viewpoints, and thus all the other histories of the battle. What happened to the soldiers? What did soldiers on the field of battle at Waterloo, or the Somme, actually do in response to the orders transmitted down to them? How long did those activities take them, and how frequently were they performed? What were the challenges in doing so? What factors fostered success or, as so often happened on the Somme, augured poorly instead? I hope the analogy with the members of the professoriate is apt: the chairperson of my academic department could and did assign aspects of my work, and among those assignments were orders to teach a certain class at a certain time. And I followed orders: I taught classes. But what, exactly, was involved in doing so, both before and after the end of time? And that invites another question: when we came to work, what else did we do all day? Congruent with the Ladd (1979) report, I can state that I spent some hours per week devoted to research. But what exactly did my research activity entail?

Bastedo (2012) has recognized this gap between theory and educational practice in the traditional literature of higher education, stating frankly that "we have poor quantitative data" (11), while citing the potential for rich studies, as well as for "deep studies of faculty scholarly learning, research, cognition, and work" (11).

Bastedo's position enables me to make a very important point about *A Professor at the End of Time*: one of my objectives is precisely to break down the disciplinary boundaries that have contained the kind of work that I accomplish herein. In other words, some of the book's power resides in the fact that I am not one of those researchers in higher education who operate with their own lenses and biases, and who might be more likely to have the general's perspective on the issues. The Waterloo analogy seems apt in another way, too. Those of us who were actually delivering the educational product can attest to both the extreme conditions of the battlefield (that is, the limitations under which we delivered that product) and the changing dynamics of the warfare we waged, the process by which that delivery was transformed forever.

If I am correct about the technological watershed that has occurred, the structural and economic changes that have occurred in the last several decades, and the threats that such developments pose for the professoriate, then, as we drive deeper and deeper into the twenty-first century that detailed knowledge will begin to slip away. *A Professor at the End of Time* is a book about time, and it is a book about work. It is also a time capsule to be opened in the future: to help the Keegan-esque scholar of higher education in that time recover the knowledge of what we did as professors in our time. And with that knowledge, such a scholar might also recover the knowledge of what it was like to do that job.

The level of detail that I intend to provide does not exist in any account that I have been able to locate, at least not in the form that *A Professor at the End of Time* will reveal. In addition to the aggregated accounts of professors' time allocations written before the end of time (for example, Fairweather, 1996; Tierney, 1999), which I will make use of in my own work, there have been some diary-type studies. For example, James Phelan (1991) kept an impressionistic and yet reflective diary of fifteen months of his work in the English Department at a research institution. There have also been generalized, somewhat idiosyncratic, accounts of what professors do, also written before the end of time (for example, Falk, 1990). While such works are helpful, it is still the case that there has been no attempt to create a detailed, data-based narrative based on a case study of a single professor who worked in the transitional time from the golden age to the present, at one of the industrial-scale universities in the twentieth century. In addition, each of the works mentioned above is a snapshot of its time. There will be something more here. For *A Professor at the End of Time*, in addition to being a book about time, work, and details, is a book about change—turbulent change.

MY ROLE AS A PROFESSOR

A Representative of My Time

There are many members of the professoriate who function as public intellectuals in the United States today. Their writings may appear in the popular press on any number of topics, from economics or foreign policy to issues of personal health and wellness. Newscasters may seek them out for television interviews; their books may be on the best-seller list for months. In addition, there are many more members of the professoriate who share their scientific findings with the general public, sometimes stunning and spectacular findings that foster changes in how we view the universe, our planet, our health, and our behavior toward each other. Many of these professors become well-known figures in the contemporary American landscape of notable people. Like most professors, though, I am not like that. For example, I have never written any of the opinion pieces that I alluded to above, nor have I been asked to do so. I have not led any national organization of professors or been interviewed on television. My research findings have been read (if they have been read) by a very tiny group of people who share my interests, probably no more than fifty or a hundred people on the whole planet. So my qualifications to tell the story that I have to tell do not rest on my fame or my stature in my academic field. Rather, I think my main qualification is that I am representative of my era in higher education. In stating that, however, there is no doubt that the performance of my academic work has depended on aspects of my being over which I have not had control. I recognize, as have numerous other scholars (for example, Diggs, Garrison-Wade, Estrada, & Galindo, 2008; Park, 1996; Ropers-Huilman, 2008; Zackerman, Cole, & Bruer, 1991), that other professors, including people of color and women, would probably have a different perspective on those factors that enabled me to carry out that work.

Although I am not at all famous or even well known in my own time, my lack of fame might actually be an asset, as far as the validity of my data is concerned. There are no indications to believe that my work was very much different than that of any other one of the hundreds of thousands of professors who had jobs in the sector of the industrial-scale schools that I inhabited for most of my career.

There is another facet with regard to my being a representative specimen: throughout my career, I simply went about my business in my own department as a cognitive scientist. That meant that I was largely immune to or ignorant of the realities of the changes that were occurring in higher education. As I've learned since, I was all too typical in this regard, too. Tarah Wright and Naomi Horst (2013) conducted a study in which they demonstrated that professors can respond appropriately to questions about the financial barriers to sustainability in higher education. But they also found that most of the professors reported that they had never thought about it prior to their participation in the study—despite, one might think, the extreme salience and vocality associated with this problem.

I Was the Last and the First

In addition to my typicality, I have another qualification for writing about the end of time, which has to do with the timing of my entry into the ranks of the professoriate. My generation of professors, the ones from the birth cohort that included people born on the leading edge of the post–World War II baby boom, was the last generation to operate in the pretechnological era that occurred immediately after the golden age. Recognizing that the terms "technological era," "pretechnological era," and especially "golden age" are relative and somewhat loaded, I will state that I used plenty of technology of the time to help me in my job as a professor throughout my career. Nevertheless, there seems to me to be a gigantic divide between using e-mail as a communication tool now, at the end of time, and using e-mail the way I did for the first time in 1984, when I had to ask the four professors who shared a party line with me to please stay off the phone for the next twenty minutes or so.

While I am old enough to remember episodes like that, I am young enough to be in the first generation of professors to operate the sluices of the waterworks admitting, at a certain pace, all that technological innovation into the mainstream of American academic life now. Or at least we may have had the illusion that we were controlling the pace of admittance.

I watched a brief interview with a farmer on the news the other night. He was discussing all the changes in farming that had come about as a result of the technological revolution that had occurred in agriculture. I remarked to my wife that he might consider writing a book called *A Farmer at the End of Time*. It is true that probably every worker in the United States could point to technological developments that changed their jobs or professions profoundly. They might also validly assert that this fact alone does not establish that now is the end of time for those professions. The size and scope of technological import alone might not necessarily spell the end of time for any given career, although I have seen quite a few jobs or professions—elevator operator, typist, calculating machine operator, and TV repair person—meet their end of time by changes in technology that occurred during my lifetime. But the point that I want to establish here is that even if we cannot know in advance whether or not a given profession is doomed by technological developments, it is still the case that being the last and the first confers a unique position on those observers who manage to document the changes in those professions that do succumb.

SITUATING MY CAREER

In the previous sections, I have made some references to my work, its locale, the timing of my career, and so on. Some of those elements and circumstances of my work are more easily thought of as external from my perspective, as they have to do with places I worked and the timing of my being there. Other circumstances are more easily framed as being internal: the putative characteristics of my birth cohort, for example, and its timing and role in American life as it made its way forward.

External Factors

After earning a PhD in experimental psychology from the University of Cincinnati in 1977, I was employed as a professor at two institutions of higher education. I worked in the Psychology Department (as it was known then; it is now called the Department of Psychological and Brain Sciences) at Indiana University in Bloomington for two academic years, until 1979. Indiana University is a great example of a large, public, research institution. It admitted a relatively small proportion of its applicants; the accepted undergraduates came from every state in the country and from around the world. The size and scope of its graduate education was proportionately large. The permanent faculty members were dedicated and diligent in their production of advanced and high-quality research. And the Psychology Department had what I would call a fairly large cadre of non-tenure-track professors, or contingent faculty members, of whom I was one. One of the most commonly offered choices in a student's general education curriculum both now and then is an introductory psychology course, and Indiana was no exception in providing it (in fact, as was typical in psychology departments at that time, there were two introductory courses). The contingent faculty member's principal role was to staff one of those two introductory courses.

In the spring of 1979, I interviewed for and was offered a tenure-track (or permanent) position in the Psychology Department at Eastern Illinois University (EIU) in Charleston. I worked there for the next thirty-four years, until my retirement in 2013. Like Indiana University, EIU is a great example of its kind of institution: a regional, comprehensive, public university. As I was fond of saying during the time I worked there, EIU belonged to all the people of the state of Illinois. Approximately 97 percent of the undergraduates had gone to high school in the state, a percentage that stayed remarkably constant across the span of years I worked there. At EIU, the teaching mission was the faculty's primary focus, although many of the departments had a research mission that was clearly stated as second in importance, following teaching. Like many public comprehensive institutions, both permanent and contingent faculty members at EIU were represented by a union (University Professionals of Illinois), which we authorized to bargain collectively on our behalf as our sole representative or agent in all matters of salary and working conditions. This arrangement had existed at EIU and several other public campuses in Illinois since the mid-1970s, following the big push for faculty unions that occurred in the 1960s when unions acquired the ability to bargain collectively for faculty members (Cain, 2011).

EIU was not unusual in having this kind of arrangement. Nationwide, 35 percent of all public universities had faculty unions as the twenty-first century began (Cain, 2011), and this percentage was almost certainly higher at the comprehensive public institutions than it was at the public research institutions. There was also some geographic variation: faculty unions were more commonly found in community colleges and four-year schools in the Northeast, Midwest, and West than they were in institutions in the South and Southwest. Illinois was typical in this regard. Of the twelve public four-year campuses that the state of Illinois owned and operated at the end of time, faculty members were unionized, in whole or in part, at eight of them. But among those eight schools, only the University of Illinois–Chicago was classified as a research institution. While the percentage of unionized faculty members has either stayed constant or risen during the period from the end of the golden age until now, the percentage of unionized workers in the United States has declined over the past thirty years, from 20.1 percent of all workers in 1983 to 11.3 percent in 2012 (Bureau of Labor Statistics, 2016).

To sum up, I spent the bulk of my career as a professor at a regional, comprehensive, public university whose faculty members were represented in their salary negotiations by a union. There were several hundred such institutions of higher education in the United States at the beginning of the twenty-first century.

Internal Factors

In addition to these factors of the institutional matrix (the differences between the public comprehensives, with their strong faculty unions, and the research institutions) that were present throughout my career as a professor, there was also the fact that the raw ingredient—the personnel—who were added to that matrix also may have had some distinguishing features that shaped the way the professoriate went about its work in the pretechnological era. And that suggests that it is important to consider some factors about the generation of people who went on to serve as the professors as the technological era dawned.

I was born in 1950, part of the cohort that has been referred to as the baby boom generation, in reference to the relatively high birth rate that occurred in the United States in the years following World War II—specifically, from 1946 to 1964. Actually, the birth rate in the United States began to fall precipitously in 1960, and by 1964 it was no higher than it had been in 1942. Nevertheless, the name and the defining years have both stuck. "Boomers," especially those born in the period's earlier years instead of in its later ones, have regarded themselves as having a number of special characteristics. There does not seem to be any overwhelming empirical evidence to suggest that leading-edge boomers really possessed the characteristics attributed to them. But despite the absence of what such evidence, as a member of that cohort, I can state that the terms that are often used have become elements of our narrative history—the story, or schema, that we, as part of a generation, have constructed and used to interpret our lives. At that level, the characteristics we are purported to have may possess a different kind of reality, a kind of lived reality, even if the empirical basis is not there.

Baby boomers were the first American generation to go to college *en masse*, right out of high school. And in 1968, I became part of that mass. While many of us thought of college as a conduit for our career aspirations, we had many other reasons for going. For example, we were frequently regarded as idealistic by our elders, which for us meant that many of the public and personal institutions of contemporary American life, including government, marriage and the family, and education, were seen as imperfect and in need of change. To be a college student in those years was to gain entry into the public dialogue about how these changes might be enacted. There was also a collective search for identity among college students—nothing new there. But the identity we searched for seemed to us to be very different from the one that our parents had adopted. Given the absence of anything like the World Wide Web, being in college was a way to be exposed to more ideas, more concepts, and more ways of living, all of which could be used to build that identity. And related to both the idealism and the search for identity was the concept of "changing the world"—if not perfecting it, then at least making it better. We believed that we could.

There were some other attributes that boomers brought to the professoriate as they did to the workplace in general, including a willingness to adopt to the goals of the institution, to have loyalty to that institution, and—perhaps especially—to work hard for its success (Staley, 2011). There is some evidence to suggest that these characteristics might be just as true of the members of other birth cohorts who have since entered the professoriate as they were of the boomers. The generation of Americans who were born after the baby boom, in the years from 1965 to 1984, is referred to as Generation X (Masnick, 2012), or just Gen X. Given that Gen X is now the largest birth cohort in the United States, with eighty-six million members (Masnick, 2012), and given the length of time required to complete a PhD and possibly postdoctoral training before getting on the tenure track, it is not surprising to find that many current pretenure faculty were born in that cohort.

Ann Trower (2010) has determined that there is a substantial amount of continuity in values or orientation toward the profession between boomer and Gen X faculty members. For example, similar to boomers, pretenure Gen X faculty members do not envision themselves leaving their institution once they attain tenure: only 13 percent of pretenure Gen X faculty thought that they might do so (Trower, 2010). Despite that, Gen X faculty members are apparently more willing to leave the ranks of the professoriate than baby boomer faculty members were, a factor that I explore in more depth in chapter 7. Gen X faculty members are also somewhat more likely to consider and strive for a work-life balance than were boomer members of the professoriate, a finding that has been interpreted to mean that faculty members in Gen X faculty are somewhat less likely than their boomers peers to aim for a somewhat early retirement from the professoriate (at which point, presumably, boomers thought they might have their personal lives returned to them).

In summary, I was born into a cohort of Americans who regarded themselves as idealistic and on a mission to change the world. We brought the values of institutional loyalty, hard work, and career commitment to our roles in the professoriate, work that many of us felt we were called to do.

VERBAL DOCUMENTARY, AUTOBIOGRAPHY, MEMOIR

The Method

As mentioned above, in writing *A Professor at the End of Time*, I based my methodology on the technique used by Keegan (1976), who analyzed the contemporaneous recorded observations made by soldiers on the battlefield, participants whose military rank was usually well below that of a general. By comparing accounts and resolving differences in perspective, Keegan was able to piece together a coherent narrative of a given battle from the standpoint of the participants, thus providing details of the action that may not have occurred to the generals.

To carry out a similar analysis of my work as a professor, where and how would I obtain those corresponding details that would enable me to synthesize an account of my doings across the entire arc of my career? Just as Keegan looked at various accounts, I have various sources of information: records, official documents, paper and electronic files, notes, memos, and more, created for different purposes and at different times, that I compare to each other to draw detailed conclusions concerning activities about which the professoriate is notoriously vague—such as giving tests. For example, I have a copy of virtually every test that I ever gave in any class during my career at EIU. I must not get too far ahead of the story here, but in revisiting class notes, class logs that I kept, and tests from 1979, I was shocked to find some of the questions, prompts, and testing practices that I used before the end of time, compared with what was to follow. And that story is more nuanced that one might think: it was not simply a case of creating and administering difficult tests earlier in my career versus easy tests as my career ended. In the appendix, I have provided a more complete description of the materials that I have used for this purpose, a body of materials that I refer to as the corpus, and there I explain the uses of its various components in more detail.

Verbal Documentary

For the past couple of years, when I described this book to people who asked about it, I have used the term "verbal documentary" to encapsulate what I hope the above method will produce: a vivid, unrehearsed, detailed, and easily visualized depiction of my professional life and times. In this section, I explain my use of this term in a positive sense, clarifying what it means, but I also want to distinguish the verbal documentary format from other forms of reporting with which it might have some kinship.

First, the analogy with a documentary film is intentional: like a documentary film, what I have written about here is factual and can be verified. I have used the phrase "documenting my work" as a shorthand expression for this kind of writing. The expression is borrowed from the official contract language that the faculty members at my institution used to describe the process of building their retention and promotion portfolios. The idea is that the portfolio represents the applicant's claim for retention, tenure, or promotion, and the documentation is the evidence in support of the claim. There are a number of facts or claims that I could document, but the facts that I document in this book are the ones that will support the narrative about teaching or doing research that I wish to construct. Like a documentary film, (but not necessarily like the portfolios I built when I worked as a professor) my account documents events that were unstaged, at least as far as the book is concerned. That is, when I was a professor, one of my objectives was actually to teach students, not to gather material for a book about being a professor teaching students. However, the process of writing brings some order to these inherently unruly processes of teaching and doing research. Again, there is a similarity with the documentary film process here. Even documentary films are constructed and orderly in the sense that they are edited for coherence, clarity, and narrative cohesion. I have done that, too. And like a documentary film, the nature of this construction and editing process has occurred after the fact, sometimes long after the fact. In some cases, I have documented aspects of my teaching or research that occurred thirty-five years ago.

Most of the time, in a cinematic sense, the camera will stay focused on me: I intend to write about what I did or what happened to me. At times, I will deliberately shift the focus from activities to experiences—that is, what those events felt like. But I plan to hold such shifts to a minimum; I do not want my account to be overtly didactic. Perhaps the most important characteristic of a documentary is its ability to impart a reality that enables the viewer (in the case of film; here, the reader) to go beyond the facts and thus to know what it may have been like. When the documentary technique is successful, viewers (or readers) know what it was like without being told. Consistent with this idea of a camera focus, I do not intend to make comparisons to other professors I know or knew, or anybody else such, including members of the staff or administration. But I will have some things to say about those partners who were the yin to my yang professionally— that is, the students.

Memoir, Autobiography, Autoethnography

In *Palimpsest,* Gore Vidal (1995) writes about the first forty years of his life. In that work he provides a personal definition of the art of memoir and offers a distinction between it and another form of writing: "A memoir is how one remembers one's own life, while an autobiography is history, requiring research, dates, facts double-checked" (p. 5).

A Professor at the End of Time is neither a memoir nor an autobiography, although it has some similarities with both forms. For example, my book is not a memoir, in the sense that its wellspring is not my constructive memory of events in the experiential domain. Although I will rely on my memory at times, just as a memoirist would do, there are also thousands of printed and electronically saved documents that I will use to describe my job and analyze my work. In some cases I have found that those materials actually contradict my memory of events, and because the data cannot lie, what is written in those materials therefore supersedes my memories. Similarly, the book is not really about my experiences per se. But as I alluded to above, I intend to present the information in a way that I hope will enable readers to accurately reconstruct something about those experiences. The fact that the book is not a memoir also means that I will not have too much to say directly about either the faculty members or administrators with whom I worked, other than to admit that in general I loved the bonhomie and persiflage that came with being a professor. Readers looking for an account of all the other gears I meshed with, or those listening for the grinding noise of the gears I clashed with, might not see or hear that. But they will see and hear something about how many other gears I was engaged with, and therefore how many other moving pieces there were in the apparatus of higher education.

However, despite its emphasis on facts, *A Professor at the End of Time* is not an autobiography, either. That term implies that I intend to write about, and document, my entire life. But even though I have been freely using the terms "data," "verification," and "documentation," it is not really the details of my entire life that will be documented, and not even all the details of my professional life. The mere idea of a professional life implies that some sense making, and therefore some abstraction of the events involved, has already occurred. I want the account to be closer to the facts than that; I intend to document my professional activities themselves. At points where it seems that valid inferences about those activities can be drawn, I will do so in part 2.

Finally, *A Professor at the End of Time* cannot exactly be characterized as an autoethnography, although, once again, there are some points of contact. Autoethnography is a research technique in which one's personal experience is described and systematically analyzed as a way of approaching and understanding the experience of a culture (Ellis, Adams, & Bochner, 2011). This investigative method grew out of a dissatisfaction that emerged in the twentieth century when it became increasingly clear that the details, facts, and truths that were unearthed using more conventional techniques were nevertheless bound to the procedures and processes that were used to find them in the first place (Kuhn, 1996). This realization in turn led scholars to the stark impossibility of finding or even creating some overarching or universal narrative that was independent of its creators or of the time in which it was constructed (Rorty, 1982). Like an authethnographer, I recognize the impossibility of either discovering or otherwise creating a completely objective account of objects or events. I have to face, and write in, a reality in which I am culture-bound, cohort-bound, and finally time-bound. However, unlike an autoethnographer, my objective is not to capture my experiences, but rather my behavior and actions as they bore on the discharge of my responsibilities. And my behavior and doings are substantially more susceptible to the kind of empirical analysis to which I will subject them than my experiences are. Rather than pointing to the experience of a culture, I will use my analyses to understand how it was that not only my behavior, but also the behavior and practice of an entire cohort was eventually diminished and lost.

There is another, more positive, aspect to this inability to escape my own time: it means that there is a story right here, a narrative with a beginning, a middle, and an end. I also believe that it is a compelling story, one I am eager to share, about my time in a place called industrial-scale higher education, whose machinery and objectives changed dramatically and, I believe, permanently through the decades that I worked as a college professor.

PART 1

A PROFESSOR AT WORK

"They think how one life hums, revolves and toils,
One cog in a golden singing hive."

—Stephen Spender, "The Funeral"

"I make a living playing rock 'n' roll. I'm not going to complain about
anything."

—Taylor Hawkins

The British poet Stephen Spender was adept at creating subtle contrasts that illustrated the numerous paradoxes of modern life. Even in the brief snippet above, Spender creates an interesting juxtaposition of words associated with the impersonal and the mechanistic ("hums," "revolves," "cog") and the organic ("life," "toils," "hive"), as well as finding a counterpoise between the solitary ("one") with the numerous ("they," "hive"). I think both themes and their contrasts will be relevant in part 1 of this book. The following four chapters focus on my work as a member of the professoriate, and I use my voice to tell that story. But I will also gradually pull the lens back until that singular portrait becomes just a tiny portion of a larger mosaic in which the details of the business of higher education come into view, details to which I and all the members of my cohort were obliged to conform.

If Spender celebrates the bending of one life's needs to the requirements of the many, Taylor Hawkins, perhaps best known for his work as the drummer of the rock band Foo Fighters, celebrates the joy of getting to do as one wishes. And that quote is apt here, too. Like Hawkins, I feel privileged to do the work I did, to be a member of a very special workforce—one that enjoyed unusual perquisites and prerogatives. And perhaps because of all that, I too feel simple gratitude for the role that was mine to play in the professoriate, at the end of time.

2 · THE WORK OF THE TEACHING COLLEGE PROFESSOR
In (and out of) the Classroom

If we were to make a movie with a college professor as its lead, and the script involved filming a scene in which our protagonist arrives at a class and prepares to teach, what would the screenplay for such a scene look like? We can easily imagine the college students of traditional age seated in rows of desks in a classroom or, if the students are more numerous, seated in chairs in a theater-type room with an inclined floor. When the professor arrives (probably after most of the students), he or she might be carrying a large notebook of some sort, which is then laid flat on a table or lectern at the head of the classroom or theater and opened to a particular page. At the appointed time, the professor begins to speak. But what comes next? And to the considerable extent that whatever comes next represents *work* on the part of the professor, how did the professor conceptualize that work?

As clichéd and stereotyped as these elements of the imaginary screenplay are, there is also a kernel of truth to them. In this chapter, I discuss that reality as well as discussing "what comes next," at least as I carried out that role for the thirty-six years that I was in the business of educating college students. My objective is to provide the reader with a clear idea of the diversity and demands of the teaching work of the professoriate, at least to the extent that my behavior was typical, during the latter part of the twentieth century and in the beginning of the twenty-first. The overarching theme of this and the next chapter can be stated as follows: the members of the professoriate approached their work having built, during their own education, a cognitive framework or mental organization for teaching (I use the cognitive science term "schema" or "scheme"), which can also be characterized by its flexibility. In the next chapter, I will show that the increasing reliance on technology in teaching that occurred in the 1990s and beyond insidiously altered the teaching process of the professoriate, changing it from a service to a product. Along the way, the relationship or context in which its service was rendered—the professor-student relationship or alliance—was subverted, broken down, and gradually marginalized. That is not to imply that excellent college teaching is no longer occurring, or that it will no longer occur in the future. But I do want to strongly suggest that whatever form such teaching takes, it will be different from the form I used. Going forward, the professoriate will need to find its own voice once again, and that voice will be different from that of my cohort.

A discussion of college teaching at the beginning of the twenty-first century inevitably invites at least a mention of its now-paired term: learning. Indeed, as Mary Burgan (2006) has noted, "an insistence on this term [learning] is so obligatory as to have become politically correct in educational circles, where 'teaching' is seldom mentioned without being yoked to 'learning'" (p. 28). Although I agree that the two terms are now apparently permanently harnessed (as, frankly, I think they should be), nevertheless I will not have much to say in this chapter directly about learning. To a certain extent in higher education, the quantity and quality of the students' learning has become politicized or, to use an even stronger word, weaponized under the aegis of reform-minded policy makers and others who wish to use society's legitimate interest in accountability implied by the term "learning" to impose control over higher education's directions and practices. The fact that learning or other similar terms are considered as outcome measures that would ultimately be linked to funding decisions is evidence of this movement—an approach at change by those from without, rather than from within, higher education. To those who worked within higher education, as I did, learning means something else.

To paint the picture of my work as a teacher, I begin this chapter with a discussion of the underlying conceptual framework or model that I and many others, I believe, used as an effective schema for organizing our college teaching. I also explain the generality and flexibility that I think made this schema as useful as it was. I taught in a number of different physical settings, and the parameters of those physical settings imposed themselves on the teaching that occurred within them, sometimes positively, sometimes not. I have also tried to encompass the size and scope of my classroom teaching—what I taught, when, to whom, and to how many. Most of my classroom teaching took place during the long-established academic year (beginning in August or September and winding up in May or June). But I was an active classroom teacher in the summer months as well, and the range of my teaching portfolio shifted and took off in some surprising directions in the summer. Most of my teaching time was spent in the classroom or an organized lab setting. But one of the most striking aspects of my work as a college professor is the amount of time, and the number of different ways, that I engaged in teaching outside the classroom—and I discuss those settings and the range of teaching skills and attributes that they called for.

In addition to making a distinction between teaching and learning, I have also made a distinction between the work or labor of the professor and the technique that he or she may use to accomplish that work, and my focus will be on the work itself. There are many useful books that have been written to help new faculty members learn about teaching, or even how to teach in a college setting (to name just a few, Bain, 2004; Brookfield, 2006; Filene, 2005; Ramsden, 2003). I find just a bit of irony in the existence of such a plethora of books on that subject, given the name of the degree that most members of the professoriate hold: doctor of philosophy (PhD). The term "doctorate" is derived from the Latin verb *docere* (to teach), suggesting that doctoral degree holders do not need any tutelage in instruction. But the reality is that most recently minted PhDs are far more proficient, and probably more comfortable as well, in their role as researchers and scholars rather than in their teaching role. Most professors are expected to simply find their way as teachers; certainly I did plenty of that and found myself lost on many occasions.

A COGNITIVE SCHEMA FOR COLLEGE TEACHING

In this section, I suggest that the baby boomer professors who arrived for a college class ready to teach at the end of the golden age (circa 1980) and beyond did so with a particular cognitive framework, or schema, that they had built for that purpose, one that they had themselves learned from their professors although it was seldom explicitly taught. I have chosen to refer to it as the compression-expansion model, because in the process of transmitting it, the professor's knowledge undergoes a series of diminishing and augmenting transformations. This schema begins with a proposition that the mind of a professor is enlarged with the specialized and technical knowledge that he or she acquired as both an undergraduate and a graduate student. And the professor expands and builds on this knowledge base to an increasing extent across the course of his or her professional career. Let me illustrate this with just a couple of examples. Right now, if I were asked to write essays in response to two academic test questions, one asking me to detail the political landscape of England in the 1640s, and the other asking me to explain the process by which leukocytes arrive at an infected site, I might write a passable answer to the first question, and I would certainly fail the second one. I acknowledge the risk that I am being too obvious here, but we all know that the hypothetical professors who might have posed these questions could talk all day long about those subjects. For the professor in any course, then, one task consists of imparting the relevant contents. Given their vastness, to transfer them completely is probably impossible within the constraints of a typical college course, although there are some professors who try nonetheless. To accomplish this export process, the professor first creates a vehicle that might be referred to in a number of ways—notes, outlines, exercises, and so on—each of which refers to an encapsulation of some of the professor's knowledge. The creation of this vehicle is a process in reduction, and it therefore represents the first compression in the compression-expansion model. In the classroom or lab, the professor uses this reduction and—through a process that might involve oral or visual presentation, explanation, discussion, responding to questions, or working through examples—expands and inflates the original material back out to something like its original size, or into an object that more closely approximates the size of the original in the professor's mind. The professor's exposition therefore becomes the first expansion in the model. Meanwhile, the students have likewise been busy: while the professor is engaged in the process of expanding, the students (theoretically) are creating a product all their own. By applying their own cognition to the professor's work, and by representing this real-time cognitive activity in a physical form, perhaps by creating written notation, the students create their own reduced-size copy of the professor's activity. This note taking becomes the second compression of the contents of the professor's mind. Finally, the students use the representation they have created—that is, the notes they have produced in class—along with other materials that have been provided and, through a process of study, create a durable and expanded representation in their own minds. Figure 2.1 shows this process in a schematic form. Each cognitive or physical object is shown in a larger or smaller box as it is compressed (using the greater than symbol to show that the material is moving from a larger space to a smaller one) or expanded (using the less than symbol to show that the material is moving from a smaller space to a larger one).

When this schema is executed over and over again across all the sessions of the course and replicated in the many other courses that the student completes over the arc of the college career, the result is the college-educated person. There are numerous ways to define this person. I suggest there are two critical components. First, the educated person is one whose mind has been enlarged and therefore furnished with the materials that he or she has studied. The person has represented a number of cognitive objects in the form of integrated knowledge, and that knowledge may make the learning and incorporation of future knowledge somewhat easier. For example, knowing some aspects of the political landscape of England in the 1640s that led to the emergence of a right-wing dictator's rule may help me understand some of the dynamics in the otherwise

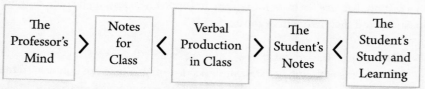

FIGURE 2.1. Basic Compression-Expansion Model

bewildering political landscape of post–World War I Italy, as it is depicted in the biography of Benito Mussolini that I happen to be reading. The second component is somewhat more subtle, and I gave a hint of it in the example I offered. It is important to note that the use of the compression-expansion schema does not imply a passive process, such as simply transferring a file that is intact and complete between two computers. In and out of class, both the professor and the student are engaged in an active and dynamic exchange involving sustained cognition to make the compression-expansion model work successfully.[1] Thus, not only does the educated person become an individual who knows things, but he or she is also a person who knows how to apply cognition to make that knowledge a reality. That is, the educated person becomes a problem solver, an individual who can apply learning schemas in new situations to attack and reduce problems and thus find answers.

However, it is plausible to argue that in some worst-case scenarios, which may have been more likely to exist before the end of time than after it, the compression-expansion schema may have been used by professors in a format that implied more passivity than I am suggesting here. Such a passive format may have emphasized the students' roles as receivers of knowledge, and it may have relied on some easy metrics to see if the appropriate quantity of knowledge had been thus moved from professor to student in the form of tests that measured merely the retention of relatively isolated facts, tests based on the verbatim regurgitation of information. As I have described the process here, college courses with those qualities would represent a corruption of the compression-expansion schema.

THE PHYSICAL LOCATIONS OF MY COLLEGE TEACHING

I have described the cognitive model that professors might have and use for their teaching. But where is this model implemented? Before discussing the details of what I taught at the two institutions for which I worked, the details of the physical locations in which teaching took place deserve some mention. I taught in a number of different environments, some of which were considered to be state-of-the-art at the time I taught in them, and some of which created teaching challenges all their own. I was not alone in finding myself assigned to teach a course in a setting that was far from ideal. Burgan (2006) has described some of these locations and their issues in exquisite detail:

> Most regular classrooms these days are spare, fluorescent-lit boxes with industrial-strength, tubular student desks that may or may not conform to the student body. And even relatively modern classrooms are likely to have a ratty old instructor's desk—its lectern missing or stolen for use in another classroom. There are also green chalkboards in various shades of dust, a pull-down screen for slides or other media. . . . Some classrooms even exhibit the failed technologies of yesteryear: the dangling brackets for TV monitors, the grimy carts for overhead projectors, the empty sockets and tattered speakers for defunct sound systems. (p. 29)

I can attest to all of that, even to the extent of sometimes chasing down the grimy cart with the overhead projector that had been borrowed by another professor teaching in another classroom because, grimy though it may have been, I still had my favorites among the overhead projector carts. But not all of the classrooms I used were like that. Before I became a professor I taught as a graduate student in some wonderful facilities, including Zimmer Hall at the University of Cincinnati. At that time, the room, whose capacity was perhaps 1,000 students, was equipped with three large back-projected screens and a rock-concert-level public address system. There was a technician on duty for my Introductory Psychology class (for those wondering about the circumstances of all this: in my final year in graduate school, as my assignment for my teaching assistantship, I filled in for my professor and mentor, who was on sabbatical). When I arrived backstage for class (and it was a stage at least thirty feet across), I handed the technician the carousel of slides that I would be using for class that day. All I had to do was press a button on the lectern to advance them. I did not realize at the time that I would never again teach in a facility that well equipped or that well supported.

As I stated in chapter 1, I spend the majority of my career teaching psychological and cognitive science in the Psychology Department at Eastern Illinois University. The Psychology Department at Eastern occupied approximately 12,000 square feet in a structure named the Physical Sciences Building, whose capacity was approximately 70,000 square feet. As suggested by the building's name, it was common knowledge on campus that psychology's inclusion in the building had been an afterthought. The classrooms, even the new ones in the wings, had obviously been designed for the teaching of natural science courses: each room was equipped with a solid, massive, demonstration bench whose dimensions of ten feet by four feet (and probably about four feet high!) dwarfed the student desks. The bench was furnished with active gas and oxygen jets, a built-in vacuum, a deep sink, and hot and cold running water piped in through high-topped chromium faucets. Some of my colleagues found ways to subtly protest their teaching environment by pretending to wonder in class if the lab equipment was really still functional, then twisting a knob or handle and apparently discovering that in fact it was. Occasionally a faculty member might find a more creative way to spoof the room's facilities, as was the case with one colleague who hopped up on the bench, took off his shoes, and washed his feet in the sink.[2] Although the bench created a barrier that might have hindered some professors' teaching styles (standing behind it, the professor was remote; in front of it, too immediate), at least it did not create physical discomfort for the students.

Our only dedicated lecture hall was located on one of the oldest corridors in the building. The student seating arrangement consisted of rows of unpadded wooden seats and seatbacks, each of which was supported by an elaborate wrought-iron frame bolted to the floor and attached to its neighbor. The amount of space allocated to the seat's occupant, both in terms of width and pitch (the distance between the seat back and its counterpart in the rows ahead and behind) was much less than that of a typical airplane seat in economy class on a domestic flight. If the prospect of teaching in these kinds of environments sounds demoralizing, or if reporting these conditions sounds disparaging, I can also attest that most of us found ways to become great teachers despite the challenges offered by the environment.

TEACHING AT INDIANA UNIVERSITY

Although most of my comments and analysis in this chapter focus on my time as a professor at Eastern Illinois University, I also have some comments about my work at the beginning of my career. In my first job as a professor, I taught psychology as a contingent faculty member at Indiana University–Bloomington (IU) from 1977 to 1979. Most of my writing about my time at IU has been drawn from my memory—my record keeping in those days was not nearly as comprehensive as it was to become in the next phase of my career.

What Did I Teach There?

In common with a number of other flagship campuses of public universities in that time period, the Psychology Department at IU had a cadre of perhaps six or eight faculty members who staffed the Introductory Psychology course, thus freeing up its tenured or tenure-track faculty members to teach more advanced undergraduate and graduate courses. It was a symbiotic relationship for the contingent faculty and the department. At that time, I enjoyed teaching Introductory Psychology, and I was able to get some valuable teaching experience in larger classes. And our presence enabled the department's permanent faculty members to spend their time on the more advanced classes. The typical Introductory

Psychology class size of 250 students did not scare me; I had taught a couple of Intro Psych classes as a graduate student in which the class size was 600 or 800 students (in the aforementioned Zimmer Hall). At that point in my career, I also did not mind teaching the same course over and over again; once I had the content of the course mastered, I was able to devote more time and effort to learning what it was that made some presentations seemingly more effective than others.

Almost all of my Intro Psych teaching at IU took place in a large auditorium or lecture hall. As I recall from the looks of it, the auditorium had been designed in the 1950s—that is, it was not terribly old at the time I taught there. As would be the case at Eastern, the students sat in rows of attached chairs, each of which had a small writing table that folded out from a space between the seats. As I remember it, each row consisted of approximately fifteen seats, and there were perhaps fifteen or more rows in the room. The room itself may have been forty feet wide by sixty-five feet deep. It was equipped with a microphone, which was necessary from a practical perspective. There was also a large chalkboard and a motorized movie screen.

High and Low Technology before the End of Time

As implied by the previous comment, prior to the existence of the World Wide Web and its relevant content that could be projected onto a classroom's screens, one of the main ways that professors had of bringing the outside world into the classroom consisted of showing films. Classrooms varied quite a bit in their adaptability for showing films. When I taught as a graduate student in Zimmer Hall, the technician on duty handled the details of getting the film ready to go. At a prearranged cue from me, the film would magically begin rolling on one of the overhead screens. At Indiana, things were a little different. There was no projection system permanently installed in the room. As a professor, I was permitted and authorized to check out a film projector and a film from the library. Or it may have been the case that the department owned one or two projectors. In either case, after lugging the 16-millimeter projector into class and balancing it one of the student chairs six or seven rows back from the screen (there was no stand installed for the projector), the professor was responsible for threading the film. Despite the apparently simple threading instructions printed directly on the projector, I was not very skillful at snaking the film leader through the complicated sprocket system, nor did I improve much over time. But my big problem stemmed from how I used the film itself. I was not the kind of professor who let a film roll on for its full length, which might be thirty minutes or more. My much preferred method was to interrupt the film several times to expand or elaborate on points that I did not think had been made in sufficient detail, or to connect a point that the film was making with another that we had already discussed in class. But using the film that way created at least two kinds of difficulties for me.

First, I needed to learn the skills of a contortionist, because the microphone cord was just barely long to reach from the stage back to the projector. It was possible for me to lean out over the projector, stopping it with one hand while I held the microphone in the other, and address my students from the middle of one of the rows of chairs. Or I could put the microphone down, stop the film on a particular frame, return to the stage, and teach from there. But that involved correctly stopping the projector, which was my second problem. Stopping the projector on a particular frame for anything more than a few seconds required throwing a certain lever on the projector that lowered an opaque shield in front of the film, darkening the frame and—crucially for the integrity of the film—reducing the heat from the projector's bulb. On a few occasions, I threw the wrong lever on the projector and, in the middle of my gesturing at the screen, found myself helplessly watching as the projector bulb visibly and audibly burned a hole in the celluloid, much to the shrieking delight of my students. After making this mistake several times (which was easily discernible to the library personnel, in light of the fact that I was returning the film in pieces), I was no longer permitted to operate the projector without supervision from the library staff. But if I was less than competent in the use of the so-called high-technology teaching demonstration tool of its day (showing films in class), I became proficient in another form of demonstration—the low-tech one: using the chalkboard.

It might be hard for readers twenty-first century and beyond to imagine illustrating a point to an audience by drawing it on a chalkboard, but this is what I and other professors typically did in the 1970s. And I learned there was a subtle and valuable art in using the chalkboard effectively. Primitive though the diagrams may have been, the fact that their pieces and labels were often created sequentially, in real time—thus layering the diagram with shades of meaning— had several positive effects. First, the students usually endeavored to re-create the diagram in their note taking. And the act of doing so meant that the students engaged in a creative cognitive process all their own. Sometimes during a visit with a student during office hours, it was fun (and illuminating) to see how the student's version of the diagram I had drawn was similar to or different from the one I had created. The importance of producing a diagram that could be duplicated by the students should not be underestimated. I recall a conversation I had sometime in the early 1980s, when I was a junior faculty member, with a much more senior colleague about using the chalkboard. Somewhere, somehow, I had scrounged up a set of colored chalks, and I was raving about their diagrammatic possibilities. But my older colleague demurred. On what basis, I asked? It was the fact that, using only ink, the students could not readily duplicate the chalk colors—a point I had not thought about. In a very subtle, nonobvious way, my senior colleague's unwillingness to use colored chalk implies something about the power of the compression-expansion model: if it was to work properly, apparently a good level of fidelity was required between the material that appeared on the chalkboard and the notes that the student took. After this revelation, I decreased my use of the colored chalks (although I kept the set until I retired).

There were some other disadvantages in using the chalkboard, too. For example, to get the interactive effect I just alluded to, the diagram that I drew in a 9:00 A.M. class had to be erased at 9:50 when the class concluded, and then redrawn in the 10:00 A.M. class. If the diagram was complicated, this was definitely an extra bit of work. But even this disadvantage created teaching possibilities. Redrawing the diagram showed the students in the 10:00 section that I was working in the here and now to reach them rather than relying on something I had already created, which, from their perspective, had been done for someone else. Thus re-creating the diagram accomplished at least two things for me as a professor. First, it showed the compression-expansion model in action: the diagram was a compression of some knowledge that I possessed that I was then expanding in an active way in the classroom. Second, the fact that the students could validly infer I was creating something explicitly just for them was an important element in fostering the professor-student alliance that I was seeking to establish.

TEACHING AT EASTERN ILLINOIS UNIVERSITY

The Credit Unit Calculation

Before I can discuss the number of courses that I taught and their nature, there is some context that is important. As I explained in chapter 1, the faculty at Eastern was unionized, and we worked under the terms of a collective bargaining agreement. Because the collective bargaining agreement stipulated everything about our teaching assignments and working conditions as professors, and because our union agents had negotiated our payment for all the aspects of our work for the university, it was necessary for all of our academic work to be quantified. This quantification was expressed on each faculty member's Assignment of Duties (AOD) form (which we knew informally as our workload document). All of our teaching responsibilities, in their sundry forms, were considered primary duties, so those assignments always appeared on our AODs. At the most basic level of the contract, teaching a typical three-credit course—that is, a course that met three times per week for a total of three hours—earned for the faculty member three credit units (CUs). The department chairperson had the authority to assign up to twenty-four CUs across the academic year, thus making it equivalent, again, at a very basic level, to the classic "four and four" teaching load (that is, four courses in each of the two semesters making up the academic year) that many or most members of the professoriate had in the industrial-scale schools, and that was considered to be the maximum that a member of the professoriate could effectively handle.

Although the local administrator (the department chairperson) might have some fixed ideas about what courses each faculty member would teach, the CU system nevertheless allowed for a great deal of flexibility in just how a faculty member might discharge his or her primary responsibilities. And this flexibility created opportunities for faculty members to strategize about their workload—that is, to think in terms of what they wanted to minimize or maximize. For those who abhorred teaching large classes, it was possible to avoid teaching them, although doing so might involve teaching a greater number of smaller classes and thus increasing the number of student contact hours during the week. In contrast, a professor who wanted to minimize contact hours during the week might do so by offering to teach large sections of the same course.

I was a rather slow learner when it came to deciphering all this, and that had some implications for me, especially in the early and middle segments of my career. When that fact is coupled with my desire to please (or maybe it was my fear of angering someone), it becomes somewhat more understandable why I typically said yes to every teaching suggestion the department chairperson made. As a result, it was not until relatively late in my career that I had established something like a teaching program—an array of courses that were related to each other in content, format, and style and that, therefore, might be expected to have a cumulative effect on students who stayed with me to complete all of them. My apparent inability to formulate anything like a teaching program meant that I ended up teaching a number of different courses, sometimes only once or twice, which in turn meant that my teaching efforts were somewhat dissipated across our entire curriculum.

Classroom Teaching: How Many Courses? How Many Students?

Face-to-face teaching in a classroom or lab, at regularly scheduled class times, was the main, but not the sole, delivery model I used during my thirty-six years as a professor. In the 1980s, I taught two courses whose content was delivered primarily by prerecorded, professionally produced TV programs. But even those two courses were hybrids, or mixed models of delivery. Although most of the content in those courses was delivered via prerecorded TV programs, there was also a regularly scheduled face-to-face meeting of several hours each month, for discussion and questions. For the members of the professoriate who were in my cohort at my institution, this pattern was typical. Most of the permanent, veteran faculty members in my department had not taught an online course, even though, by the time of my retirement, our department was among the most active in my institution in offering online courses. The resolution of this apparent paradox is contained in the words "permanent" and "veteran." Most of the online courses were taught by members of the contingent faculty, sometimes by that species of faculty person who is among the most mysterious of all faculty members—namely the part-time, contingent faculty member who works from his or her home.

To analyze my teaching effort across the arc of my career, I gathered information from the corpus, including the printed newspapers in which the course offerings were published each semester until 2007; the Assignment of Duty forms; and the teaching files that I created each semester for my courses, which housed the syllabi, tests, handouts, and other information for each course that I taught. I also gathered other relevant information from the paper and electronic files, including information about supervision of student research and other content-based individualized teaching that I did. From these sources, I created a spreadsheet showing the names of the courses that I taught, when I taught them, how many students were enrolled, and the grade-point average (GPA) that the class earned, taken as a whole. This spreadsheet also shows the names of the students whose research projects or internship experiences I supervised. The total number of students thus taught is 6,029. Turning from student numbers to courses, the spreadsheet shows that in the thirty-four years that I worked at Eastern, I taught a total of 191 classes, which includes 28 classes that I taught over the summer and 5 special theme workshops, each of which was the result of a competitive teaching opportunity. The total of 191 does not include course titles that we used for research supervision purposes, or course titles that signified student professional development, such as internship supervision. I have analyzed the summer teaching and the research supervision in separate sections. Subtracting the 28 regularly scheduled classes taught in the summer and the 5 special theme workshops leaves 158 regularly scheduled classes that I taught during the academic year.

To illustrate the pattern of my teaching during the academic year, I derived a reduced version of the spreadsheet from my initial one, which appears below as table 2.1. Table 2.1 shows the particular name of the course that I taught (for example, "Cognitive Psychology"—I will explain the course content for some of these names as I work through the table), and the semester that I taught it. Thus, the column labeled "F81" shows that I had four classes assigned to me in the fall 1981 semester: Cognitive Psychology, Introductory Psychology 1, and Introductory Psychology 2 (which I taught twice that semester). EIU was not alone in dividing the Introductory Psychology course into two different content domains at that time—both the University of Cincinnati and Indiana University had similar setups. In my first seven years at EIU (academic years 1979–80 through 1985–86) I taught some version of Introductory Psychology twenty-five, which constituted 56 percent of my teaching effort by class, since I taught forty-five classes in all during that time period. Although psychologists of any

TABLE 2.1. Courses Taught, by Fall (F) and Spring (S) Semesters

Course #	2310	2320	2390	2610	3620	3680
Name	Intro. Psych 1	Intro. Psych 2	Intro. Psych (Honors)	Statistics	Psychology of Learning	Sensation and Perception
Year						
79	3 Fall	1 Fall				
80		3 Fall			2 Spring	
81	1 Fall	1 Spring, 2 Fall				
82	1 Fall	1 Fall			2 Spring	
83	1 Spring, 1 Fall	2 Spring, 1 Fall			1 Spring	
84	1 Fall	2 Spring	1 Fall		1 Spring	
85	1 Spring		1 Fall		1 Spring	
86		1 Spring	1 Fall		1 Spring	
87			1 Fall		1 Spring	
88			1 Fall			
89	1 Fall		1 Fall			
90	1 Fall		1 Fall			
91	Sab. Fall					
92	Sab. Spring					1 Fall
93						1 Fall
94						1 Fall
95						1 Fall
96						1 Fall
97	Ch. Fall					
98	Ch. Spring					1 Fall
99				1 Fall		
00				1 Fall		
01				1 Fall		
02				1 Fall		
03				1 Fall		
04				1 Fall		
05				1 Fall		
06				1 Fall		
07				1 Fall		
08				1 Fall		
09				1 Fall		
10				1 Fall		
11				1 Fall		
12				1 Fall		
13						
Total	11	14	7	14	9	6

TABLE 2.1.   Courses Taught, by Fall (F) and Spring (S) Semesters (*continued*)

Course #	3805	3810	3820	3820	3830	4250
Name	Research Methods	Exp. Psych: Learning	Exp. Psych: Perception	Cognitive Neuroscience	Cognitive Psych.	History and Systems
Year						
79						
80		1 Spring				
81		1 Spring			1 Fall	
82					1 Fall	
83					1 Fall	
84					1 Fall	
85					1 Fall	1 Fall
86			1 Fall		1 Fall	1 Fall
87			1 Spring		1 Fall	1 Fall
88			1 Spring		1 Fall	1 Fall
89					1 Fall	
90					1 Fall	
91						
92					1 Fall	
93					1 Spring, 1 Fall	
94					1 Spring, 1 Fall	
95					1 Spring, 1 Fall	
96		1 Spring			1 Spring, 1 Fall	
97					1 Spring, 1 Fall	
98					1 Spring, 1 Fall	
99					1 Spring, 1 Fall	
00					2 Spring, 1 Fall	
01					2 Spring, 1 Fall	
02	1 Spring				1 Spring, 1 Fall	
03	1 Spring				1 Fall	
04	1 Spring				1 Fall	
05	1 Spring				1 Fall	
06	1 Spring				1 Fall	
07	1 Spring					
08	1 Spring					
09	1 Spring					
10	1 Spring			1 Fall		
11				1 Fall		
12				1 Fall		
13						
Total	9	3	3	3	37	4

TABLE 2.1. Courses Taught, by Fall (F) and Spring (S) Semesters (*continued*)

Course #	4590	4610	4666	4820	5170	5610
Name	Psychology Seminar	Advanced Statistics	Honors Seminar	Psycho-linguistics	Theory of Learning (Grad)	Research Methods (Grad)
Year						
79						
80						1 Fall
81				1 Spring		
82				1 Spring		
83						
84						
85						
86			1 Spring			
87						
88			1 Spring	1 Spring, 1 Fall		
89			1 Spring	1 Fall		
90			1 Spring			
91			1 Spring	1 Spring		
92						
93			1 Spring		1 Spring	
94			1 Spring		1 Spring	
95			1 Spring		1 Fall	
96			1 Spring			
97	1 Spring	1 Spring	1 Spring			
98						
99	1 Spring		1 Spring			
00		1 Spring				
01		1 Spring				
02			1 Spring			
03			1 Spring			
04			1 Spring			
05			1 Spring			
06			1 Spring			
07			1 Spring			
08			1 Spring			
09			1 Spring			
10			1 Spring			
11			1 Spring			
12			1 Spring			
13			1 Spring			
Total	2	3	23	4	5	1

academic specialty or subdiscipline were regarded as equally qualified to teach Introductory Psychology, those whose PhDs were in experimental psychology, as mine was, were often the real workhorses of Introductory Psychology teaching.

I was on sabbatical in academic year 1991–92, and I taught no classes that year (although I did teach in the summer sessions immediately before and after my sabbatical). Moreover, I served as the acting chairperson of the Psychology Department in academic year 1997–98, and I taught only two classes that academic year. To get a measure of how many regularly scheduled classes I taught during the typical academic year, I subtracted those classes and years from my total. In the remaining thirty-two years that I worked as a full-time faculty member at EIU, I taught 156 classes, for an average of 4.88 courses per year—a teaching load that, on the face of it, might not appear to be particularly heavy. However, there is some context that could modify that interpretation somewhat. First, several of the courses that I taught had laboratory components, which increased the number of contact hours and amount of preparation time, compared to those of a purely lecture course. Second, especially toward the end of my career, I took on administrative assignments that became part of my primary duties and thus took the place of classes that I otherwise would have taught. By the end of my career, these administrative assignments accounted for nine CUs per academic year, or the equivalent of three classes. When those are added to the classroom teaching, my teaching load approaches the equivalent of eight classes per academic year, a figure that that is recognized as something like the standard load at a teaching institution.

The administration at my institution made a strenuous effort to keep class sizes low, and I was certainly among the beneficiaries of that effort. Because Introductory Psychology was counted as fulfilling a general education requirement at my institution, as it does at many institutions, class sizes there tended to be higher than they were in the courses that were intended for psychology majors. However, during my entire career at EIU, I taught only six Introductory Psychology classes that had 90 or more students enrolled. Overall, the 5,252 students I taught in the 158 regularly scheduled classes during the academic year averages out to 33.24 students per class. The standard deviation of the class size was 23.67, which expresses the fact that there was a great deal of variability in the size of my classes. The largest class I taught was Introductory Psychology in the fall 1989 semester, with 113 students; the smallest was an Honors Seminar in the spring 1987 semester, for which only 3 students were enrolled!

Looking at table 2.1, I think the figure that will stand out the most for readers who are insiders in higher education is the overall number of different courses that I taught. During the time that I was a professor at EIU, the Psychology Department maintained approximately thirty to thirty-five regularly scheduled courses in its undergraduate curriculum (not counting courses that were designed as individualized research or internship supervision courses). The sixteen different undergraduate courses that I taught during my career therefore represent approximately 50 percent of all the regularly scheduled courses in the department's undergraduate curriculum. Dividing the 158 classes that were assigned to me by eighteen (the sixteen undergraduate courses plus the two graduate courses that I taught) shows that, on the average, I offered each semester-based course 8.78 times. Given that my career at Eastern spanned seventy-two semesters, the fact that I taught each of my courses fewer than nine times on average suggests that I was probably teaching too many different courses, too few times. For example, although it is true that I taught Cognitive Psychology thirty-seven times, Honors Seminar twenty-three times, and Statistics fourteen times, table 2.1 also shows that I taught ten different courses no more than nine times each during my career at Eastern.

To get a somewhat different perspective on this, I computed a transition number for each academic year at Eastern by noting two kinds of differences in my course offerings compared to the previous academic year. I counted each course in the current year that I had not taught in the previous academic year as an "addition," and I counted each course that I had offered the previous year but was not offering in the current year as a "deletion."[3] For example, in academic year 1981–82, I taught three courses, Introductory Psychology 1, Psychology of Learning, and Cognitive Psychology, that I had not taught in the previous academic year (1980–81), which I counted as three additions. I did not teach the graduate Research Methods course that I had taught in the previous year, and I counted that as one deletion. I carried out this computation for each of the academic years that I worked at EIU. Then I added up the number of transitions, both additions and deletions. Across the span of my time at EIU, there were twenty-nine times (that is, on average almost one per year) when, at some point in the academic year, I taught a course that I had not in the previous year. Similarly, there were twenty-seven times when I had dropped a previously taught course, at least for one academic year. Adding the kinds of transitions together for a total of fifty-six and dividing that by the 158 classes assigned to me shows that 35 percent of my courses changed on a yearly basis. That fact may have had some positive consequences for me, but it certainly had some negative ones.

What conclusions might be drawn from this analysis of the courses that I taught and their number, frequency, and size? First, although I did not necessarily have a huge number of classes assigned to me, nevertheless the CU system ensured that the overall contribution of each member of the professoriate at my institution remained close to the "four and four" teaching load that characterizes the work at many or most industrial-scale schools. Second, my average class size, although substantially higher than the average class size appearing on my institution's website, was still much, much lower than the average class size of the research-based schools in the elite system. I am sure that the members of the professoriate at those schools expect their typical undergraduate classes to be several times larger than the average of such class I taught. But if not number or size, what then was the main source of the weight in my teaching load? Probably it was a feature of my teaching that was under my control to a certain extent, although I did little or nothing to control it until the end of my career: the year-to-year variability in my teaching schedule. That was a problem because the preparation involved in teaching a college class is probably the most time-absorbing activity for the professoriate, and thus the time invested in such preparation almost invariably must be drawn from time that would otherwise be spent on different valuable activities. As I show in chapter 4, although I probably became a better, more complete professor with my willingness to take on and give up most of the courses in which I had invested myself, I definitely created difficulties for myself in developing or even sustaining my research program.

CLASSROOM TEACHING IN THE SUMMER

There might still be quite a few people who believe that college professors, like elementary or secondary school teachers, enjoy a summer vacation of several months' duration. But in reality most public universities offer extensive summer course programming, and the institution's permanent faculty members usually are the first ones who are offered the opportunity to staff such courses—at a salary that may vary quite a bit from the one earned during the academic year. I certainly availed myself of the opportunities I was given. Technically, I was eligible to teach at least one regularly scheduled course in each of the thirty-four summers that I was employed at Eastern, beginning in 1980 and ending in 2013. But when I became the assistant chairperson of the department in 2010, a position that extended my contract basis from nine to ten months, I no longer made myself available to teach, tending to the assistant chairperson duties exclusively during the summer months. Of the remaining thirty summers, I taught at least one of our regularly scheduled face-to-face courses twenty-eight times, earning at least one full month's pay in every case except one.

The Number of Students and the Number of Classes

In those twenty-eight summers that I taught one of the regularly scheduled courses in our curriculum, I had 567 students enrolled, which averages out to be approximately 20 students per class—substantially smaller than the size of my classes during the academic year. The same sort of scattershot pattern of courses offered that I observed in my academic year teaching was replicated, even more viciously in the summer. From the summer of 1996 until the summer of 2009 (which was the last summer in which I taught a course), I had begun to get some control over my course offerings, teaching just one of two course titles (either Psychology of Learning or Cognitive Psychology) for eleven of those thirteen summers. But before then, my summer teaching efforts were all over the map. From the summer of 1980 until the summer of 1995, of the fifteen times that I taught a regularly schedule course in the summer, I taught six different courses, usually teaching each course just two or three times.

Even though the pay for summer teaching was generous at my institution, and the class sizes were smaller than I taught during the academic year, it may have been a mistake for me to teach as much as I did. First, I committed the same error in the summer that I did during the academic year: I did not exercise, nor did I even attempt to exercise, much control over which course I would be teaching, especially in the early and middle parts of my career. Though I taught a wide variety of courses during the academic year as well, at least most of them were courses for which my graduate school training had directly prepared me. During the summer, I taught at least two courses (Child Psychology and Theories of Personality) that I had never taught during the academic year, and for which I had only a minimal academic background. Second, even with all the relentless detail about the numbers of students involved, I may have failed to communicate one very important fact: college teaching is an exhausting profession, and as I aged, the summer months became increasingly important as a time for me to renew myself to meet the demands of the upcoming academic year.

TEACHING OUT OF THE CLASSROOM

Classroom teaching, with or without a laboratory component, was certainly the most prevalent form of teaching that I did, at least in terms of the numbers of students whom I served. For most of those classes, the format of the class would probably be described as a lecture, even though that term is a misnomer for the interactive, multimedia presentations that most members of the professoriate led in classrooms by the end of time.[4] But even this degree of prevalence is a bit of an illusion about college-level teaching. By the end of time, the members of the professoriate were called on to teach in a number of settings, many of them outside the typical classroom and with each setting requiring its own set of skills or talents. This is not to suggest that classroom teaching was the merely tip of the iceberg or to imply that I did more teaching out of the classroom than in it, but a good deal of my work involved a number of forms of teaching outside the classroom, whose format and activities I describe next.

Teaching Content out of the Class

Sometimes the out-of-class teaching involved duplicating the content of a regularly scheduled course but with many fewer students—generally only one. There were a number of reasons for doing this: for example, students may have documented a particular kind of hardship, financial or otherwise, that had delayed their graduation. If they needed only one regularly scheduled course to graduate, and that course was not being offered in the current term, then the department chairperson might try to make an arrangement with a faculty member who usually taught the course. That is just one of the numerous scenarios that could arise. Our department (like every department at my institution) had a recognized Independent Study course that could be used as a template course for almost any academic purpose. Generally, the procedure for using the Independent Study course involved a meeting or conversation between the student and the professor to set up the terms of the Independent Study. The result of the meeting was a contract signed by the student, faculty member, and department chairperson stipulating what academic assignments the student would undertake to receive the right amount of academic credit. On completion of the agreed-on academic work, the student filled out a waiver form to have the Independent Study count with the registrar for whatever the original unavailable course had been. The waiver form was processed through people at several levels, including the college dean, and required a signature at each level. Writing the process out in detail like this might create the impression that Independent Study was a rather a complex work-around. In practice, the whole process went smoothly enough, although it required a significant amount of effort on the part of the professor to plan the instruction for and keep track of his or her Independent Study student. The fact that we were willing to engage in this kind of work is a testimony to how important we felt it was to make accommodations for students who were close to graduating.

Remote, Individualized, Content Teaching

The type of individualized, course-content teaching that I described above could be delivered in either of two formats: it could be accomplished remotely (in which case, the content turned into something very similar to a classic correspondence course) or in a face-to-face setting. Looking at the corpus shows that there were two instances, once time in the early 2000s and once later in that decade, when I reworked the content of one my regularly scheduled courses into the remote-learning—or, as it was often called, distance-learning—format for an individual student. There are two points to make regarding this kind of teaching. First, having converted my existing course materials from their face-to-face format into something each student could use on his or her own, I think it is plausible to say that I could have gone on to offer each of those courses on a more regular basis online had I chosen to do so. But because I did not do that, the amount of time involved in creating equivalent materials that could be used by the student as the basis of an authentic and meaningful learning experience was probably not accurately represented by the CUs that appeared on my workload document for having taught the course the way that I did. That amount was 0.3 CU. Second, because I never met either student personally, forming the teacher-student relationship was more challenging than it would have been in a face-to-face class. At least, I found it to be a challenge. People who regularly taught in the online environment may have developed particular techniques that were useful for building that relationship, or, as I suspect was often more likely to be true, the professor simply abandoned many aspects of the teacher-student relationship.

Face-to-Face Content Teaching out of the Classroom
For the same reasons I outlined above, sometimes there was a need to offer a reg-ularly scheduled, but not currently offered, course to an individual student who was present on campus. Another look at the original spreadsheet of my teaching activities shows that there were two instances, once time in the mid-1980s and once in the late 1990s, when I taught one of my regularly offered courses to a sin-gle student, who met with me in my office for that purpose. The academic credit was transmitted using the same Independent Study mechanism we used for the remote teaching. Although the data set of these instances is too small for me to be able to draw any conclusion with authority, the timing of these two instances in comparison with the timing of the two that I taught remotely suggests to me that, as time went on, we became more likely to use our more advanced tech-nology to teach content-related courses outside of the regularly scheduled class. This phenomenon seems to be part of a more general pattern that I observed—namely, that students enjoyed the flexibility in their own schedules created by online teaching and hence may have been somewhat reluctant to appear in per-son for a class, once it was possible to get the same credit for an online course.

EMPIRICAL RESEARCH SUPERVISION

One of the tremendous changes in higher education that occurred in the waning decades of the twentieth century was the increasing inclusion of undergraduates in the production of empirical research at nonelite schools. Graduate education in the social, cognitive, and natural sciences had always been marked by a defi-nite research component, and this emphasis was undiminished by the inclusion of the undergraduates. The picture thus being sketched shows the professoriate learning how to adapt its research supervisory skills to a new and somewhat less sophisticated (although no less eager) audience of undergraduates. As the fore-going suggests, in contrast to the other forms of nonclassroom teaching that I have described, the supervision of empirical research, both graduate and undergraduate, was a much more consuming facet of my teaching, both in terms of time and effort.

By the time I retired, there were at least three forms, or levels, of empirical research supervision in existence in our department in the undergraduate curriculum. First, in the late 1970s, just prior to my arrival at EIU, the Psychology Department had developed an Honors Program for academically talented students. I have reserved some space in chapter 6 to discuss what turned out to be my extensive role in this program. However, it will suffice here to say that the completion of the Honors Program involved the student's enrollment in a year-long research course sequence requiring faculty supervision. Outside of the Honors Program, students could enroll in a course specifically designed for them: Supervised Research. Finally, and perhaps indicating a somewhat lower level of student involvement, students could enroll in the same all-purpose Independent Study course that we used for so many academic functions at my institution.

Supervising the empirical research of undergraduates was necessarily different from supervising graduate students' research. Undergraduates usually did not start out with a research idea that was as well developed as those offered by graduate students, nor were undergraduates' skills at developing their ideas, theoretically or methodologically, as advanced as those of graduate students. Despite those differences, the outward form or structure of the supervision process was often similar for both groups of students. Students could be individually supervised as a consultative process in the faculty member's office or the lab. One common supervisory format involved the creation of a lab group. As implied, in weekly meetings in the lab, each member of the group might take turns to present the progress of his or her research project to the other members of the group, whose questions sharpened and focused the research process. For graduate students in the behavioral and natural sciences at elite institutions, the lab group was probably the dominant research supervision paradigm in use at the end of time. And perhaps because so many members of the professoriate had themselves been trained to do empirical research that way, it became a common supervision paradigm for undergraduates in the industrial-scale schools as well.

But there were also huge differences between the two settings that complicated the effective use of the lab group approach. In the labs at the research universities using the lab group approach, the professor (in this context, sometimes simply referred to as the "principal investigator" or PI based on his or her official designation in the grant application process) functioned as the head of a research program, and each student's project was a piece or element of a larger enterprise whose individual elements were mutually supporting. This arrangement created a synergy for all the individual research projects from which each project benefited. But this kind of mutually supporting research was seldom undertaken by all of the undergraduates working with a professor at the industrial-scale schools—and never in my case or that of any professor whose supervisory work I knew of. Rather, because the individual students were much more likely to be working on their own projects, the overall work of the lab's personnel had a fissionable rather than a coherent quality.

The nature of the empirical work at industrial-scale schools and its supervision thus imposed an altogether different burden on the professor, compared to that of professors at research-primary institutions. Whereas successful supervision in the latter case required depth of knowledge and command of the entire research process to produce high-quality publications from the students' work, successful supervision at the industrial-scale schools was more likely to involve breadth of knowledge and an ability and willingness to shift gears on demand to help students in the lab group meeting. In this regard, as a result of teaching so many different courses, at least I could legitimately say that I had a big-picture view of the science of psychology, a discipline whose breadth was truly breathtaking.

Supervision of Honors Program Theses

In 1984, at the request of the department chairperson, I switched administrative assignments with another faculty member and became the departmental coordinator of the Psychology Honors program, a position I was to occupy until my retirement in 2013. Part of that job involved tracking students who were recruited to the program and their progress and completion rates, among numerous other details of their participation. I created a spreadsheet for that purpose, which I used to compute the numbers that appear in this section. Beginning in 1986, when the students I first recruited into the program began to work on their theses, until 1989 or thereabouts, when we changed the program to enable students to seek supervision from other faculty members, I supervised the honors theses of all eighteen students who completed the program. From 1990 until I retired I supervised ten more, for a total of twenty-eight undergraduate honors theses. Given that in this period (1986–2013), there were 111 graduates of the program, my supervision represents about 25 percent of the total—a percentage that I am sure will not be equaled any time soon by any of my remaining departmental colleagues.

How was this work accomplished? I think it is telling that in the earlier days of the department's Honors Program, I could build a research supervision day into my work schedule, and I was confident that the students of that time period—the late 1980s and early 1990s—would be able to accommodate themselves to it. On those days, ideally, my preference was to simply stack up the individualized research meetings with the students in a three- or four-hour block of time,

usually on a morning or afternoon of a day on which I had no regularly scheduled class meetings. That is, I was able to stipulate the day of the week that we
would meet. I did not always achieve that degree of compression in my schedule.
For example, my daily planner for Thursday, February 23, 1989, shows that of
the eleven tasks, meetings, or appointments that I had scheduled for that day,
five of them involved meeting with students for the purpose of research supervision. These five meetings were spread out across the day in thirty-minute
increments, beginning at 9:00 A.M. and extending to 2:00 P.M. That pattern is
duplicated for the following Thursday, March 2. Of the fifteen tasks or meetings
that I had scheduled for that day, eight of them involved supervision of students
in research, and these meetings extended from 9:30 A.M. until 3:30 P.M.

By the 2000s, though, I was no longer able to implement that system. The students were often too busy with all their other commitments (frequently including jobs with a regular commitment during business hours on weekdays) to
enable me to stipulate a day of the week that I could devote mainly to the supervision of student research. By the time I retired, it was a much more common
practice for the student to supply me with his or her most convenient research
meeting times across the semester, and my role consisted of building a schedule
that would enable me to meet with each one on a day and at a time that he or she
had indicated availability.

Supervision of Other Undergraduate Empirical Research

Earlier in the chapter I discussed the use of the generic Independent Study course
that the professors in my department used as a portmanteau to carry a large number of otherwise different academic experiences. In the late 1990s, the members
of the department craved greater precision, and for the sake of the student's cre-
dentialing process, there was a need for the student's transcript to indicate that
he or she had actually been involved in empirical research, as opposed to purely
library research (whether conducted remotely or on campus) that might be the
case with the creation of a term paper. Accordingly, the faculty created another,
more intense, level of independent study in the form of a second course known as
Supervised Research. As I recall, there was no operational difference between this
course and Independent Study, whose title we also retained. Both courses produced the same amount of academic credit for the student, and the CUs that the
faculty member earned were the same for both. The courses were intended to be
functionally different, however. Students in the Independent Study course might
work as researchers in a professor's lab, especially on projects that the professor
had designed. But students in the Supervised Research course were required to
design and implement an empirical project of their own. Thus, the Supervised
Research course was basically the equivalent of an honors thesis experience for
students who were not officially admitted to the department's Honors Program.

I supervised one student using the Supervised Research course number, but I also persisted in using the older Independent Study number, especially if a particular student was working a higher-level empirical project with another professor at the same time she or he was working on a different project with me. During my time at EIU, I supervised the empirical research of eleven undergraduate students in addition to the honors thesis supervision that I described above. These eleven students' projects were spread out fairly evenly across my career, with three students completing their work in the 1980s, five in the 1990s, and three in the 2000s. Approximately half of these undergraduates presented the results of their investigation at a conference, with the most likely outlet being a conference designed specifically for undergraduates. Four of the eleven students went on to publish their research, with me as a coauthor.

I used the other research supervision course number, Independent Study, on my AOD to indicate the supervision of empirical research that was carried out in my lab. Generally, I used this number to indicate an entry-level research participation experience, one in which the student expressed an interest in wanting to help with, or get involved in, research or get some experience in doing research. Often this help was offered in the hope, sometimes directly expressed by the student, that by virtue of this assistance, I would be in a better position to write a letter of recommendation as part of the student's graduate school application process in the next year. Most often, these students helped me by becoming experimenters in my lab for a semester or two. In every case, they were engaged in a project that was part of my research program—that is, the project was intended to become part of a publishable paper. Sometime in the mid- to late 1980s I learned through a process of trial and error that undergraduates were capable of this work. Their usual tasks consisted of administering experimental protocols to human volunteer participants, making sure the materials for an experiment were organized, and organizing raw experimental data for analysis. To make their participation a learning experience, the students read background literature, which they discussed with me on an individual basis at several meetings prior to their work in the lab. And at the conclusion of the project, each student and I discussed the findings directly from the statistical package printouts to determine what the study had shown us. Based on an analysis of my AODs and reprints of published articles in which their contributions were gratefully acknowledged, I supervised fifteen students who worked as experimenters in my lab.

By the end of time, adding up all the CUs allocated to the faculty members in our department for research supervision of undergraduates in its various forms would show that this work could have created a full-time teaching load for two or three professors out of the twenty faculty lines, permanent and contingent, that we generally had allocated to our department. Thus, by CU count, such supervision probably accounted for 10–15 percent of faculty teaching effort. But in this case, the CU count probably significantly underestimates the time and effort involved in this type of teaching. While it was true that the work of these fifteen students helped me immeasurably in my research effort, freeing me from the time I would have needed to administer the experiments myself, it is also the case that getting the background studies ready for them to read and explaining those studies to them, unpacking the details of the protocol step-by-step for them, and making sure that they understood the findings required an additional set of teaching skills that I would not have had to develop had I simply administered the protocol myself.

Graduate-Level Empirical Research Supervision (Master's Theses)

I have focused on the supervision of undergraduate research, but our department also offered two graduate-level programs that I would define as preprofessional. Despite this designation, each program nevertheless required the demonstration of research competency in the form of a thesis. I was not primarily affiliated with either program, and that may be the reason why I supervised only three graduate theses in the twenty-three-year period from 1979 to 2002. But in the early 2000s, I was asked to help directly by the faculty member who was the coordinator of one of the programs. Each of the graduate programs had only a small number of faculty members in the department who were its primary affiliates, and they were often overwhelmed with the need to supervise their graduate students. I responded that I was willing to do so, and from then on, each of the graduate program coordinators advised their students that I was available to supervise theses. Accordingly, in the final eleven years of my career (2003–13), I ended up supervising six more graduate theses, for a total of nine students across my thirty-four-year career at EIU.

Although our departmental policy enabled students to approach and choose faculty members for thesis supervision, in practice, some professors put limits on the topics they were willing to supervise, sometimes limiting their supervision to topics in their primary, programmatic, research line. As I discuss in more detail in chapter 4, that approach was probably the right way to go about it, at least from a career perspective. Limiting the students to a topic in one's own programmatic research greatly increased the likelihood that the thesis could become the basis of a publishable paper with relatively little additional work from the student and, especially, from the professor. However, I was not convinced about the wisdom of this approach from a departmental standpoint. At least in my case, my programmatic research area was relatively narrow and focused on basic research on cognition. Consequently, there were not too many immediate implications in my research for students in the applied, practitioner-oriented programs in our department to pursue. If I had put those same kind of constraints on my willingness to supervise, it almost certainly would have resulted in the students whom I did supervise simply being channeled to another professor and thus not reducing the bottleneck in faculty supervision of theses. Handling it the way that I did had some potentially deleterious effects for me, too: the upshot was that supervising graduate work required me to learn about quite a few things that I had not previously known very much about, including depression and memory, religiosity and attitudes toward domestic violence, and the visitation and use of suicide promotion websites by adults and adolescents. And it might be significant to note that I did not succeed in publishing any thesis research with the graduate students whom I supervised, despite the fact that their projects were often better from a scientific standpoint than those created by the undergraduates with whom I worked.

What did supervising graduate-level research entail? The graduate students were expected to have a much greater command of the previous scientific literature than were the undergraduates, along with a more sophisticated research design and data analytic techniques. For me, learning about the previous research was probably the most time-consuming element. Sometimes the students had already attained a good level of familiarity with the previous literature at the outset of the supervision process, and that helped me. When that was not the case, the student and I began a search for the major pieces of research in the area to orient ourselves. It was interesting to me to note that, over the years, both as my knowledge of the discipline of psychology grew and as I had more experience teaching our Research Methods class, I became somewhat better at finding recent, key references to articles that might help me begin to unlock a particular research domain. And the emergence of the Internet and the Web eased the dynamics of the search process too, relegating those visits to the deepest stacks in the library to the dustbin of history. At their base, however, the processes involved in graduate thesis supervision were remarkably similar to those used in supervising undergraduates. In both cases, the compression-expansion model was still on view, albeit sometimes in the opposite direction as it might be in the nonempirical research supervision. As my files suggest, during my meetings with all the students whose research I supervised, I was the one who took notes, often in my own handwriting, on a clipboard while facing the student. After the meeting, I usually tried to allocate some time later that day, even if it was little as fifteen minutes, to fleshing out or elaborating on the notes that I had made. This later writing represented my attempt at an expansion of the product that I had created during the meeting, and I often found that this writing produced both learning on my part and some questions I realized that I needed to ask the student to keep the project going smoothly.

In explaining how I operated in this learning domain, I believe and hope that some of the hidden work of the professoriate becomes more visible. What is required to occupy the professor's seat at those moments when research is to be supervised? All of the professor's content knowledge, all of his or her skills in knowledge working, and all of his or her acumen in knowledge transmission are routinely on display in the process of research supervision. Whether or not the American people or the American higher education system can financially afford to continue to sustain this form of teaching is a valid and important question that I take up again in chapter 7. But there can be no question that without the highly trained corps of intellectual knowledge workers that is the professoriate today, this complex form of teaching will certainly wither.

SUMMARY: THE WORK OF THE PROFESSOR AS A TEACHER

To my students, and probably to many of the stakeholders or constituents of public higher education in the early part of the twenty-first century, teaching in a classroom was the typical professor's most visible work. In this chapter, I provided some of the details of that work, focusing on some of its external aspects: the number of different courses, their size, and the physical layout of the spaces in which they were taught. I also suggested that those teaching professors who strode so boldly into those often-dingy spaces during the golden age and beyond were fully equipped with a powerful cognitive apparatus that I labeled the compression-expansion model. Despite the facts that most college professors then and now have no formal training as teachers, and that their teaching expertise was therefore built on the job, the existence of this scheme suggests that most of the members of the professoriate might have been more ready for college teaching than they realized.

Moreover, this cognitive scheme seemed to dovetail with or mutually reinforce the formation of a particular kind of relationship, the professor-student relationship, whose existence in turn created a communication channel across which particular sorts of academic and other information could flow. The compression-expansion scheme itself was flexible enough to be useful in the many teaching settings in which I and other members of the professoriate found ourselves: not just large and small classroom settings, not just the lecture and seminar or laboratory formats, but also in the numerous nonclassroom environments. One of the overarching points in this chapter was the variety of such teaching: like other professors of my time and cohort, I developed practices for supervising research of various sorts and people with widely varying levels of expertise.

The end of time, as I have been using that expression, was not caused by the arrival of technology beyond the technology of the chalkboard. Technology had been present in the golden age of the professoriate and probably before. But the end of time was certainly signaled by the arrival of a certain type of technology.

The technology of the 1970s, 1980s, and even the 1990s to a certain extent was mechanical, rather than an electronic or virtual. In the next chapter, I deal with the effect that switch had on the teaching work of the professoriate, and I argue there that the electronic technology was subtractive in certain respects, to a far greater extent than mechanical technology had ever been. In brief, I maintain that technological aids that can be used remotely detract from the here and now and the give-and-take of teaching. By doing so, these technologies also remove an opportunity for students both to witness and be a part of the process in which the professor is seen to be working for them. And with that lost opportunity, the formation and maintenance of the professor-student relationship is similarly impaired.

3 · TECHNOLOGY CHANGING COURSES, STUDENTS, AND PROFESSORS

I used a cinematic metaphor to open the last chapter, complete with an imaginary professor arriving at a college class and then "setting up shop" to teach. But at the moment the class was to begin, I froze the frame on the scene. With the professor about to speak, I went on to discuss my work as a teacher, beginning with the cognitive scheme that I used to organize my teaching efforts, continuing through the physical settings, and on to all the forms of teaching in and out of class that I did.

I want to return to that frozen frame again in this chapter, but with a different set of questions in mind. For example, at the moment class is due to begin, how does the professor know what he or she is going to say? In trying to answer that question, what guidance might we receive from some of the artifacts that we imagine are in the room? The professor may have a physical notebook sitting on the lectern (or perhaps an electronic notebook or tablet). What might we glean from its contents? Similarly, what means will the professor use to illustrate and share knowledge? A chalkboard (still present at the end of time in virtually every college classroom)? Or perhaps a PowerPoint slide show? And if there is a physical notebook of some sort that accompanied the professor into class, how might technological forces have changed its contents? Finally, suppose we could insert ourselves into that frame, and move around on the set of the hypothetical movie while the frame was still frozen. In turning to look at the students, who might we see?

These are some of the questions that I explore in this chapter. My objective is to provide the reader with a clear idea of what went into the teaching work of the professoriate, at least to the extent that my behavior was typical, during the latter part of the twentieth century and in the beginning of the twenty-first.

As implied by this chapter's title, this chapter has a persistent drumbeat for a theme: technologically driven forces made subtle incursions into the teaching process of the professoriate that insidiously altered its behavior, changing teaching from a service-oriented activity carried out in the context of a particular kind of relationship or alliance to a set of products that could be sold and bought by anyone.

What I did in the classroom or other setting was hugely dependent on what I had done before I arrived, and I discuss this important and mostly invisible work of the college professor in detail. Like the work in the classroom, the essence and appearance of that preliminary work were also ductile, and they were hammered into their shape by the force of whatever technological aids were then prevalent. In this chapter, I depict a veritable march of technological devices and other aids that refigured whatever it was that accompanied the professor as he or she strode into class.

This complex interaction of professional expertise, delivery technology, and preparation medium was complicated by one other supremely important agent: the student. As I stated in chapter 1, the professors who were teaching at the end of time—that is, the ones who introduced and navigated what became the technological supernova in higher education—had been born before any of it began. But that was not the case with the students. One of the interesting things about teaching as a profession (at any level) is that, even as one ages, the students do not, so the age gulf between the professor and students must continually increase. For a professor, the task of orienting oneself to the technological and cultural reality of the students involves keeping sight of a moving window of technological change that extends backward in time by approximately twenty years. Any kind of innovation occurring prior to that time will have been something new for the professor to learn about, but the students will not have any knowledge of what it was like prior to the innovation in question. Because so many of the basic electronic communication technologies have been in widespread use for at least twenty years, it is now the case that the cohort of current college students has always used them, and those students are consequently fluent in their use. This development has led to the use of the term "digital natives" (C. Jones & Shao, 2011) to describe those millennial students who have used the many forms of technology in a way that is similar to a native language, as opposed to those who had to learn how to use those forms later in life. This phenomenon led to a turnabout in expertise with technology that occurred during my career. In the 1980s, I was the leader who was encouraging students to learn how to use something as simple (but advanced for its time) as a word-processing program to write their papers (as opposed to simply typing them). But by the end of my career, I was the one who had to learn—usually slowly, gracelessly, and laboriously—how to use new forms of technology-aided communication that my students seemed to have built into their heads. Possibly as a result of the fact that, by the end of time, the students were speaking a different technological language than were many of their professors, researchers (for example, Ophir, Nass, & Wagner, 2009) have discovered operational changes in a number of the current cohort's cognitive processes, with some obvious implications for the process of teaching such students. There were also changes in the students' behaviors and changes in the communication pattern between professor and student that made college teaching a very different proposition by the end of time, compared to what it had been in the golden age.

It is quite possible that the students were not the only ones who changed. In addition to the processes of technological innovation intruding themselves on the activities of the professor, there are also some basic facts about human development across an individual's life span that must be recognized. When I started my career as a professor I was a young man, but by the end, I was a senior citizen, father, and grandfather. In brief, I was no longer teaching from the same place, psychologically, that I had been thirty-six years earlier. In what ways did those psychological realities of human development across the life span influence my activities as a teaching professor? There is no doubt more to the changes within themselves that professors may experience across their career than the simple fact that they are aging and presumably developing, while the students are the same age every year. The professor is far from being immune or otherwise cognitively insulated from his or her interactions with the students, which occur on a daily basis. There is a gemstone analogy to be made here: as gemstone polishes the others in the same tumbler, so interactions with each student continue to polish the professor. To respond directly to this question of the students' role in changing their professors, I conclude with a case study of my teaching in a particular course that shows how I may have changed as a result of my interactions with students.

THE PROCESS OF COLLEGE CLASSROOM TEACHING

Building a Course

I use the expression "building a course" to refer to those cognitive processes by which the professor makes a series of decisions about the face-to-face courses that he or she is about to teach, including decisions about the content or material to be taught, the organization and sequencing of that material, the format of the in-class contact time with the students, as well as the cognitive processes involved in the creation of any tangible, external representations of those previous decisions. For example, and congruent with the compression-expansion model that I detailed in the previous chapter, the professor may create representations of those decisions tangibly in a set of notes that might exist in a printed or electronic format (and by the end of time, certainly in both formats).

This work has gone by other names: there are professors who might prefer to name all of this work "preparing a class." I have no dispute with that terminology, although the term "preparing a class" may mean something like getting ready to go into class, which could be a different set of processes. At the least the term "building" connotes the idea that something residual and external to the professor exists after his or work has been completed, something tangible that survives and can serve as the basis for analysis. In this section I present the results of such an analysis of some of my own building efforts.

There are many variables—too many to fully discuss them all here—that might have an influence on these cognitive processes of deciding and assembling. Each variable might send the building process in a somewhat different direction, with varying results. For example, a professor who is assigned to teach an existing course that is new to him or her can rely on colleagues to help with ideas and even concrete materials. That should not imply that any professor can adopt the results of another professor's course building unchanged. When I taught as a graduate student in the 1970s I tried that approach and performed rather poorly. It took me some years to realize that each professor or teacher must teach a course several times, in a sense inhabiting it with the results of his or her own decisions and planning, to be effective. Still, building a course that already exists in some form is a different enterprise than building a course that does not already exist, as I did half a dozen times in my career.

An examination of the elements and the structure or organization of the notes themselves sometimes reveals facts about the format or use of time in class with the students. For example, my notes use the term "presentation" rather than "lecture" to describe my doings in each class on a daily basis. Moreover, each presentation always contained some of the same elements. There was always an exposition of some material to be learned: this exposition was factual, detailed, and often accompanied by—or, as I prefer to say, supported by—some other element such as a particular sequence of PowerPoint slides, a video clip, or (going further back in time) a transparency shown on an overhead projector or (even earlier) a hand-drawn figure on a chalkboard. There were always an explanation and interpretation of the material, and there were always questions, some of which I prompted but which could also arise spontaneously from the students. Some questions were simply requests for clarification (or repetition, as I described in the previous chapter, although those questions seldom occurred after the technological era began). Finally, some of the questions came from me, as I asked students something to check their comprehension of what had been presented. These could be questions in which I asked the students if they were still following what I had said or questions in which I asked the students deliberately to take a more active role in the class by explaining a concept in their own terms.

In terms of their appearance, I found it congenial to cast my class notes in a numerical outline format. I indented each new subsection, giving my notes the superficial appearance of paragraphs that segmented the subtopics in any given day's presentation. I exploited this appearance sometimes by allocating portions of time (in minutes) to each segment. Sometimes students in my class might hear me say "So, what did we establish in this segment?" or "How does this segment connect with the previous one?" without my necessarily having made them aware of the basis for those comments. Still, the students seemed to learn the content in response to this kind of organization. If I paused during class and asked the students what was going to happen next, sometimes a student might look at the clock and say, "You are going to ask us what we learned in this segment."

In spite of the fact that I will be comparing my course notes to a fossil record of an animal species a few paragraphs below, it is worth remembering that those fossils were once dynamic animals that moved and changed, and so it is with course notes. There were several circumstances that could result in the alteration or complete renovation of a course's notes, including changing textbooks. The more time that I had spent teaching a particular course, the more of its content I had committed to memory and so the less I relied on the actual notes. There is a well-known finding from cognitive science that pertains to what might happen when I redid the notes from such a course: the notes themselves had a tendency to become more and more abstract or schematic as I redid them after becoming more and more familiar with the material. Consequently, before the end of time, when a student who had missed class talked about "getting the notes" and asked to copy mine, I usually told the student that my notes might not do her or him much good. What might have started out in my Cognitive Psychology course as a paragraph with numbers, details of the procedure, and so on might end up as a simple statement such as "discuss Neisser and Harsch study."

My particular conceptualization of the phenomenon of course notes—as a representation of a thought process, not intended for public consumption, and therefore retaining some of the characteristics of its fragmentary interiorness—is just one way of thinking about them. There were professors at my institution who assiduously prepared and distributed to the students outlines of their presentations, and sometimes these professors would refer to this documentation as their course notes. But most of the time, I found that, behind those distributed documents, was another set of notes with the characteristics I alluded to above. Consequently I believe that the distributed outlines called course notes that we sometimes saw should be more correctly understood as one more form of expansion from the professor's initial compression of the material.

Building Courses before the End of Time: The Analysis of Notes and Outlines
In this section, I have analyzed several sets of course notes, built at various points in time from the early 1990s to the early 2010s. The overarching story here is that the technology that we used to distribute or expand the materials in the course notes came to supplant one of the initial steps in the compression-expansion model, thus changing its characteristics over time.

To show this, I turned to the corpus of materials described in the appendix to identify sets of course materials, including course notes that were current as well as older sets of course materials. When I stated that any given set of course materials is like the fossil record of a species, I meant that by comparing a course's notes from several notebooks it might be possible to trace the evolution of the college course, at least as I taught it. In my case, creating this fossil record involved comparing the notes and materials for any course that remained intact in the format in which I had last taught it prior to my retirement with whatever previous forms of course materials and notes that I could identify and locate. First, I located the course materials, including notes, for five courses that I was either still teaching at the time of my retirement or had put away intact when I stopped teaching them. The courses were Advanced Statistics, in use from 1997 to 2001; Cognitive Psychology, from 2003 to 2006; Research Methods, from 2002 to 2010; and Cognitive Neuroscience, from 2010 to 2012. I counted and categorized the materials in each case in the last year of use. Each one of these sets of course materials contained all the notes and supporting materials that I distributed to students. In the case of the Advanced Statistics and Research Methods courses, the sets of course materials also included homework assignments, worked-out answers to problems, and so on. These particular materials are not included in the analysis that follows.

In addition to those courses, which are still encased in their own loose-leaf binders, I looked into the corpus for sets of notes and supporting materials that I had used prior to building the sets listed above. These were notes that I had stored in manila envelopes or file folders and put away in a file cabinet. I was able to locate the materials for all or parts of nine courses, of which I selected five for which the information appeared to be the most complete. Those courses, and the time period in which the notes were used, were Cognitive Psychology, from 1992 to 1994; Theories of Learning, from 1993 to 1995; Cognitive Psychology, from 1995 to 1998 and again from 1999 to 2002; and Statistics, from 2000 to 2002.

Next, I counted and categorized each piece of paper or transparency in each file. I counted those pages as "notes" that were clearly directions for me that I created as a compression of knowledge and intended for use in the classroom: they were handwritten or printed pages in a reading-size font, and using the case-numerical organization that I came to use for course notes during this period.

Each plastic acetate slide was counted as a transparency page, even though in some cases the transparency was not the same size as a printed page. After I developed PowerPoint presentations for courses, I printed them out in outline format—three PowerPoint slides per page, which is generally how the students seemed to print them out as well. I counted each such page as a unit, but to actually compute the number of PowerPoint slides (to compare them directly with the number of transparencies, for example), the PowerPoint pages should be multiplied by a factor of three. I used the expression "other paper" to refer to pages that were not readily categorizable but were nevertheless used directly in the teaching mission. Beginning in 2009, each of the classrooms to which our faculty members were assigned to teach was equipped with a document camera, whose function I will explain in more detail in a later section. For the courses that were built or were in use from that date onward, most of the other pages were materials that I shared directly with the students in the class. In those cases, the image projected from the document camera was functionally equivalent to a transparency, except that the document camera projected a much sharper and brighter image than any overhead projector could ever hope to do. Prior to 2009, the pages categorized as "other paper" were most likely to be some raw material, such as a photocopy of a page from a book or a scientific journal that I used directly in presentation—that is, without the benefit of constructing any actual notes ahead of class. In those cases, which are few, it is safe to say that there was no initial compression of the material that I was teaching; in a way, what came out of my mouth in those classes was much closer in form and content to my own knowledge level.

Tables 3.1 and 3.2 show the results of this categorization and counting, in two formats. Table 3.1 shows the raw page count for each of the ten courses analyzed (the five courses still intact in their binders, plus the five courses whose materials I located in my files) in roughly chronological order. In table 3.2, I converted the raw page count to a percentage of the total for each of the categories of materials. For this table, I collapsed the printed and handwritten notes into a single category.

Looking across the approximately twenty-year period depicted, there are some unmistakable trends in the data from the courses shown, and I have some comments on those trends in the next section. But first, I wish to discuss the final course I developed and taught, Cognitive Neuroscience. It deserves some special consideration: it is an anomaly in the sense that it is the only course I built after the end of time, as defined here, had clearly begun.

Building a Course at the End of Time

As shown in tables 3.1 and 3.2, and consistent with the compression-expansion scheme that I described in chapter 2, to build the courses that I had started to

TABLE 3.1. Materials Used in Teaching Courses: Annotated Page Count

Course	Year shown	Notes printed	Notes hand-written	Transparencies	Power-Point slides	Other paper	Total
Cognitive Psych	1994	23	14	28	0	13	78
Learning Theory	1995	24	6	5	0	0	35
Cognitive Psych	1998	16	2	23	0	2	43
Statistics	2002	35	1	123	0	1	160
Cognitive Psych	2002	29	3	64	0	0	96
Advanced Statistics	2001	6	13	146	0	0	165
Cognitive Psych	2006	35	0	129	2	16	182
Research Methods	2010	41	1	97	101	31	271
Statistics	2012	31	2	31	72	155	291
Cognitive Neuroscience	2012	0	0	1	172	12	185

TABLE 3.2. Materials Used in Teaching Courses: Percentage of Total Pages Devoted to Notes and "Support" Mechanism

Course	Year shown	Notes	Transparencies	PowerPoint slides	Other paper	Total
Cognitive Psych	1994	47	36	0	17	100
Learning Theory	1995	86	14	0	0	100
Cognitive Psych	1998	42	53	0	5	100
Statistics	2002	23	77	0	0	100
Cognitive Psych	2002	33	67	0	0	100
Advanced Statistics	2001	12	88	0	0	100
Cognitive Psych	2006	19	71	0	9	99
Research Methods	2010	15	36	37	11	99
Statistics	2012	11	11	25	53	100
Cognitive Neuroscience	2012	0	0	93	6	99

teach prior to 2010, I began with the contents of my own mind, as these contents had themselves been assembled and organized by decades of intellectual activity—both reading and writing—in the discipline of cognitive science, added in the contents of the textbook and some other printed materials, and then reduced the resulting amalgamation into manageable and tangible representation in the form of printed notes. Consistent with the schema for college teaching that I have proposed, the notes represent the professor's initial compression of the available material for teaching.

Once the set of notes exists, two processes come into play—one necessary, one somewhat optional. To carry out this expansion, professors need a mechanism to distribute, broadcast, or otherwise disseminate the notes. Typically, this mechanism of expansion was the professor's presentation, lecturing, discussing, or using some other form of speech in real time. This initial expansion—the professor's speech—may have been accompanied by an additional support process. Support could be accomplished by any physical apparatus that could depict those aspects of the notes that were more easily shown than explained, if the notes contained any elements like that. For example, in my oldest notes dating back to the 1970s, which I no longer possess, I am sure I could find the drawings and diagrams that I drew on the chalkboard at the appropriate point. In that case, the chalkboard was the mechanism of support. In the 1980s and to an even greater extent in the 1990s, the support mechanism became the overhead projector, which was omnipresent—each of our classrooms had at least one such projector. In the 2000s, other professors and I began to engage more completely in a task that may have appeared to be that of a simple conversion from one graphic format (transparencies) to another (PowerPoint slides). Based on the details of table 3.1, I began this process in earnest soon after 2006. The Cognitive Psychology course that I taught that year contained only one presentation that was supported by PowerPoint slides. But, as table 3.1 also shows, by the time I had concluded teaching Research Methods in 2010, the PowerPoint slides were entrenched as the mechanism of support, taking up 37 percent of all the teaching materials I used in the course.

I stated that the Cognitive Neuroscience course that I began to teach in 2010 was a bit of an anomaly, and table 3.1 bears this out: I deviated very substantially from the process that I had used to build virtually every course I had made and taught in the thirty-five years that I had been doing so. Rather than first create a set of notes that represented a compression of my knowledge and then, in class, bringing another visual process to bear in which my verbal expansion was supported, I skipped the note creation stage. Cognitive Neuroscience, which was the last course I designed and built, was also the first course I taught that had never existed in any other format besides the PowerPoint slides. Hence, because there was no foundational object in the course (the notes), the visual support mechanism (the slides) was not really supporting anything. This phenomenon was both an effect and a cause. It was an outcome of the fact that the PowerPoint slides could be shared with the students much more easily than could the products that were created using the previous support mechanisms. And it produced some changes in the nature of the compression-expansion model.

Changing the Characteristics of the Compression-Expansion Model

I stated that the data in tables 3.1 and especially in 3.2 present us with some clearly identifiable trends. First, the percentage of my course materials devoted to notes declined steadily across the final twenty years of my career. For the three courses shown in table 3.2 that I built and taught in the 1990s, on average notes accounted for about 58 percent of all materials. But for the three courses shown that were the final ones that I built, in the 2000s, notes made up only about 9 percent of the materials. The four sets of course materials for Cognitive Psychology show the same phenomenon: each time that I redid the materials for the course, the percentage of the course materials devoted to notes declined, going from 47 percent in 1994 to 19 percent in 2006. One of the reasons for this decline has something to do with the effect of memory schemas that described earlier: the longer I inhabited a particular course, the more I could rely on a brief cue in my notes to trigger the expansion that I wanted to produce in class. But the bigger reason has to do with the increased role of the supporting materials. In the early 2000s, most of the support materials were transparencies. By the later 2000s, transparencies represented a much smaller percentage of all the course materials, because I was no longer using them almost exclusively. Rather, the 2000s became the decade of the PowerPoint as those slides made up at least 25 percent, and, in one case, fully 93 percent of all the course materials.

But there is a bigger difference here that needs to be discussed: PowerPoint slides originated in my classes as a support mechanism. I used them (I thought) to help me make more understandable some things that were hard to describe but relatively easy to visualize—the same way that I had used the transparencies and the chalkboard. But while the previous support mechanisms not very easy to distribute to or share with the students, the PowerPoint slides were. Considering the compression-expansion model as it existed in the 1990s and earlier, there was a clear line between the original distribution mechanism (the professor's voice) and the support mechanism (chalkboard and so on). But with the onset of PowerPoint technology, what I have been calling the support mechanism became part of the distribution mechanism. And with that blurring of the lines, the PowerPoint slides began to supplant the original distribution: the professor's verbal presentation had become part of the visual presentation that previously was simply used in support.

I have added some lines to the representation of the compression-expansion model I used in chapter 2 to show these characteristics of support and distribution. Figure 3.1 shows how the support mechanisms (chalkboard, overhead projector) seemed to operate in the model in the pretechnological era. Essentially, the mechanism of support is always on the expansion side of the model and is linked temporally to the distribution mechanism (the professor's presentation).

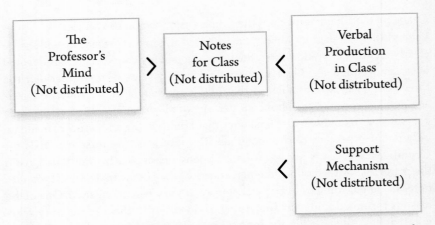

FIGURE 3.1. The Compression-Expansion Model Showing the Support Mechanism in the Pretechnology Era

That is, prior to the end of time, the use of the support mechanism is synchronized with the distribution mechanism, as indicated by the fact that the support mechanism appears in the same "column" as the distribution mechanism. However, whatever the support materials are, they are not themselves distributed. The students are left with the task of reducing or compressing them once again in their notes.

But with the arrival of the PowerPoint slides, some of this changed quite a bit. Figure 3.2 shows how the model seemed to operate in the technological era. I have shown the professor's presentation as an "expansion," but because the notes are the original and only form of initial compression, it is not clear that the professor's presentation is really an expansion of anything. The support mechanism is likewise still an expansion, although once again, it is not exactly clear what it is that is being expanded. But it is clear that the support mechanism is no longer temporally tied to the original distribution (the professor's presentation). The students always had an opportunity to print the PowerPoint slides in any format they chose, prior to their arrival in class, and most of them did so. Whatever cognitive work the students had been required to do to compress the contents of the previously used support mechanisms into their notes, they were no longer required to perform it. Finally, as implied by the previous sentence, in the technological era, the support mechanism itself is distributed, which had not typically been the case using the old-style compression-expansion model.

If it is granted that the model changed significantly with the use of presentation software such as PowerPoint, then the next question becomes what effects on the professoriate and its work those changes had. First, if nothing else, the use of PowerPoint or other presentation software represented a movement of

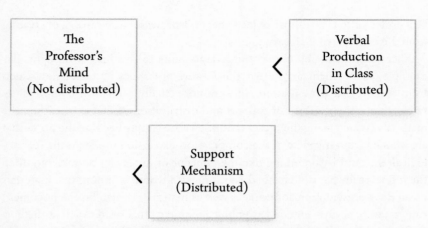

FIGURE 3.2. The Compression-Expansion Model Showing the Support Mechanism in the Technological Era

the border between the public and private zones of the professor's work. Heretofore, almost all the contents of the professor's teaching work, the artifacts that he or she made to teach, existed in a private and ephemeral zone, even though the presentation was public, as was the use of whatever support mechanisms the professor may have chosen. But both the distribution and the support belonged to the professor, and they were both gone when the professor left the room. That implicit ownership might be the reason why, for example, until the 2000s, students routinely asked my permission if they wanted to make an audio recording of my presentation. This ownership also had some implications for intellectual property rights: it was much easier to argue that a professor owned the notes, supports, and entire course before the existence of freely available supports on the Web. In turn, this availability opened the door for the concept of a college course becoming more public, more available, and therefore more like a commodity than it had ever been before.

Beyond changing the boundary of ownership in the typical college course, the use of presentation software changed the process of college teaching in at least one other important way. The use of presentation software apparently offered the professor the option of teaching a college course without first creating a set of notes that represented a compression of the knowledge that resided in his or her head. But the act of compressing this knowledge into the form of notes is one of the essential acts of the professoriate because it is an expertise-based act of deciding what should be included and what might be excluded from all the concepts, ideas, and so on that could be presented. The ability to create this private set of notes, and the opportunity to do so, are therefore indications of the privileged position of the professor's knowledge in all of this: one has to be a professor to create those objects that only professors are capable of creating from the contents of their own minds.

There are, no doubt, some counterarguments to this line of thought. For example, some might argue that the PowerPoint slides or materials created from some other presentation software are actually a form of compression, rather than simply a form of support and distribution. If that is true, then the materials created using the presentation software simply become the notes that are missing from my view of the compression-expansion model in the technological era. And if something like the concept of notes can be restored, then the model really has not changed. In response, I would point out that materials created via presentation software, as well as materials shown on the document camera, were always intended as public documents that resided across the border or boundary from the professor's private personal knowledge. That makes such materials very different from the true compressions (the notes), which were never intended as artifacts to be shared with the students. A second difference is an outcome of the first difference between the notes and the Power-Point slides. Because the notes function as something like stage directions in a theatrical play and are not shared, they enable the professor to extend the presentation in a number of different directions, if the professor decides to do that on the basis of contextual clues that members of the class may be providing. In the absence of that ability, the PowerPoint slides or other previously shared materials establish a certain ballistic quality to each class: once launched on the PowerPoint slides, it is much more difficult for the professor to change direction in any given presentation.

TECHNOLOGY CHANGING THE CLASSROOM ENVIRONMENT IN THE 1980s AND BEYOND

Technological forces changed the way we went about our business—the sharing or transmitting of knowledge—inside and outside the classroom and the means of interacting with students as we did so. The phrase "classroom environment" in the subheading above has an almost literal meaning for me: with the appearance of each new device or other innovation, whether hailed or derided, a sort of climate change occurred in the classroom, a change that reduced the salience of the physical or bodily aspects of my interaction with the students in the class, creating distance in its place and thus subtracting the inherent warmth, or at least the emotionality, that results from communication on a human verbal and visual scale.

Above I discussed the use of the chalkboard in its role as a support mechanism in my exposition of what I have called the compression-expansion scheme, that cognitive metaplan that professors used to build their courses. I am going to return to the chalkboard, but this time I use it as a springboard for a discussion of the role that technology played in changing the classroom environment—how professors and students dealt with each other—as the bewildering and mind-numbing streak of innovations, like the splintered broomsticks in the Disney adaptation of *The Sorcerer's Apprentice*, continued their inexorable march. So back to the chalkboard we go: to circa 1977, when I used the chalkboard to illustrate the knowledge that I had programmed into my courses. In other words, to diagram a concept or simply to show how a possibly unfamiliar term was spelled, I began, as Plato may have done circa 350 B.C.E., by scraping two minerals together, one harder than the other.[1] As primitive as that might sound, there was nevertheless a subtle and reassuring physicality about constructing material on the board: the professor had to move away from the lectern, turn his or her back to the students, and use large muscles to write on the board. And the benefit, however small it may have been, accruing to this display of the professor's physical presence was its reminder of his or her humanity, and with it the notion the professor and the students were simply people engaged in a common pursuit. I do not wish to appear overly wistful about using chalkboards—I sharply curtailed my use of them as soon as the obvious successor (the transparency projector) appeared—but they did have their advantages. One was that, with the size of the chalkboard, which might consist altogether of an array of separate boards totaling 80 to 100 square feet, nothing the professor constructed needed to be erased until the end of class. There is also the concept of scale: if a professor wanted to create a time line or other display that was twenty feet long, it might be possible to draw one on consecutive panels of a chalkboard that spanned the entire frontage of a classroom, but that would be less feasible using almost any other medium.

Still, I relinquished the chalkboard when the next thing seemed to come along. I was allured by the apparent labor saving involved in the use of the transparency, or overhead, projector. With it, I would no longer be compelled to draw—rather crudely, I must admit—everything on the chalkboard. By the mid- to late 1980s, many publishing companies were producing sets of transparencies to accompany their Introductory Psychology textbooks, and the projection machines were not necessarily expensive. Within no more than one or two years, every psychology classroom—indeed, virtually every classroom—at my institution was equipped with its own resident overhead projector, invariably resting high atop its own portable cart. That arrangement was not quite good enough for me. At the beginning of each semester I hunted down the cart that I wanted to use, based on its height (taller was better) and overall state of repair. I tried to make sure that this cart would be the one kept in the classroom where I was teaching most or all of my courses. I also arranged for the department mental office manager, who doubled as our commodity agent, to lay in a supply of high-powered projection bulbs. Finally, I selected the projector with the clearest lens, and then I mated all the elements up. I referred to the result as my "hot rod projector." The resulting machine enabled me to project larger, clearer images without having to turn out the classroom lights, from a vantage farther back in the classroom than the conventional projectors could match. But the real heyday of the transparency projector began a few years later, in the early 1990s, when transparencies could be made directly by the professor using the more sophisticated photocopying machines that were then available. Looking back at table 3.1, I note that several of the twenty-eight transparencies associated with the 1994 Cognitive Psychology course were of this type, so I know I was involved in using this form of technology by then—if not sooner, given that those notes had been in use for several years by 1994.

As a form of technological assistance in the classroom, the overhead projector had quite a few positive features. For example, the professor could face the class while using the transparency projector, which was not the case with the chalkboard. Moreover, the professor could build some surprises into the transparency by covering and then uncovering parts of the projected transparency with another technological innovation of the period, the sticky-backed, repositionable piece of paper known as a Post-It Note. The emergence of photocopiers in the early 1990s that could produce transparencies also coincided with both the widespread appearance of high-speed Internet connections and the students' mass gravitation toward e-mail as a medium of communication. These developments enabled professors to easily circulate their transparencies among their students via the mechanism of the e-mail attachment. On the debit side of the ledger, although the use of transparencies definitely enabled the pace of the typical course to quicken, professors were required to learn the art of pacing to use the transparencies. Their chalkboard work required enough time to create that the students could almost always keep pace with the professor, and most of the time, the material stayed on the chalkboard for the entire class. It was a different story with the transparencies, whose duration on the screen might range from just a few seconds to a few minutes. Students were sometimes challenged to extract all of the information they wanted. For the first time in my classes I began to hear questions like "Could you go back to the previous overhead?" or "Could you leave that up a little longer?"

Although the use of the overhead projector was gradually being supplanted by the professoriate's increasing reliance on PowerPoint slides as the decade of the 2000s began, probably the final nail in the overhead projector's coffin was the arrival of the final real-time display mechanism that I have considered here—the document camera. The document camera was a lectern- or table-mounted device that could be patched into the permanent projection system in the classroom that had been dedicated to the computer—both the computer and the projection system being omnipresent in classrooms as the 2000s opened. The document camera operated in a way similar to an overhead projector: there was a lit table and overhead lens, whose focal length could be altered to zoom in or out on the object on the table. But whereas the overhead projector required its projected image to be based on a plastic transparency, there was no such limitation with regard to the document camera: a page from a textbook or other source or even a three-dimensional object could be projected equally well, and with a brightness that was superior to the best hot rod I had ever been able to build. By the end of my teaching career in 2013, the overhead projectors, still to be found in some cobwebby corner of nearly every classroom, were hardly ever used.

All three of these technologies (chalkboard, overhead projector, and document camera) were essentially interactive devices that were used mostly or exclusively in real time in the classroom. As I discussed above, their role in the compression-expansion schema seems clear: each technology was a support mechanism, something that directly aided the professor in the expansion process and only there. Generally, whatever materials were used in this way were private and could not be detached from the professor's intellectual work in creating the course. But that was not quite the case with the next float in the parade: the PowerPoint slide. Although the PowerPoint presentation system was officially launched on May 22, 1990, the same day that Microsoft released Windows 3.0, it took some time to catch on in the academic arena. It may not have been until the early 2000s that many professors were using PowerPoint extensively. As its use became more widespread, controversies about PowerPoint quickly began to simmer in academic settings (Voss, 2004). As I stated above, using PowerPoint seemed to change the academic climate, or the ecosystem of the classroom, and its ability to be embedded in other technologies marked the first real step toward the commodification of the professor's work.

The reasons for this may lie in the facts that the sequence of slides was no longer necessarily the professor's private work, and because of that, the slides could be detached or separated from the professor's in-class distribution. Although I was not a particularly sophisticated user, the textbook publishers made it easy to create PowerPoint presentations for their courses by providing the professors who had adopted their book in courses with password-protected access to each and every graphic element used in the book. Sometimes I might want to use a graphic representation that had appeared in some other location: in those cases, it was easy to send an e-mail to myself with the image attached directly from the photocopier. In a few cases, I created PowerPoint slides by simply cutting and pasting the content from some other application I had on my machine (such as the Paint program that was standard equipment on all Windows-based machines throughout the 1990s and early 2000s). The PowerPoint program was a flexible and accommodating importer of images in almost any format.

What enabled these characteristics to alter the classroom climate? First, there is the point that the students generally had access to the PowerPoint slideshow ahead of the class session, which was not the case with the previously discussed support mechanisms. And the fact that the students already had the PowerPoint slides meant that the professor could not easily use any of the surprise strategies with Post-It Notes that became part and parcel of the overhead projector demonstrations. The dramaturgy became very different: rather than becoming a part of some mise-en-scène, the students in class were simply watching a movie that they had already seen once. Second, using PowerPoint required the presence of a reasonably up-to-date computer in the classroom, and certainly by the 2000s that fact alone meant that whole world was potentially present, visible, and almost palpable in every professor's classroom. The concept of a closed-door college classroom as a place where a private, human-scale transaction was taking place between professor and students had vanished by then.

Perhaps the final step in this evolution, and the one that most strained the compression-expansion model, was the creation and development of entire computerized environments for classroom teaching such as those obtainable with electronic content managers like WebCT, Blackboard, or Desire2Learn. By the end of time—really, throughout the 2000s—most professors in my department at least were using WebCT to send out the PowerPoint slides; administer tests; set up, maintain, and listen in on interactive discussion rooms; and perhaps other things too. The students referred to the availability and preclass reception of the PowerPoint slideshow as "posting the notes." But it was definitely not that. This is not the place for me to discuss these and other features and options of these electronic content managers in depth; other commentators (for example, Donoghue, 2008, pp. 105-110) have already told that part of the story very well. In most accounts of their use, there are underlying themes of commodification (the notion of the course's being detachable from the professor's delivery of it), the emphasis on the delivery of content, and the hybridization of the face-to-face classroom experience as the professors in those courses took on a greater and greater supplementary electronic presence.

In summarizing this part of the story, it is not my plan to rail against these developments or to deride or decry them. It is true that almost from the inception and release of these technological innovations, the professoriate seems to have had its share of members who are more than ready to criticize the use of each of them, and I cannot dispute the validity of many of the critics' arguments (see Mason & Hlynka, 1998). Despite that, I was not a member of the resistance movement. But neither was I a wholly active participant in the use of the new classroom environments. Instead, I used what was by then very basic technology to send out a mass e-mail to my students on a daily basis, with PowerPoint presentations attached. This practice suited me better than a wholesale involvement in the electronic content managers would have done, and there were some findings suggesting that a daily e-mail from a course's professor may have had some motivational properties (Legg & Wilson, 2009).

TECHNOLOGY CHANGING THE TEACHER-STUDENT RELATIONSHIP

As we have seen in this chapter, technological forces seem to have had their way in changing the characteristics of the compression-expansion scheme and the classroom environment or climate. Finally, in this section, I plan to examine the role that technology played as it influenced the communication patterns and, consequently, the relationship patterns among both professors and students.

The Ever-Changing Medium of Communication with Students: Office Visits, Letters, Phone Conversations, and E-Mails

When I began my career as a professor, I was inexplicably proud of the facts that I had a private office assigned to me, in the building where I taught, with a listed address: these facts seemed to be markers of my arrival in the profession. I also had a phone, and I had publicly posted office hours in which students and others could feel free to drop in. Taken together, there were then at least three channels of communication by which students or others could contact me: in person, by mail, or by phone. Each medium was used: students occasionally sent me letters from off campus or via campus mail. They stopped in during the office hours and at other times, and telephone calls to my direct office number occupied me for up to an hour per day. The passage of time and the invention of newer means of communicating would change this pattern. By the end of time, even though I could still be contacted via any of the channels that were functional in 1977, on a practical basis, there was a marked change in the percentage of contacts that were initiated using any of those original means. In my final year, I could count on the fingers of one hand the number of phone conversations that I had with students—that usage had declined precipitously—nor were they likely to send letters with any measurable frequency. This movement away from the telephone as a medium of communication was not particular to me. By 2012, three academic departments at my institution had removed the private faculty telephone lines from their offices in what was promoted as a cost-cutting move (Deters, 2012). When I had an opportunity to ask a faculty member how that move was playing out, he reported that neither he nor, apparently, his students missed the desk phone at all. In place of phone calls, students vastly preferred using e-mail to contact their professors, via either the professor's direct e-mail address or the e-mail-like shell that was embedded in the professor's electronic course manager. Based on an analysis of the tasks that I duly listed in my daily planners at the end of time, I spent upward of 10 percent of my time every workday responding to or initiating e-mail messages.

Questions of Availability

The use of e-mail and its even less articulate cousin, the text message delivered via a smart phone, increased the potential for connectivity among faculty and students, certainly a desirable outcome. However, the typically asynchronous nature of e-mail and texts also increased the need for a person's availability on and attentiveness to those channels. And that may have created a strain on the professoriate overall, as it did on me. For example, Ann Austin (2011, p. 149) relates an anecdote of the student who sent a professor an e-mail at 3:00 A.M., which contained a question requiring immediate attention that the student apparently thought would be directly forthcoming. I use the expression "the" student here, because every professor or former professor of a certain age with whom I have spoken can recount a similar anecdote, accompanied by a chuckle by which the professor intends to communicate the student's misapprehension of the start and end of our workday—itself a term that was soon obsolete.

How did this change of primary communication medium, from telephone to e-mail, produce changes in the professor-student relationship? One clue can be found in the term I used to describe the e-mail channel in the paragraph above: the speed and ease of e-mail mimics conversation, but the verisimilitude breaks down if the recipient is not attending and responding. The introduction of potentially asynchronous forms of communication as a replacement for telephony required a constant monitoring of the new forms for them to work. Thus I went from a pattern of checking my e-mail in 1993 at irregular intervals to just leaving the program running in the background on my computer twenty years later. Asynchrony refers to occurrences at different points in time, but the term also implies being without time, outside of time, or outside the boundaries of time. And so it was with the asynchronous e-mail communications. Without anyone's intention that it should happen, the concepts of temporal boundaries or borders began to break down, including the concepts of the "business day," the "workday," or the "close of business." Whereas a student at the beginning of my career may have had a very reasonable expectation of my not answering my office phone at 6:00 P.M., one at the end of my career may not have had any reason to believe that I would not respond to an e-mail at 10:00 P.M. And as those temporal boundaries and expectations about them disappeared, the professor's apparent unavailability may have been read as a lack of commitment, caring, or even professionalism.

Perhaps thoughts like those are the ones that animated professors' change in how they used e-mail. My preference in writing *A Professor at the End of Time* has been to keep the focus on data that I have and can use to document and support the assertions that I make. But in this case, although redolent of memoir, one anecdote might illustrate my point. In my final year as a professor, I chaired a search committee for the position of dean of the Honors College at my institution. I have included a discussion of the details of such search committees in chapter 5, and here I will say only that the job involved exchanging torrents of e-mails with the other members of the committee, most of whom were faculty members. Frequently during the months-long process, I found myself preparing and sending e-mails at 10:00 P.M. or so, a rather late time for me to still be working at that point in my life. If I had to request some information from the committee members, be it about a question of scheduling, a room preference, or something else, I generally phrased the request as something that would require action at some time in the future, perhaps the next morning when the faculty member arrived at his or her office and read the e-mail that had built up overnight. But I found that was not the way these committee members were working: most often, *all* of the committee members had responded to such requests within thirty to forty-five minutes of my sending them out, regardless of when I did so—a fact that astonished me. When I complimented them on their responsiveness later in a group setting, they all told me that they used any pretext, such as a momentary period of wakefulness, to read and respond to their e-mail all night long. And several of the committee members were people who were well into the middle years of life. The inference I drew from this episode, aside from the one in which I determined it was time for me to quit, was that professors risked being left behind or feeling as if they had been left behind by their students and their colleagues if they did not simply accede to the reality of the absence of temporal boundaries around the concept of work.

Changes in Patterns of Communication

I am using the expression "patterns of communication" as shorthand to describe the flow of electronic information among professors and students, but especially among the students themselves. Around 2010, one of my departmental colleagues carried out an informal electronic survey among his students to learn which forms of electronic communication the students were using. He found that the overwhelming majority of them had an account on the social media site Facebook (which had been launched in 2004), and they were often very active there. A far smaller percentage of students had a Twitter account, and only a very few were using an RSS feed to read updates on web pages or blogs (which implies that any students who were following a particular blog were manually logging into the site each time they visited). Broader surveys that have been done more recently (reported in Widrich, 2013) seem to support my colleague's findings: 67 percent of all Internet users were also using social networking sites, and Twitter was still being used to a greater extent than were other sites such as Pinterest, Instagram, and Tumblr. Several years earlier, in 2007, the departmental honors students, whom I regularly taught, reported spending an average of two hours per day using their Facebook accounts—this date shows how quickly and completely the site caught on with college students, who were, after all, probably its initial intended target audience. By the time the honors students and I did a unit on communication in interpersonal relationships in our Honors Seminar in 2011, the discussion turned, disappointingly from my perspective, into a conversation about how to best manage one's Facebook account.

But this intense and sustained interest in Facebook, at least, reveals some interesting phenomena about the pattern of communications among students in the technological era, compared to previous times. First, no longer is the professor necessarily at the hub of communication about the class (as he or she had been in the pretechnological era). Students can, and do, circulate information about the course among themselves, a fact that paradoxically might do more to establish the concept of community among the students than any of the university's formal programs. Second, the prevalence of Facebook and other social media sites means that when a professor enters a college classroom on the first day of class, he or she is also, probably unknowingly, setting up a petri dish in whose rich broth a unique culture will grow exponentially across the academic term. Finally, as implied by the previous sentence, the professor needs to be aware that he or she is not actually in the petri dish along with the students: the social networking exists on a channel that functions independently of the professor's use of electronic media for teaching such as the chat room, discussion boards, and so on in WebCT or Desire to Learn. That communication or networking among the students probably goes on via a number of back channels that are independent of whatever use of Facebook the professor might make in teaching the class as well.

DID STUDENTS CHANGE? OR DO WE NEED TO CHANGE?

In the previous sections, I showed how advances in technology altered the classroom environment, changed the relationship between the professor and the student, and established alternative channels of communication on which the professor was not necessarily invited to participate. In this section, I intend to turn the focus directly on the people who were my partners in the educational process—that is, the students whom I served. As I stated in chapter 1, *A Professor at the End of Time* is a book about the wholesale changes created by technological innovations and other forces that have remade the structure, process, and product of higher education. I believe the reality of this assertion is never plainer than in discussing the cognitive and, ultimately, behavioral changes evinced by college students at the end of time.

To be sure, like most cognitive scientists (for example, Pinker, 2010), I do not believe that technological forces or innovations alone have altered, or will alter, every fundamental aspect of human neurology and hence the basic functional properties of human cognition: the biological structures that enable the neural computations underlying adaptations such as language, memory, attention, and reasoning will not be vaporized by technology. But I also do not believe that the apparent inalterability of such fundamental biological structures offers any reassurance that nothing is going to change, or that nothing has changed. The shape or characteristics of each of those cognitive functions may change, and there is certainly a plentitude of research (for example, Ophir et al., 2009) to suggest that those characteristics have changed and will continue to change. The reason for that assertion has to do with the nature of the events in the environment that the brain uses to build those neural networks in the first place—they are not there at birth; only the raw neural materials and the capacity to make them are. From the amount and nature of the environmental stimulation provided, the brain builds networks that can localize, extract, and organize information in ways that are functionally adaptive in that environment. At the risk of oversimplifying, in language learning (for example), if the environment is syntactically complex, contains long sentences such as those found in many books, and presents many novel or unusual words, then the brain will develop the ability (that is, build the appropriate neural networks) to both decode and deploy those features in its own linguistic work. If the linguistic environment is simple, then the brain will build networks for that world instead.

There is ample evidence that students of the millennial generation are far less bookish than were their baby boomer or Gen X forebears. In one study among many showing similar findings, Victoria Rideout, Ulla Foehr, and Donald Roberts (2010) found that people ages eight to eighteen spend an average of seven hours per day engaged with some form of Internet-enabled, electronic apparatus, an amount of time that is probably more than they spend in any activity except sleeping. What might happen to the human brain when it is immersed in such a bath of web-based content? Nicholas Carr (2010) believes that Internet use interacts with the brain's plasticity, resulting in neural circuitry that seems to mimic the properties of the Internet. And finally, how might neural circuits designed by the Internet operate? Developed as they have been from screen-based forms of information, those circuits would want to move quickly, and they would want to extract information presented in visual and spatial formats rather than in the slower, sequential, sentential, and deductive formats that one might associate with conventional, book-based text. While that statement is hypothetical or speculative, if true, it would nevertheless explain some things that many researchers and scholars have observed about many of the millennial students in universities today.

Nelly Stromquist (2011) surveyed professors at a prestigious university in Peru and found that they frequently reported effects of the students' immersion in the virtual environment, with shorter attention spans, inability to attend to lectures, and the desire for more interactive classes chief among them. Actually, I do not believe that the millennial students necessarily have short attention spans for all forms of stimulation. The mention of more interactive classes may be the key: students may experience difficulty in sustaining their attention in a typical college class, given that the class may be organized for the exposition of information in ways that they (that is, their neural circuits) are no longer programmed for.

The student's attentional capabilities are also on the front line of one of the latest battlegrounds in the never-ending campaign to enforce suitable classroom behavior and etiquette. This battle concerns students' apparent need to use their smart phones to tap out brief text messages while the professor is engaged in the a priori more serious business of teaching. This student practice, which by the end of the first decade in the new millennium had reached crescendo levels, never bothered me particularly, although I tried to be very sensitive to the non-texting students who were distracted by it. But many or most of my colleagues made in-class texting the centerpiece of their disciplinary programs, calling out the texting student in class, confiscating his or her phone for the duration of the class period, and levying huge grading penalties on any and all offenders. On one occasion, a colleague who burst into my office after the most cursory of knocks on the door simply could not contain his utter disbelief at and, it must be stated, his contempt for the behavior of a second texting student who had just seen him publicly impose these severe penalties on a classmate a few minutes previously. When he barged into my office, I think the colleague was looking for my sympathy and approval, but I withheld both: I think he missed the point of the second student's behavior. Sometime earlier that year, in my Statistics class, I had noticed the fairly incessant texting of a student who was struggling in the class, despite some other indications that she was actually fairly bright. When she came by during office hours to discuss her grade, I took the risk of bringing it up, suggesting that she might help herself by refocusing on the material in class. Her response hit me like a blow from a maul: "Your class isn't that bad, you give us chances to talk and do different things. But I have to text because, no matter what, I can't listen to one person for more than a few minutes." After that episode, I realized that for those students, whatever their number, whose brains have been reprogrammed by their immersion in the electronic world, there is no possibility of unmaking or reversing the way their brains operate for the sake of a professor's preferences, no matter how extreme the penalty the professoriate exerts. And at the risk of being too polemical, surely those professors who insist that their students devote sustained attention to their densely built and finely argued lectures whose pace matches the processional speed of some royal pageant must know that such presentations, the kind that we were taught to take pride in our ability to build, may actually reach only a vanishingly small proportion of their students in the future.

TEACHING AS A JOURNEY: THE HONORS SEMINAR EXPERIENCE

One of the most commonly adopted tropes at the end of time consists of describing a process of change as a "journey," with its implications of arduous and uncertain passages, stages, and—one hopes—a triumphal arrival at some planned and sought-after destination. The journey thus becomes a trial or a test, in which only those who develop new strengths or summon previously unknown ones will advance and prosper. I have been tempted for some time to use this trope to describe my college teaching career, but I am also ambivalent about the idea for a number of reasons. Like a journey, my career gave me some experiences and sights that I had not known existed. And I was deeply changed as a result of some of those experiences. When I earned my PhD, I could not foresee that sometime in the future a student in my office would express her gratitude at the simple pleasure of being in college by contrasting it with the life she had lived up until the previous year as the girlfriend of a gang leader on the south side of Chicago, who, as she sat by his side, negotiated into the night with his customers from a kitchen table laden with only three things: packets of cocaine, firearms, and "more money than you make in a year" (in her memorable phrase). But unlike a journey, my career did not have a destination; I did not know where my career as a college professor would lead me, physically or psychologically. So I never had a sense of arriving at a particular ending point. My students knew that I referred to the work of teaching as "the beautiful mystery": its parts were exquisite, but it could never be solved or even mastered. At the end of my career, I simply stopped at what seemed a suitable place along the trail far from the place where I had begun. In this section, I want to use my experience in teaching the Honors Seminar, a course I taught twenty-three times over a period of twenty-eight years, as a case study, hoping to put some of these developmental processes from my time as a college professor on view.

The Honors Seminar was intended as a capstone course for those students who had been admitted to the department's Honors Program, a number that usually hovered around ten upper-division (junior- and senior-level) students. When the Honors Program was initiated in the late 1970s, the course was intended to function as a special topics course that focused on some issue in the professor's area of expertise.

That is where things stood in the spring 1993 semester, when I taught the course for the seventh time. That year the special topic was reasoning and problem solving, and the letter grades assigned to each of the nine students in the class were based mostly on their written responses to essay test questions that I made up. Seven of the nine students earned an A in the course, and the other two earned a B. I was smugly happy with the fact that almost all of them students had earned an A. But then something happened on the last day of the course, when I asked the students what, and how much, they had learned. Following a series of tepid responses, one brave student, who had done very well on the tests, stood up and stated, "It was okay, but really, only you and [another student whom she named] actually understood the material"—a pronouncement that produced a rising murmur of assent. I remember that student fondly and with gratitude: she helped me to see that my smugness needed replacing. When I thought about her comment at greater length, I became more convinced of the essential correctness implied in it: being bright, the students could always supply me with good student behaviors and thus earn high grades. But those grades did not imply that there was any genuine learning taking place. And really, as I mulled it over, why should the students want to learn and own the material just because it was something that I loved?

The following year (1994), I made what I still regard as one of the most momentous decisions I ever made as a professor. I defined some broad areas within the broad discipline of psychology and informed the students that, within those broad areas, they would be the ones choosing and presenting to the class the content, in the form of scientific journal articles. It was my colleagues' turn to be smug with me as they listed the many reasons that this format would not work, chief among them being that the students would turn the course into a simplistic game by choosing only very easily comprehended articles. That fear was never realized. I was initially amazed that the students, when provided with a modest amount of guidance, could and did choose interesting and complex articles that challenged everyone, including me at times. I had taken a big step on my journey as a professor when I realized that, at least with this admittedly bright and motivated group of students, they were capable of so much more than I may have been willing to concede, when they were offered an opportunity to make choices they could own.

The journey did not end there. The course happily unfolded year after year on the terms that I described, with almost every student continuing to earn an A on the essay tests I was using. It was this uniformity of grades that caused me to begin to question the point of the essay tests that I was using as the grading basis. One of the criteria for admission to the Honors Program was that the student's grade point average had to be at least 3.5 (an A minus). In other words, the students had already proved that they knew how to earn an A in a college class, so, I reasoned, what was the point of making them do that again, especially in a class that was designed as a special opportunity? This time, I did not wait for the students to question the testing and grading practice. In spring 2003, I informed the students that, rather than taking tests, they would receive four writing assignments over the course of the semester. Their objective on these assignments was not to arrive at correct answers to questions, but rather to respond to a set of prompts or stimuli that I would create and that would enable them, I hoped, to document their learning. Here are two examples of those prompts from the first writing assignment: "9. How did your learning in this unit relate to your learning in other classes? 10. What about your own use of time in the seminar itself? Are you 'working' the seminar the way you wanted to? If not, what needs to change?"

Once again, I was impressed with the seeming care and responsibility that the students showed in responding to prompts like these. Of course, because I was still grading them, it might be argued that the students recognized that it was in their best interest to lavish their attention on the writing assignments. But there was something else about the students' responses that made me think there was more than that going on. As the semester proceeded, the students became increasingly candid about what they had not learned, where they had had setbacks, what they had done to overcome some of their own perceived shortcomings as learners, and so on. In this way, the students were providing me with the evidence I could use to lower their grades, if I chose. And their evident trust that I would not do that put me on the horns of a dilemma.

I could assign lower grades to the students who honestly admitted their challenges and defeats on the ground that they had not documented as much learning as the other students had. But to lower the grades of the honest students meant that I was penalizing them for trusting me to honor the teacher-student relationship that I stated was my goal. Dissatisfied with either of my options, I wavered unhappily between them for at least a few years. At last, in the final years of my career, beginning around 2007 or 2008, I arrived at a peaceful place on this issue—the place where that I think was destined to land, given the whole trajectory of my thought and work as a professor. At that point, I began the Honors Seminar with a discussion of grades and the grading scale that was still included on the course syllabus until the end of the semester. But I also told them that, unless there was some egregious breaking of the faith that we would establish, their grade was already a given: it was up to them to determine how much real learning they would accomplish when they knew in advance the grading process was already taken out of the equation. And each student and I would find out the answer to that question together over the semester.

That is the place where my journey as a teacher came to a halt. In that one course, I had given away almost every traditional professorial function: setting the agenda, determining the content, leading the class, and assigning grades. Yet there was no course in which I felt more teacherly. Consistent with my view of teaching as a beautiful mystery, I learned that when the traditional roles are given away, there was a new and even more intriguing set of teacherly functions and roles to play.

Over the space of two chapters, I have documented as best I could changes in the teaching work of the professoriate. And I have tried to show how those changes produced by forces outside the professoriate have become increasingly turbulent, diminishing, and subtractive. This section offers a corrective. It shows the cognitive developmental changes in my work that have often been additive: working with the students as I aged enlarged me and enabled me to find ways to bring out the best in my students, as they had succeeded in bringing out what I considered the best in me.

4 · RESEARCH
The Barren Victory

Teaching in all its diverse forms may have been the most visible of the professoriate's activities in the workplace. However, many members of the professoriate, including many of those who worked at industrial-scale institutions, faced the obligation of producing works of original research, scholarship, or creativity. And "obligation" is probably the correct term: advancement, or even survival, for a professor at the end of time often depended on his or her achieving some measure of success and accomplishment in those activities.

Several themes about doing research emerge in this chapter. As is true of teaching, research and scholarship take place in many forms, each of which requires its own combination of knowledge, ability, creativity, and perseverance. That diversity of activity and the concomitant requirement to stay engaged in a number of its forms constitute the first theme of this chapter. Across my career, I engaged in grant writing (both for internal and external funding), reviewing prospective textbooks, and reviewing articles for publication in scientific journals. I also presented the results of research at scientific conferences, and I wrote several editions of a textbook in my area of expertise. These activities were in addition to what is probably, for a member of the professoriate whose work occurs along any of the broad avenues of science, the most elemental of all units of scholarship: the publication of original empirical findings in a scientific journal. To be productive meant keeping all of these various activities moving forward, and that in turn required diligence, a perpetual vigilance about commitments that could represent a threat to one's use of time, and constant attention to detail.

The volume and nature of the resources needed to sustain the professoriate's research productivity is the second theme that emerges in this chapter. This need for a diversity of resources may have been particularly true for research in any of the sciences. By the end of time, the distinction between what might be called

Big Science and other forms of scientific engagement was no longer as profound or meaningful as it once had been. Simply put, almost all science had become Big Science: work that both required the collaborative efforts of a large number of people over increasingly large dimensions of time and space and was intensive in the physical equipment or apparatus that was required to do it and the physical space that needed to be permanently allocated to its conduct.

The final theme in the chapter has to do with the value—that is, the benefits as well as the costs—of carrying out research (scientific research especially, and perhaps scholarship more generally) at institutions that have not been designed and developed with that as the foremost goal. In this chapter, possibly more than in any other chapter in the book, I intend to raise what I believe are significant questions about that value. For many or most industrial-scale schools, the research mission has mushroomed as the schools have grown up—this was certainly the case at my home institution. In acquiring their research missions, industrial-scale schools may have been simply mimicking the schools of the elite system (at which a good proportion of the professors in the industrial-scale schools probably earned their degrees). I want to strongly suggest in this chapter that many industrial-scale schools may now be being hurt by the absence of a carefully thought out policy concerning what they hope to accomplish with such a strategy. In the sense that industrial-scale schools are putting forth "a great deal of research" (the expression used on my former institution's web page banner), the sum of all those activities represents a victory of sorts at those schools that transformed themselves by aping the research university model. But a victory for whom? At what cost? And to what effect?

VARIETIES OF RESEARCH AND SCHOLARSHIP

I have been using the expressions "research" and "scholarship" somewhat interchangeably. In fact, although they are clearly related, "scholarship" is probably the broader of the two terms: when a member of the professoriate uses his or her depth of knowledge, deeply ingrained disciplinary practices, and the standards in his or her particular area of expertise to write about or to discuss a relevant topic for an audience of peers or other knowledgeable people, the professor's scholarly abilities are in play. Thus, writing a review of a manuscript that had been submitted for publication in a scientific journal involves scholarship; writing a letter to the editor of a newspaper may not. When these attributes of depth, disciplinary practices, and standards are brought to bear in an attempt to discover or create new knowledge through a rigorous process of investigation, then scholarship becomes research. Writing a manuscript based on a scientific investigation to be submitted for publication in a scientific journal is definitely research—and research of a certain species, too: empirical or observational research. Although the boundary between these two terms is considerably more squishy in practice than I may have implied here (any faculty member who has ever served even one minute on a tenure and promotion committee can attest to that), the larger point is that during the golden age, and at the end of time, professors typically found themselves engaged in a variety of such pursuits, mixing dollops of scholarship, research, and sometimes creativity together as the task at hand demanded. Whatever the validity of this distinction, however, I am going to use the narrower expression, "research," as a simple stand-in and umbrella term for all the kind of work I did that was neither clearly teaching nor service, on the basis that the most prototypical and time-consuming of my scholarly works was that of scientific or empirical research. In the following sections, I will elaborate on these forms of research, beginning with the form that often sets the stage for all the research and scholarship that is to follow in the career of the typical professor.

Grant Writing

As mentioned above, at the dawn of the twenty-first century almost all science had become Big Science. And as this concept of (or, more accurately, this way of doing) science became more prevalent, external financial support (at least, more formal institutional financial support) became more important in all the sciences. The foregoing sentence should not be taken to imply that only the sciences were propelled by grants; my colleagues in the humanities and in the arts also spoke of the importance of financial support. Regardless of the area, the implication should be clear: without the money, it became very challenging to do first-quality research.

How does having a grant make such a big difference? The professor who writes the grant and who takes the responsibility for meeting its terms assumes the role of principal investigator (PI). The grant may offer the PI the possibility of being paid a salary during the summer months—money that could buy the PI out of the necessity of having to teach during the summer. As will be shown later in this section, my relative inability to acquire such grants left me on the hook for summer teaching. As chapter 2 showed, I engaged in that activity for twenty-eight of the thirty-four summers that I was employed at Eastern Illinois University—and doing so clearly detracted from the time that I had to devote to the research process. Grant money can also be used to hire other professionals, graduate assistants, postdoctoral students, and numerous other people who might assist in the conduct of the research. And grant money can be used to buy equipment whose cost would otherwise be prohibitive. In the case of human subjects research, which was the type that I was most often engaged in, grant money can be used to reimburse participants or provide a monetary incentive for their involvement in an empirical study. Not necessarily finally, but importantly, grant money can reimburse the PI's travel expenses to conferences where the findings of the work will be presented.

As all this suggests, successful grant writing was a crucial skill for a professor who wished to prosper at a research institution, and a highly desirable one for professors who worked at non-research-intensive schools as well. In this section, I will attempt to answer what I know at the outset is a difficulty and somewhat tricky, but still important, question: based on the totality of my research effort, what proportion of that effort did a typical professor at a subdoctoral, nonresearch institution devote to grant writing as the golden age of the professoriate came to a close? To respond to this question, I used the corpus of personal data that I describe in detail in the appendix. From the corpus, I located and bundled the twenty-three paper files detailing my grant-writing program. Their total volume was 2,808 pages (estimated or actually counted). The files themselves contain an intriguing mélange of paper records including handwritten notes made in my office or in meetings; carbon copies of forms, brochures, and other public information from the granting agencies; and copies of the grant applications or proposals themselves. Most of the time, the grant application was a document of twenty to twenty-five single-spaced pages, so the actual applications make up a relatively small proportion of the overall volume in the files.

In table 4.1 I have arranged the files chronologically (by year), noting the agency to which I applied (using "EIU" to indicate that the source was internal instead of external) and the outcome. As the table shows, I applied for grants (or pursued them in some tangible way involving writing) thirteen times in a seventeen-year period. I was successful in all three internal grant applications. But I succeeded only one of the ten times that I applied for or pursued external funding.

Table 4.1 also shows the amount of cash I was awarded from internal sources ($5,472) across my career, an amount that will not carry a professor's research program very far, even after an adjustment for inflation resulting from the fact that those internal awards were granted in the 1980s or early 1990s. The amount I was awarded from external sources was $74,434.77—a significant sum, but still only a relatively small proportion of the almost $338,000 dollars that I pursued altogether. The actual amount of cash that I was awarded would be a paltry sum for a professor at a research school, where a seven-figure amount might be required to earn tenure, at least in some disciplines.

To arrive at an estimate of the work or effort involved, at least in some volumetric sense, in applying for an external grant, I went back to another basic element of the corpus: the daily planners that I used to track my work and appointments. I chose the daily planner from 1993 because that was the first year that I submitted a grant application to the National Science Foundation (NSF) in the Instrumentation and Laboratory Improvement program, an enterprise

TABLE 4.1. Internal and External Grants or Proposals Submitted

Year submitted	Agency	Requested amount	Result
1979	National Institute of Mental Health—Small Grant Program	$4,910	Not funded
1980	National Institute of Aging	Not known	Not funded
1986	EIU: Presidential Summer Research Award	$2,000	Funded
1986	National Science Foundation—Research in Undergraduate Institutions	$37,681	Not funded
1987	US Army Research Institute	Not known	Not funded
1988	EIU: Council of Faculty Research	$1,472	Funded
1989	Spencer Foundation	$7,320	Not funded
1990	EIU: Presidential Summer Research Award	$2,000	Funded
1990	National Institute of Mental Health	$19,640	Not funded
1993	National Science Foundation—Division of Undergraduate Education, Instrumentation and Laboratory Improvement	$36,848.56	Not funded
1994	National Science Foundation—Division of Undergraduate Education, Instrumentation and Laboratory Improvement	$73,969.86	Not funded
1995	National Science Foundation—Division of Undergraduate Education, Instrumentation and Laboratory Improvement	$83,119.19	Not funded
1996	National Science Foundation—Division of Undergraduate Education, Instrumentation and Laboratory Improvement	$74,434.77	Funded

Note: EIU is Eastern Illinois University.

that proved successful on the fourth attempt. Looking at the specific entries in the planner, I determined that I began to work on the grant application, which was due in mid-November, in August 1993. That is, I determined from the planners that I scheduled some time during the day to work on the grant application. And for each day, I noted whether or not I succeeded in getting some significant amount of work completed (that was not always the case with assignments that I had programmed for myself because sometimes my colleagues, my students, my department chairperson, and even people from my personal life presented their own intervening and urgent needs). I scheduled myself to work on the grant on thirty-seven of the fifty days in the workweek leading up to the submission deadline. I actually completed some significant work on twenty-eight days of the thirty-seven that I had scheduled. The 76 percent success rate that might not seem that wonderful, but I am positive there were some areas of my academic work where my rate was much lower. To get an estimate of the overall proportion of my time that I was devoting to this effort, I counted the total number of academic tasks—anything related to my teaching, research, or service—that

I had scheduled for myself in the ten-week period from Monday, September 6, 1993,[1] to Friday, November 12, when I noted that I had completed and mailed the grant application. That number was 468. To get an admittedly crude estimate of the proportion of my total time and effort that I devoted to the grant application during that window of time, I simply divided my scheduled grant tasks (37) by the total number of scheduled tasks (468) to arrive at a proportion of about 8 percent, which seems subjectively close to being right.

There is a larger point that I want to make in this regard. Whatever the percentage of time and effort may have been—5 percent, 8 percent, or 10 percent or more—I found it to be unsustainable on top of my other responsibilities. I recognize that my perseverance paid off in some sense; I know that the program administrator for the NSF instrumentation grants knew who I was by the time I applied in the fourth consecutive year, given the number of times I had called him over the years requesting his guidance on how to improve my application's chances. But that was my problem: it was too time intensive for me to keep submitting the grant over and over again because that time had to be taken from that I would otherwise devote to some other effort. By the time I stopped applying for grants in 1996, that amount of time, along with the effort in the 1990s that I was putting into my cognitive psychology textbook (more about that in a later section), had really taken years of research effort away from journal article publishing, so that aspect of my research and scholarship effort had definitely languished in the meantime.

Review and Criticism

The Niagara of research and scholarly work that pours forth unhaltingly from the professoriate is largely watched over, tended, and regulated by its own members. That is how the process of reviewing, criticizing, and evaluating research and scholarship becomes scholarship (although invisible scholarship) in its own right: the reviewing professor brings his or her stored knowledge to bear to determine whether the academic product in question, be it a journal article or a textbook manuscript, measures up to whatever standards are being applied. Reviewing involves criticism, which means contextualizing the current work and using that contextualization to bring to light the work's strengths and limitations. Implied in the criticism is an evaluation of quality, and that evaluation is almost always part of some type of decision: whether to publish the textbook or scientific article or to award the grant. To do all those things, scholarly knowledge is needed and used in no small measure. It is true that the textbook or journal article under examination may arrive from the author's keyboard fresh, bold, and imbued with such obvious coruscating brilliance that the review process hardly helps the piece at all. But in other cases it may be the brilliance of the review that makes the piece into something that matters much more than it would have.

My reviewing and critical work took many forms. Early in my career I reviewed prospective textbook manuscripts. Later I reviewed journal article submissions and submissions for presentation at scientific conferences. Despite the fact that I enjoyed doing almost all forms of review work, most of my reviewing seemed to fall into one of two broad categories of work, and those categories themselves fell into different portions of my career. Early in my career, most of my review work consisted of reviewing prospective textbook manuscripts that were generally, but not exclusively, intended for an Introductory Psychology course, which I taught many, many times in graduate school and early in my career. Going back to the corpus of paper files, as shown in the appendix, I located fifty-six files (the total volume of these files was 1,052 pages) having to do with textbook review, with fifty-five of them detailing a review process that occurred in a thirty-year period from 1981 to 2001. Most of this work was done in the 1980s, with thirty-six files dating from that decade. I carried out fifteen such reviews in the 1990s and four more in the early 2000s. I still occasionally reviewed a textbook review through the final stage of my career—the last such instance took place in 2008. In many of those cases occurring in the 1990s and beyond, I was more likely to be contacted as an expert, rather than as a general, reviewer.

The contents of the files are very homogeneous, consisting of the publisher's specific and general questions about the work and my specific responses. As implied by the ratio of the amount of paper to files, most of these reviews were relatively short—generally no longer than five pages. However, some reviews stretched out to epic lengths; in the files I found one review that went on for twenty single-spaced typed pages. Even in this narrow segment of my academic work, the drumbeat of technological change can be clearly heard. Prior to 1985 or so, my responses were written in my tiny, jagged, and altogether crabbed handwriting, to be agonizingly typed by some member of the department's long-suffering secretarial staff. By 1985 or thereabouts, I was writing the responses on a personal computer on my desk and printing them using the dot-matrix printer that also resided there. Still later, there was much less paper changing hands, as I simply typed and sent my responses electronically. But that the electronic process did not appear to catch on until the late 1990s or early 2000s.

As my career wore on, I began to leave the textbook reviewing behind and turned instead to reviewing of a different nature. From the corpus of paper files, I located twenty-five files (the total volume was 1,246 pages) detailing my review and evaluation of prospective scientific journal articles. Twenty-three of these were from the period 1993-2001. That year seems to be when I switched from archiving that kind of reviewing in a paper file to saving it in an electronic file.

In the corpus of electronic files, I found documentation of thirteen more prospective journal articles that I reviewed from 2002 to the end of my career. That brings the total to thirty-eight articles reviewed in what amounts to a twenty-year period—by itself, not a particularly huge volume of work considering the length of time I was involved.

Like the contents of the textbook review files, the contents of these files are similarly homogeneous. From the early 1990s to the end of that decade, the file typically included a paper copy of the manuscript. In about eleven cases, I reviewed prospective articles for the *Journal of Experimental Psychology: Learning, Memory, and Cognition,* probably the leading scientific journal of its time in academic cognitive psychology. Those manuscripts were routinely sixty to seventy pages in length. There was no standard format for this reviewing. I usually organized my reviews around clearly labeled major and minor points—and each of these points was usually a deficiency of one sort or another that signaled an obstacle or impediment to having the article published. The review might consist of three single-spaced pages of detailed comments. The letter of the deciding, or action, editor at the journal concluded many of the files. As with every other aspect of the professoriate's work, the advance of technology altered the process of reviewing. By the early 2000s, I no longer found a paper copy of the manuscript in the files—not because I no longer retained them, but because the submissions and reviews were conducted entirely electronically from that point on.

Textbook Writing

The ad hoc nature of my reviewing may imply a somewhat casual relationship with that form of scholarship. That impression is accurate to the extent that I did not create the reviewing opportunities that came to me; no matter how much I relished them, such opportunities were under the control of the editors of research journals and publishing houses, who seemed to seek out my help at regular intervals. But regardless of how relaxed or casual my relationship with reviewing may appear, that characteristic disappears from all the other forms of research and scholarship I engaged in, all of which were purposeful, deliberate, and targeted. In this section, I will discuss the first of these three forms of research and scholarship: the work involved in writing an academic book.

Actually, there are any number of species of books that might be written by a professor working in the cognitive and behavioral sciences. Just to describe a few of the more common types, a professor may write a book-length exposition of an original theory, whose contentions might be supported by original empirical research findings accrued over years or decades of work. Or a professor may assemble and edit a number of purpose-written chapters bearing on a common theme or topic. Or a professor may choose to write a textbook, and these in turn can be categorized into any number of levels of depth, methodological rigor, and sophistication. For example, a professor may choose to write an introduction to his or her academic discipline—a task that requires a great deal more scholarship and ability than might be supposed by those outside higher education. Or he or she may discover, as I did at a particular point in my career, that it was the notion of a textbook for a particular subdiscipline that had apparently been bubbling away in a cauldron on the fires of the unconscious mind until its heat and energy brought its possibilities into the open.

For me, the book that eventually emerged from that crucible was a textbook intended for the first undergraduate course in my academic area of specialization: Cognitive Psychology. I was the sole author of the book for its entire life: its first edition was published in 1986, and its fifth and last was published in 1999. The chronological details and the work process itself are easily stated: I had some aspirations to write a book in the 1970s, and I even went so far as to write an outline, the other elements of a book prospectus, and a chapter, all of which I began to shop around. But my position as an academic was far from sure at that point, and I put the project on hold. After I earned tenure at my institution in 1983, circumstances seemed more propitious than they had been. After examining my materials and reanalyzing the content and approach of existing books in the field, I revised my proposal and rewrote my sample chapter. To make an initial contact with the acquisition editor, I did what was relatively standard in those days: I approached one of the numerous field representatives who had been hired by publishing houses and who visited each professor in their sales territory on a semester-by-semester basis. My writing moved ahead under full steam after I signed a contract with a publisher in the fall of 1983, and I completed the manuscript's first draft by December 1984. The book was finally published in late 1985, with a 1986 copyright date.

Although publishing companies tended to hold the actual numbers of sold copies of textbooks pretty close to their vests—no box-office boasting there—the first edition of the textbook sold well enough to warrant further editions, which, in due course, I began. Because publishers usually aimed at a publication date by the end of a given year, as soon as possible after the fall term began but certainly before it ended, in time for the publishers' representatives to secure adoptions for the spring term beginning in January, it was important to have the production process completed by December 1 of the nominal publication year, at the latest. Because the publication of a second or subsequent edition required six or seven months of production work, the revised manuscript, with the peer review of each chapter completed and with all of its facts checked, needed to be delivered to the publisher by April 1 or May 1 of the calendar year preceding the book's copyright year. Making sure the book arrived by that date required six or seven months of work on my end, planning out the next edition, digesting the feedback from expert reviewers chosen by the publishing house, and rewriting accordingly. So altogether, given that the book was on thirty-six-month publication cycle (a timetable I managed to adhere to for three of the book's four editions after its first), I had to spend about fourteen of those thirty-six months doing little else in the research area but tending to the book. When I signed the contract in 1983, I didn't realize that I was getting married to an enterprise that would be with me so constantly for the next fifteen or sixteen years.

To estimate the work involved in any of my academic tasks and responsibilities, and by doing so to communicate something about the size of that work to those who might not have any other means of knowing it, I have been relying on what I recognize is a somewhat crude measure of workload by counting the number of paper and electronic files and counting or estimating the number of pages associated with the paper files at least. For the textbook project, I was able to locate fifty-six paper files that collectively contained at least 4,440 pages, making this task larger (in terms of page count) than all of my grant writing and all of my reviewing, compensated or not, combined. The fifty-six files contain an interesting but somewhat random assortment of materials. As might be expected there are paper copies—preliminary, copy edited, and in galley form—of each chapter from some editions. Curiously, I no longer seem to have a copy of the first edition's manuscript. There are copies of other elements, as well including the loathsome permissions log (which had to be completed by hand) and all the materials that supported it.

As I have written so frequently here, the avalanche of technology changed virtually everything about the work of the professoriate. Although I no longer have a manuscript copy of the book's first edition, I know that early in 1984 the writing was done by first making a copy in longhand that was roughly typed by me, before I handed it over to a member of our secretarial staff for a more finished product. I eventually learned how to compose at the typewriter keyboard, which removed at least one laborious step from the process. I began using a personal computer, which I bought using the publisher's advance as stipulated in the contract I signed, in May 1984, and I was probably only the first or second professor out of the twenty or so in my department to have such a tool on my desk. Its functions were limited, although I thought it miraculous at the time. The computer had sixty-four kilobytes of random access memory (RAM), thus limiting the length of each file. Like most of the personal computers of the era, mine had no built-in permanent storage device. There was an external disk drive, into which a 5.25-inch floppy diskette could be inserted. Every use of the save command was an adventure in which I remember feeling the blood surging to my head in anticipation of the tell-tale sounds of the disk's whirring that told me some tiny imperfection in the disk or vibration in the office had sent the disk head flying off the recording medium on the disk surface, losing whatever it was I had been trying to save, and possibly rendering the disk's data unreadable besides. Although the technology continued to improve, my records indicate that I was still saving at least some material on 5.25-inch diskettes until 1990 or so, when I shifted over to the much more durable (but still not completely trustworthy) 3.5-inch disks. In my files I have two complete sets of 3.5-inch floppy disks that contain the complete text of my book's third edition, whose copyright date was 1992.

Conference Presentations

One of the most fundamental responsibilities of any researcher or scientist is to disseminate the results of one's work to colleagues, peers, and any other interested consumers. Publishing articles in scientific journals remains one of the foremost ways that this responsibility can be met. But even in the technological era (or perhaps I should say *especially* in the technological era), there is an important role for spoken presentations of research findings, delivered to a live audience in real time, that afford the possibility of a spoken exchange. Unlike journal publications, in which the professor can never be too sure about how closely the article was read or what was actually learned from it, conferences offer the presenter a much higher level of control over what it is that one's listeners and interlocutors are actually taking away from the experience. For those and numerous other reasons, like most members of the professoriate, I betook myself on a regular basis to scientific conferences all over the United States.

As my curriculum vitae indicates, I was listed as an author of or contributor to forty-five papers or other presentations at fourteen annual scientific conferences across the thirty-three years that I was active in the process of presenting. In table 4.2, I have abstracted the information from my curriculum vitae and combined it with information from the corpus of paper files to show the scientific conferences, the number of presentations that I submitted to each one, the number of presentations that it accepted, and the number of those presentations that corresponded to my programmatic research areas.

Forty two of those forty-five presentations consisted chiefly of results based on empirical data gathered from human participants or from the computer simulation of human behavior. Although I was an author of papers at fourteen different conferences, there were only three conferences where I presented more than twice, and I presented only once at eight conferences.

As noted above, table 4.2 shows the number of research presentations that were programmatic—that is, presentations of a researcher's work on a topic or problem that is a sustained focus of his or her interest. Programmatic research can be contrasted with ad hoc or one-shot research projects. Discussing the concept of a research program this way helps establish what will become one of the most important themes in this chapter about a crucial difference in the

TABLE 4.2. Conference Presentations: 1978–2011

Conference	Accepted/submitted	Programmatic research
Midwestern Psychological Association	13/20	13
Psychonomic Society	13/13	13
American Psychological Association	5/5	1
Association for Psychological Science	2/2	2
Southeastern Psychological Association	2/3	0
Southwestern Psychological Association	2/2	0
Animal Behavior Society	1/1	0
Cognitive Science Society	1/3	1
Eastern Psychological Association	1/1	1
Illinois Psychological Association	1/1	0
Illinois School Psychologist Association	1/1	0
Jean Piaget Society	1/1	1
National Association for School Psychologists	1/1	0
North American Simulation and Gaming Society	1/1	0
Total	45/55	32

conduct of research between the members of the professoriate who work at a research institution and those who work at an industrial-scale school. That is, it is much more difficult for a professor at one of the industrial-scale schools to develop and maintain a research program, where the entire complex of support needed to do so is either limited or lacking altogether, than it is for a professor at a research institution, even though everyone recognizes that it is only programmatic research that has any chance of actually solving a scientific problem and therefore becoming influential among the community of scientists. As table 4.2 shows, thirty-two (or 71 percent) of the forty-five presentations with which I was involved were projects in my areas of programmatic research. In the other thirteen cases, I was occasionally involved as one of a number of coauthors on a presentation, and one or more of them was usually able to claim the research topic as programmatic in nature. In many of those thirteen cases, however, I simply teamed up with a colleague on a study that one of us had proposed, which we then executed together.

To estimate the workload involved in this particular form of research activity, I located in the corpus twenty-four paper files that collectively contained 852 pages. I noted that the page count represents the smallest of such counts that I have presented thus far, possibly suggesting that the presentation of research was only a small part of a professor's overall research activity. Actually, though, I think the relatively small number of files is indicative of a change in my record keeping that occurred in 1995 or 1996. All of the conference presentation files were dated from 1981 to 1996, but twenty-two of my forty-five presentations occurred in 1996 or later. It is plausible that around that year I began keeping the conference presentation files in with the files of manuscript submissions. For many or most professors in the scientific community, presentations at research conferences are closely linked to publication in scientific journals, with the presentation often functioning as something like a preview of the written report. This raises the possibility that the estimate of the volume or size of the effort devoted to journal article publication is somewhat inflated. Probably the total number of paper files devoted to conference presentations would be in the 45–50 range, and the total page count around 1,700 pages, making this work approximately equivalent to the work involved in reviewing, or possibly even grant writing—although certainly less than the amount of work involved in textbook writing.

Table 4.2 also reveals something that conference presentations have in common with grant writing: the unfortunate, but nevertheless common, reality of rejection. Although my acceptance to submission ratio (approximately 80 percent) was dramatically higher than my hit rate for external grants (about 10 percent), nevertheless three of the fourteen venues at which I presented rejected at least one of my proposals, and in one case, I was rejected more than twice. It might be the difference in the two hit rates that explains the fact that I sustained my rate of conference applications across my whole career, whereas I seemed to have given up on external grant applications after I received one in 1996.

SCIENTIFIC JOURNAL PUBLICATION

As I stated in this chapter's introduction, recognition of the diversity of forms or of scholarly activities that professors must master is one of the major themes that I wanted to establish in this chapter. However, some of these forms are clearly more established and more central to the professoriate's role than are others. For those members of the professoriate who are also members of the scientific community, the most atomic or elemental activity in the entire research portfolio is the publication of an article in a peer-reviewed scientific journal. Such publication is the sine qua non of a researcher's career; other forms of research and scholarship can be supportive, but they are always ancillary. Across my thirty-seven-year publication career (1976–2013), which began while I was still in graduate school, I was the sole, lead, or contributing author on twenty-seven such publications.

In this section, I will detail the nature of the work involved in authoring those publications. Unlike the other forms of research activity, there is a kind of hierarchical organization discernible in research publication: smaller units of work are gathered to form broader coherent units, which in turn are subsumed under a still larger research direction or vision. In the previous sections, I have cited the number of files and their estimated page counts to arrive at what I have been calling a volumetric comparison that can be used to provide at least a crude estimate of the size of that particular component of the research process. I have done the same sort of analysis here. I will anticipate the bottom line somewhat: the volumetric comparison shows that the size of the journal publication enterprise dwarfed the effort involved in all the other forms of scholarship that occupied me. It is this discussion of the work and effort involved in journal article publication that will provide me with the warrant I need for the questions that I wish to raise about the value of that work. After examining the magnitude of the effort in producing publication-quality research and the burden of doing so, not just on the professoriate but also on the students and the institutions, the length of time involved (generally longer than the time involved in writing the first or, certainly, subsequent editions of my textbook), we will have gained a certain vantage point. And from the height of that point, where the effort involved in journal article publication can be seen in a single gaze, we may find a surprising answer to our questions about the worth of the research endeavor, especially for the professoriate of the future at industrial-scale schools.

Some Terminology about Research

The smallest nonfissionable unit of scientific research is known as the study. Studies can be differentiated on the bases of their numerous, semi-independent dimensions (such as the species of their participants, assuming that the study includes participants), but they also have some essential similarities. Studies are always designed, planned, or constructed in advance by the researcher, and their focus is almost always on answering a primary question or supporting a primary hypothesis. In my research—all of which took place under the broad umbrella of psychological or behavioral science, and most of which was in the narrower tradition of cognitive psychology or cognitive science—the data came from observations of some species, usually our own. For the first two studies I was involved with, I had the pleasure of working with rats as participants. Most the studies I designed were experiments whose arrangement of control and treatment groups were designed to permit a clear inference about some aspect of human cognition. But not all of the studies were experimental. Sometimes the data came from computer simulations of behavior, in which the computer program simulating human behavior contained numerical controls or parameters presumably governing aspects of the cognition being simulated. In keeping with the tradition of experimental psychology, most of my experimentation involved the participation of a relatively small number of people—generally some dozens in each experiment.

At the next higher level of organization, studies or experiments could be combined after they were completed to form a project for publication purposes, and this situation was increasingly likely to be the case for me as my research career progressed.

In the first part of my research career, but especially in the 1970s and 1980s, I was content to publish the results of a single experiment in an article by themselves. In other words, in my work at that point, there was an equivalence between the study and the project. Later, and especially in the 2000s, I was less likely to publish the results of a single experiment, and that development was also very consistent with changes that occurred in the publication of research findings in cognitive and behavioral science in the closing decade of the twentieth century and opening decade of the twenty-first.

Finally, at the highest level of organization was the research program, a term meant to denote a series or set of projects designed to illuminate a specific research area. Like most researchers, I had the most autonomy over my research at this programmatic level: during the golden age and into the technological era, professors have been free, perhaps especially at industrial-scale schools, to direct their research programs to any area they wished. During the thirty-seven-year period that I was active as a research scientist, I was able to engineer two research programs. One program, in operation from the late 1970s to 1990 or thereabouts, focused on the origins and development of an individual's strategies for problem solving. The second program, beginning around 1990 and continuing until the end of my research publishing career in 2013, dealt with the ability of some individuals to reason logically—particularly in that form known variously as conditional reasoning, "if-then" reasoning, or reasoning about implications.

In discussing the publication of programmatic empirical research, one of the major points that I wish to make in this section is the difficulty and effort involved in doing so, particularly at industrial-scale schools. This difficulty is shown in the timing and numbers of publications in the categories of programmatic and nonprogrammatic research that I did. For example, eleven (nearly two-thirds) of the seventeen journal article publications of which I was an author from 1976 to 1990 inclusive focused on research questions that were not in my area of expertise and were, therefore, nonprogrammatic. Although these figures suggest that the problem may have been more acute for me than it was for other members of the professoriate, there are a number of obstacles to doing programmatic research that nearly all professors at industrial-scale schools face in one form or another. In large part, these are issues of material or intangible support. I did not have a dedicated laboratory space for my programmatic research for the first ten years of my career (from 1977 to 1987), and I was able to acquire one only because the colleague who had been working in it died unexpectedly. In addition to that and other forms of material support, there is also the intangible but crucial support that results from having nearby colleagues whose research programs are focused on similar problems, enabling some mutually beneficial dialogue and cross-pollination.

The Process of Research

Just as there is a kind of hierarchical or vertical organization in the research process, there is also a horizontal organization or sequentially based series of fairly discrete steps or stages that the researcher must negotiate. I use the term "stage" somewhat loosely to refer to some set of activities that are usually completed before another set of activities in research are begun. For example, generally, the analysis of a study's data is completed before the study is written up, so I treat the analysis of data as a stage in the research process. But it is also the case that some parts of a research article (such as the procedure that was followed in the execution of the research) might be written before the analysis has been completed. As long as that exception is kept in mind, I do not believe the following brief account, which uses the term "stages" to describe the research process, produces too much distortion. In any case, the first of these stages has to do with designing the study or experiment, which amounts to determining a question to be addressed and devising a plan for doing so. This is the stage in which the researcher expresses his or her creativity: there is certainly no one right way that a research question might be addressed. (However, the fact that nearly every Psychology Department offers an undergraduate course on Research Methods and Design offers mute but powerful evidence that there are innumerable wrong ways to design an experiment.) Skillful design requires an ability to read between the lines of previous work—one's own and that of others—to suss out what is really known and what needs to be known. When the design stage is completed, it specifies a procedure or protocol to be followed in the next stage, in which data are collected. In the cognitive sciences (but certainly not just there), these data are most likely to take the form of numerical measurements made as humans complete any one of a number of tasks that might require cognition in any of its forms. The data are then analyzed statistically, because the social, behavioral, and cognitive sciences use a fairly standardized statistical language to communicate their findings. There follows the process of writing about the design, procedure, and analysis to communicate with other professionals who are interested in reading about them. This means taking the results out of their purely statistical format, but again the behavioral and cognitive sciences use a fairly standardized linguistic protocol that specifies the content, tone, and sequence of the information conveyed. It may be at the completion of this stage that the research manuscript, which may have reached its mature length of some seventy pages, makes its first foray into the outside world—whether the immediate outside world of the researcher's colleagues or the ultimate outside world of a journal's editor and review panel. Even the best of circumstances at this stage, in which the manuscript receives a conditional acceptance, the researcher must negotiate a further series of revisions and resubmissions. It might also be the case that the manuscript is rejected, possibly necessitating that it be completely rewritten before beginning another round of submissions to different journals.

Programmatic Published Research

To launch this part of the account and enable the analysis that I want to conduct, I returned to the corpus of materials described in the appendix, and I identified all the paper files that were relevant to the programmatic, published research I had conducted. There were seventy-eight such files, comprising 6,428 pages that I estimated or counted (a figure that does not include the paper data trail created by the 1,411 human participants who were involved in these experiments). Taken together, these files constituted the main source of information for the analyses that follow. In some cases I corroborated inferences that I made from the paper files with an examination of some other information in the corpus, either from electronic files that might be relevant or from my daily planners.

The next step in analyzing my research effort consisted of creating a spreadsheet containing as many of these dated milestones for each experiment and each project that I could determine. These dates or milestones seemed to fall naturally into one of two categories: dates that demarcated the accomplishment of internal stages of activity, such as designing the experiment or analyzing its data, followed by dates designating the achievement of some external activity, such as submitting a completed manuscript or a revision of it to a journal for publication.

My publication efforts reflect the trend toward the increasing complexity and length of research journal articles that occurred from the final decades of the twentieth century to the opening decades of the twenty-first. Explaining this increase in length is not much of a challenge: the articles' lengths increased because there was a tendency to include and report a greater and greater number of experiments in each article. For example, in each of the first four programmatic research articles that I published (from 1980 to 1986), I was apparently content with reporting the results of only a single experiment. In other words, the project was a single experiment: there were four projects and four experiments. But in the next stage of my career (from 1987 to 2013), every programmatic publication except one consisted of a project containing at least two experiments, and one of them contained three experiments. In this latter time period, the total number of programmatic projects was nine, but the number of experiments reported was eighteen. These numbers tell one story, but they also mask another: the completion and publication of a multi-experiment project is invariably delayed when one of its planned experiments did not turn out as intended, and this occurrence is far from unusual. Although I published the results of eighteen programmatic experiments in nine projects in the period 1987-2013, I conducted another six experiments that were to have been included in those projects but that could not be, for a number of reasons. An experiment may produce no results, somewhat uninterpretable results, or—in the worst case—the wrong results. At the experimental level, then, my yield rate was no higher than 75 percent (eighteen usable experiments out of twenty-four conducted ones). Actually, as I will show in the next section, my yield rate was no doubt lower than this because, in a few cases, I had an entire programmatic project that failed to ignite and lift off because its initial experiment simply did not work.

Earlier in this chapter, I referred to both the vertical and horizontal aspects of the research process, the former term referring to the higher-level banding together of experiments that bear on a common issue and thus making up a project, and the latter term referring to the more or less sequential activities of design, data collection, and analysis that define the borders around a single experiment. I will use both of these organizational schemes in the analysis that follows, which focuses on the time required to conduct activities at the experimental and project levels. Before starting on this particular analysis, I will acknowledge that the precision that I show in my reporting is certainly somewhat exaggerated: in some cases, there was no direct statement in my research journal about the beginning of some particular activity, and I fell back on making an inference based on the comments that were present. In still other cases, a given activity, such as data analysis, was reopened at the request of an editor or reviewer, and the spreadsheet did not take that sort of return into account. Still, despite its obvious flaws, I believe my analysis is nevertheless pathfinding in the sense that I am not aware of any other member of the professoriate attempting this type of analysis based on the work of an entire career, the vast majority of which was spent working at a nonelite university.

All except one of the twenty-eight studies that I reported in my research program were experiments, so they required the phases of design, data collection, and analysis. A completely accurate rendition of the time required for these activities would require knowing the dates on which each of these three phasic activities commenced, for each of the twenty-eight studies or experiments reported—that is, eighty-four points in time. From the corpus of paper research files, I was able to harvest these dates for sixty-nine of those points (82 percent) by noting, usually from my research journal, the time in months between the beginning of the design phase (for example) and the beginning of the data collection phase. I then computed the elapsed time in months for each of the three listed activities for each of the twenty-eight studies, to the best of my ability to do so, given that some of the dates were no longer recoverable. This analysis shows that on average I spent 2.64 months designing an experiment, which involved thinking about the theoretical implications and developing an experimental protocol that could be used to test a given hypothesis. The design phase also involved developing the materials to be used in the experiment—usually certain materials were carried over from one experiment to another within any given project, but a new project invariably involved the creation, development, and testing of new materials. Data collection was a lengthier process, taking on the average 11.08 months, although that figure includes two outlier experiments whose data collection was extended over a few years. Even with those two experiments out of the calculations, however, the average is 7.85 months, which translates to nearly one academic year per experiment typically spent in data collection. For the data analytic phase, I calculated the average time to be approximately 8 months (after excluding one experiment whose analysis I apparently did not undertake until five years after I had concluded data collection).

Obviously, the experiment had to be written up before it could be published, but that writing did not always occur, especially if the analysis showed that the study did not work and it was unlikely to be publishable. I have the dates on which I commenced the writing process in earnest for thirteen (59 percent) of the twenty-two experiments whose results were eventually written up. That analysis shows that the writing of the manuscript for initial submission was the lengthiest of the activities I have recorded so far, occupying 20.75 months on the average.

At this point, with the experiments designed, conducted, analyzed, and written up, the project's external life is about to begin. When an article is submitted for publication to a scientific journal, it may be accepted, accepted pending revisions, or rejected while inviting the submission of a revision, or rejected outright, based on either the editorial review or the peer review.

I was able to track the amount of time involved in these external processes for twelve of my thirteen published projects. The average time from a project's initial submission to its publication date was 33.58 months—on the face of it, suggesting that nearly three years were required to shepherd a completed manuscript through the publication process, a longer period than that required to conduct the research itself. Actually, that figure of 33.58 months includes the time the article is in press, awaiting publication. That period of time could last up to twelve months, and during it no real work is required on the author's part.

Programmatic, but Unpublished Research and Nonprogrammatic Research

Limitations of space will preclude my treating the other categories of research with the same level of detail or precision that I allocated to the programmatic published research. These categories are the programmatic research projects that I conducted but never published and the nonprogrammatic research projects that I did publish. There is even a category for nonprogrammatic research that went unpublished. Table 4.3 shows the number of projects, the number of overall experiments those projects entailed, and their publication fates, as well as the total number of coauthors (or collaborators in the case of unpublished research) who were involved in those projects. Even a brief synopsis of this other research work will reveal both similarities and discontinuities with the programmatic published research.

First, as table 4.3 shows, I designed and conducted research for six additional programmatic research projects (including one project that I abandoned at the design stage) that consisted of ten experiments, on which the light of day never shone. In some of these cases, the initial experiment may have produced usable data, but they were simply not compelling enough to warrant continuing. In other cases, I failed to find a way to fit the results of the individual experiments together to tell a coherent and meaningful story when those results were examined in the context of the overall project. As with the published projects, I tended to work alone on these projects—a practice that became increasingly at variance with that of other researchers in the cognitive and neural sciences as the twenty-first century progressed.

I did not work alone when conducting research whose objectives were outside those of my personal research programs. For the eighteen such projects I attempted or completed, there was always at least one coauthor or collaborator, although they were not necessarily eighteen different people. However, although I had a great deal of enjoyment in collaborating with another professor or a particularly able student on a research project, I nevertheless began to eschew nonprogrammatic research as my career went forward. Fourteen (52 percent) of the twenty-seven published research projects were nonprogrammatic, but eleven of those fourteen occurred in the first stage of my research career (from 1976 to 1990). Only three of them occurred in the period 2000–2013. Table 4.3 hints at some of the reasons for this. As it shows, all of the nonprogrammatic collaborations—published and unpublished—were single-study or single-experiment projects. As I stated above in this chapter, there are limitations

TABLE 4.3. Summary of Scientific Journal Article Publication Activity

Research category	Projects	Completed experiments	Published experiments	Project coauthors
Programmatic research				
Published	13	28	22	1
Unpublished	6	10	0	2
Nonprogrammatic research				
Published	14	14	14	14
Unpublished	4	4	0	4
Total	37	56	36	21

in the amount and quality of knowledge that a project consisting of one study can hope to provide. Rewarding though it may have been to work with a colleague, the effort may not have been justified by the results. Moreover, it was, and presumably still is, immensely challenging for a professor to sustain a research effort across multiple experiments, when the resulting project does not bear on the intellectual problems that the professor urgently wished to investigate in the first place.

Finally, as table 4.3 shows, I conducted a total of fifty-six experiments or studies, thirty-eight in a programmatic area of research, of which twenty-two were ultimately published. I also conducted eighteen experiments in some nonprogrammatic area of research, of which fourteen were ultimately published. While the yield rate, or ratio of published to simply completed experiments, is at least broadly comparable for programmatic and nonprogrammatic research (58 percent and 78 percent, respectively), there is nevertheless a problem with an overall publication rate of thirty-six (64 percent) out of fifty-six experiments. That means that data from twenty experiments were never published anywhere, of which an unknown proportion yielded statistically significant results but, perhaps more importantly, a certain number did not. There has been a great deal of attention devoted (for example, Ferguson & Brannick, 2012) to the problem of conducted but unpublished and, therefore, unreported experiments—a phenomenon that was christened the "file drawer problem" by the psychologist Robert Rosenthal (1979).

The existence of unreported but potentially useful findings moldering away in file drawers creates a number of problems for the scientific enterprise, not the least of which is the fact that their existence calls into question the reality or durability of those findings that actually have been published. If the published study is the only one that achieved statistically significant effects, and all the other studies that were essentially the same as the published one failed and were simply clapped into an impervious metal box, then clearly some questions need to be addressed about the reality of the findings. In raising such questions, it is crucial to know about these other studies, in particular how many there were, and what happened when they were conducted. And that is the essence of the problem: those questions are next to impossible to answer because those other studies have simply gone into the file drawers of professors across the nation and the world. The size and reality of the file drawer problem have been verified recently in a counterintuitive, but nevertheless predictable, way. Attempts to replicate previously established findings—a practice that has not generally been followed, at least in the cognitive and behavioral sciences—have found such established findings to be sometimes maddeningly elusive (Lehrer, 2010). This outcome is consistent with the notion that there are numerous experiments that did not produce significant effects to be found in the file cabinets of professors everywhere. However much it might pain me to admit it, my analysis suggests that I contributed, albeit unwittingly, to the file drawer problem by caching away the results, significant or otherwise, from over one-third of the experiments I conducted.

RESEARCH AT THE SUBDOCTORAL, NONELITE UNIVERSITY: A CASE OF MISSION CREEP

The expression "mission creep" is thought to have originated in the US Army to describe certain aspects of its operations in Somalia in 1993. Specifically, units were sent to Somalia to participate in a humanitarian relief operation. When the situation on the ground became an active war zone, the units were expected to defend themselves and US interests in the region, a mission for which they were ill-equipped. Far from being an anomaly restricted to military operations, the term has come to refer to a seemingly unpreventable tendency on the part of groups or organizations to find the boundaries of their effectiveness by relentlessly adding activities to their portfolio without necessarily considering the resources required for success in those endeavors. Mission creep is a characteristic of an organization or institution, but its consequences, particularly its costs, are chiefly borne by the individuals in the organization.

In this section, I am going to argue that the research mission was not part of the higher education landscape during the golden age for those institutions that could not support it. As an ingredient in the recipe for creating a member of the professoriate at such schools, the conducting of research and the creation of scholarly writing in all its forms were added to the mixing bowl only after the golden age came to an end. And to the extent that I have succeeded in documenting its pressures on my career in this chapter, the conduct of research was an ingredient that needed to be added in generous dollops to succeed, at least at some industrial-scale schools. I will conclude this section with some suggestions concerning the reasons, both stated and covert, for this change, along with some comments about its effects on the current members of the professoriate.

Jostling for Prestige

While doctoral-level institutions had become conscious of their obligation to teach well by the end of the golden age, it was also the case, ironically, that at the same time many of the subdoctoral institutions began to institute their own publish-or-perish mechanisms for advancement, based on those already operative in the doctoral-level schools. There are no doubt many factors that combined to produce this change. However, one salient explanation has to do with an institution's willingness to pursue an elusive commodity known as prestige, a willingness that marks the school as a striving institution. By encouraging its faculty members to maintain a high level of activity in research and scholarship, and in turn holding them to higher publication standards in terms of both quantity and quality of publications at tenure and promotion time, it is widely believed that an institution may gain in prestige, whether overtly in the yearly rankings published by the periodical *US News and World Report*, which are keenly scrutinized even as they are derided, or covertly, in the form of increased brand recognition on the part of potential students or potential faculty members. Despite the fact that this exclusionary game of ranking institutions has been going for some time, there is still relatively little known about its effects on the professoriate.

Kerryann O'Meara and Alan Bloomgarden (2011) interviewed a number of faculty members occupying positions at nonelite liberal arts institutions and found, first of all, that faculty members at striving institutions (as evidenced by recent movement in national rankings, among other measures) were acutely aware that their institution had embarked on such a course of action. Furthermore, faculty members at such institutions often reported feeling pulled in a number of different directions, because the time and effort required to maintain a high-profile research and scholarship agenda must almost perforce be taken from the time and effort devoted to the institution's very local goals of high-quality teaching and loyal service. Finally, the authors noted the tendency of some faculty members to resist the conflict by simply landing on one side of the divide or the other and accepting the sacrifices that their position entailed. For example, in a book about the work of the professoriate, it seems very appropriate to cite the example of one interviewed professor who reported arriving at the office at 7:30 A.M. and staying until 10:00 P.M. to devote enough time to scholarship to "keep up" with perceived peers at research-intensive institutions (O'Meara and Bloomgarden, 2011, p. 59).

The Busy Professoriate

But despite the seemingly wide-scale belief that institutions may actually gain prestige (as opposed to simply maintaining the prestige they already possess) by encouraging their permanent professors to simply publish more than they did prior to the technological era, it appears that many of the institutions that take this route to prestige lack the necessary infrastructure needed to sustain their faculty members' high-quality research efforts. Bruce Henderson (2011) studied faculty research productivity at state-assisted, comprehensive universities (SCUs), a category of institution that is particularly likely to attempt to emulate doctoral-level research universities. He noted clear increases in research productivity at the SCUs in the forty-year period beginning in 1970. But he also found that the increase in research productivity at such institutions was not nearly as great as the increase at the research universities or even at the nationally known liberal arts institutions: "The results indicate that while faculty members at SCUs have been publishing more over time, the changes have been small increases on a small base. Moreover, the gap between publishing rates at research universities and comprehensive universities has been large since the 1970s and has grown increasingly larger. In terms of publishing rates, it appears that state comprehensive universities are becoming *less* [italics mine] like the research universities" (p.35). In their attempts, however futile, to catch up to their colleagues at research schools, faculty members at industrial-scale schools have added approximately ten to twelve hours to their workweek (Schuster & Finkelstein, 2006) since the beginning of the technological era. A great deal of this increase is spent on the need to document research productivity, a focus that "reaches well beyond the research university," as Jack Schuster and Martin Finkelstein (2006) noted.

Just how far beyond the research university this focus extends was documented by Peg Downes (2010), who analyzed faculty members' responses to queries about their teaching, research, and service in the English departments at ten Council of Public Liberal Arts Colleges (COPLAC). Downes noted that in addition to sterling teaching credentials and the possession of a portfolio showing an extensive record of public service in the community, each of the ten institutions required its faculty to achieve a "substantial record of scholarly accomplishment" (p. 299). Nevertheless, although Downes reported that achieving quality teaching and scholarship meant that the lives of faculty members in these English departments were marked by sleep deprivation, with fewer than 31 percent of the faculty believing they were getting enough sleep (p. 311), COPLAC English faculty members appeared to be energized by the challenge this state of affairs created.

Finding or Making the Time for Research

Are the members of the professoriate simply adding ten to twelve hours to their typical workweek, apportioning this time equitably among three traditional areas of faculty work (teaching, research, and service)? The existing empirical evidence suggests that is not the case and has not been the case for a long time. With regard to the ever-more precious time allocated to research and teaching by the increasingly harried members of the professoriate, the demands of research productivity and engaged teaching apparently are fighting a relentless battle with each other. James Fairweather (1996) cited figures from a 1987–88 study of postsecondary faculty showing that the professoriate's time spent on teaching is nearly perfectly inversely correlated (0.83) with time spent on research. What this means is that for every additional hour that a given professor spends on research, it is most likely that the hour has been taken away from the time devoted to another activity, and that activity is probably teaching. Confirming that interpretation, Fairweather (1996) also studied the correlations between the time devoted to teaching and the time devoted to either administrative work or service responsibilities. These correlations were essentially zero, suggesting that professors who spend additional time on their teaching duties are not consequently neglecting any administrative or service responsibilities. Instead, when an institution emphasizes research productivity, as more and more institutions have done over the past thirty years, the reallocation of time comes from teaching, not from the professoriate's other core tasks.

THE BARREN VICTORY

Somehow inducing the members of professoriate to participate in the elevation of an institution's prestige by virtue of lofting their publication record is a victory for the institution, or so it could be argued. And consistent with the sometimes insidious influence of mission creep, the acceleration of faculty research efforts seems to be a relatively recent institutional victory at that. More than thirty years ago, Finkelstein (1984), the well-known scholar of the professoriate, wrote that "the majority of faculty at universities, especially research universities, publish; the majority of faculty at other types of institutions do not" (p. 90).

But in addition to the concept of institutional striving, there are other considerations to be dealt with, such as the price of victory. Studies like that of O'Meara and Bloomgarden (2011) and others (for example, Ward & Wolf-Wendel, 2005) show that faculty members are often acutely aware of the stress produced by the need to remain productive in research and uncomfortable with that stress, even as they increase the hours they work. In addition to that problem, the victory may be one without any meaningful effect, after discounting whatever gains in prestige accrue to those institutions whose faculty members display their effulgent erudition so well. While empirical research has shown that faculty members at industrial-scale schools are more productive than ever in publishing the results of their research and scholarship, other indicators suggest that they are nevertheless falling further behind faculty members at the schools in the elite system, based on both the number and influence of their publications.

As I stated in chapter 1, *A Professor at the End of Time* is a book both about the work of the professoriate and about the effects of change on that work. As dramatic as those changes have been for professoriate's teaching efforts, they have been no less so for the professoriate's work in research and scholarship. In the sciences, certain structural factors have moved some of the basic landmarks and other features of the research terrain, creating tough and uncertain going for faculty members working at schools where research is not particularly well fostered, and doubly so for those faculty members who try to create research that actually matters—research or scholarship that is read, used, and thereby becomes influential in its community. Faculty members who become aware of these changes, and who view them as obstacles, may have developed strategies in response—some of which resemble defense mechanisms. In this section, I will detail some of these structural forces and their effects, as well as the professoriate's responses, both adaptive and otherwise.

Soccer Science

"Soccer science" (Shrager, Billman, Convertino, Massar, & Pirolli, 2010) is a term used to describe the highly interactive, fluid, motion- and team-oriented way that science is done in the twenty-first century. The comparison between science and soccer seems apt: as soccer players may either advance with the ball in their possession or advance without it toward a location on the field to which they anticipate that a teammate will pass the ball, so scientists report their own findings directly and anticipate how their results might be assembled together with those of colleagues at other institutions whose work relates to their own. As Jeff Shrager and coauthors note, doing high-quality scientific work in the soccer science environment requires a continual commitment on the part of researchers to stay alert with regard to ongoing early developments produced by researchers in distant labs, and this commitment might be almost all-consuming.

But this is not the way high-level research was formerly done, at least in the behavioral and cognitive sciences: soccer science is a recent development that relies on the speed, ease, and ubiquity of electronic communication channels. For example, a paper appearing in one of the leading research journals in psychology in the 1950s, such as the *Journal of Experimental Psychology*, might have been authored by a single faculty member, who possibly designed and executed a study, analyzed the results, and wrote the entire paper—which consisted of the results of a single experiment. To see some of the differences in current practice, I examined the May 2014 issue of an equivalent successor journal (*Psychological Science*) and counted the number of authors responsible for the ten research articles or research reports appearing there. The average number of authors was 4.5; there was no single-author article included (the fewest number of authors for any article was two, and there was only one such article in that issue).

It may be the case that the decline of the lone wolf researcher with his or her single-investigator-organized lab has been accelerated by the interdisciplinary nature of the problems that the cognitive and behavioral sciences have taken on (Ivry, 2013), but the effects on the professoriate at industrial-scale schools would probably be the same regardless of what factors produced the change from the previous model, which might be called baseball science (one hitter up at the plate at a time, who has little interaction with any teammates during his or her time at the plate), to soccer science. Because the completion of high-quality research requires the attention of devoted, networked researchers, it has become, and will continue to be, difficult for the solitary researcher at an industrial-scale school to participate in research at that level, or to be competitive with the researchers at elite schools in securing journal space. Even when they team up with colleagues at their own institutions, as I did for virtually all of the nonprogrammatic research that I completed, researchers at industrial-scale schools will still face the requirement of making an all-out commitment to the research process, which they are simply unable to do.

The Influence of the Research

Because researchers at industrial-scale schools are simply not in a position to make that all-consuming commitment required for publication in the highest-quality journals, the research they actually complete tends to appear in journals that are regarded as low-impact—journals containing work that is less likely to be read and cited than that appearing in top-quality journals. Consequently, little of the research carried on by researchers at industrial-scale schools is likely to become influential.

There are numerous ways of gauging a given scientist's influence and productivity. Perhaps the most basic involves using technological aids, such as Google Scholar, to count all the citations of a scientist's work—each citation marking an occasion in which that researcher's work has been referred to by another researcher in his or her work. As a measure of influence, a simple citation count has some flaws, but the underlying logic of it remains clear enough: one's research influence rises with one's citation count. Using Google Scholar, I set the controls to find all of my published articles, and I included citations to my Cognitive Psychology textbook.

Google Scholar located a total of 721 citations to my published work, but the majority of them (442, or 61 percent) were citations to the textbook. Subtracting those citations leaves a rather paltry 279 citations to my actual published research, certainly a meager number considering the thirty-seven years (from 1976 until 2013) that I labored in that particular vineyard. When the numbers of citations are broken down into those representing a citation of a published article on my programmatic research, versus the citation of a nonprogrammatic ad hoc article of the sort that made up slightly more than half of my published output, the pattern tells a particular story. Of the thirteen published journal articles in my programmatic areas, only one attained a double-digit number of citations, and that was for the only article that I had succeeded in getting published in what was truly a top-quality journal. Three of those thirteen articles in my programmatic area had not been cited by anyone, not even once. That means that even I did not cite my own previously published work on at least those three occasions—truly an unpardonable mistake. But what of the fourteen nonprogrammatic published articles? Interestingly, nine of them had been cited by other researchers at least ten times; and a few of those articles had been cited thirty or forty times by other researchers. I drew the following conclusion: the more specific my research became, the less influential it was. Or, phrased slightly differently, as a *soi-disant* cognitive scientist, I had virtually no influence on the research work of my peers.

Although a gross citation count cannot tell the whole story of a researcher's productivity and influence, Google Scholar provides additional measures (and there are other services that provide still more measures) that can flesh out the information contained in the simple citation count. One of the metrics that Google Scholar can compute to assess a researcher's influence is the h-index, named after its inventor, Jorge Hirsch (2005). Essentially "h" is the number denoting the largest subset of a researcher's publications that have been cited by at least "h" different sources. The h-index for a researcher who had authored twenty papers, of which ten had been cited at least ten times by other researchers, would be 10. Thus, the h-index can never be larger than the total number of papers that a researcher has authored, nor can it be larger than the square root of all the citations that a researcher has received. My h-index was 11 overall, but when considering only those citations that have occurred since 2009, it fell to only 5. Both numbers would appear to be low, given the length of my career as a researcher. Nevertheless, providing the right context to interpret the h-index accurately is a challenge. Ray Iles (2013) located the profiles of eighty-eight academics who had identified themselves as full professors at one of fifteen research universities in the United Kingdom. He found that the mean h-index for this group was 24, and the median was 20. The highest 25 percent of the professors had an h-index of 30 or more. In a comment on Iles's blog post, a self-identified full professor with a position at an American research university noted that his h-index was 58 after thirty-five years of work as a scientist. Certainly these facts are far from establishing an authoritative context, but they strongly suggest that, whatever effort and labor I put into developing my research profile and productivity, it remained the fact that my published work, especially the programmatic work that was the most difficult to execute, was seldom cited by more than a handful of researchers and was probably even read by only a tiny handful more than that.

Responses of Faculty at Industrial-Scale Schools

The founder of the discipline that became the sociology of science, Robert Merton (1949), defined "anomie" as the realization of a discontinuity between cultural goals and the legitimate means available to reach them. In the culture in which the professoriate operates, the doing of research is the goal that has been transmitted to them by virtue of their training at research institutions. But at the industrial-scale schools where the overwhelming majority of the professoriate works, the legitimate means to achieve that cultural goal and the chance to do so are present only to a limited extent. While many members of the professoriate may continue to conform to the cultural norms and to conduct their research and scholarship within the compass of resources provided for them, others may not merely conform. Merton (1949) defined several forms of institutionalized deviance from these cultural goals, which he recognized as constituting an adaptive strategy for dealing with the effects of anomie.

Joseph Hermanowicz (2011) in turn has taken the four deviant strategies Merton identified and mapped them onto career pathways, or characteristic responses that academics may make to the relatively unattainable cultural goals as they are viewed at industrial-scale schools. For example, "retreatism" is a strategy in which the professor renounces the goals of the research community and the means available to meet those goals. Retreatists might be more likely than other professors to emphasize the roles and goals of teacher, service provider, or even part-time administrator in their careers rather than the goals of the researcher, scholar, or scientist. "Ritualism" is a strategy that renounces the goals of the larger research community, even while accepting the limited opportunities for research that industrial-scale institutions may provide—an acceptance that often occurs for ulterior reasons. For example, a ritualist may design and execute the minimum amount of research necessary to procure a merit-based pay increase. Ritualists appear to be conforming to the goals of the community, and only they know they are not. This strategy can be contrasted with that of "innovators," who renounce the limited means at their disposal while still embracing the goals of the larger research community. Their motto might be "All is fair in love, war, and research." Innovators may do anything they feel is necessary to get their name as an author on the maximum number of papers they can, including promising to work as a collaborator with anyone who will have them, and then doing the absolute minimum they can get away with. In extreme cases (which I emphasize are rare), the innovator may be the academic scientist who fudges or even fabricates the data. Finally, the "academic rebel," like the retreatist, rejects both the goals of the research community and the limited means available to carry out those goals. Unlike the retreatist, though, who adopts one of the professoriate's other preexisting roles such as teaching as perhaps the main source of his or her identity, the rebel invents new goals, and often new means to achieve them, that might ensure that he or she becomes influential. For example, many of the professors who launched themselves wholeheartedly into the massive open online course (MOOC) revolution at its dawning could be considered academic rebels. As an empirical and theoretical literature about MOOCs was being erected virtually from the ground up, these professors had the opportunity to become very influential for their expertise much more quickly than they could have done by working in any preexisting research area.

In this book, I have strived to keep the focus on my own work with its attendant successes, failures, and mistakes. Here, though, I will permit myself to say that these strategies, deviant though they may be, are far from being rare or unusual. Although I cannot claim to have seen the true academic rebel in action, I have observed each of the other strategies, especially retreatism and ritualism, being used by my colleagues from time to time. Moreover, at certain times in their careers, I believe that almost every one of my colleagues—certainly at least the colleagues whom I got to know well as I worked with them over a period of years—relied on one or more of these strategies to cope with the inevitable vicissitudes of life as a researching academic. In my case, while I thought at times, especially later in my career, that I was now finally doing my best work as a scientist, and while I found myself sometimes reading a research report with excitement, I know that much of the time the next paper that I wrote was just one more hard, grinding attempt to meet a self-imposed deadline for the sake of another line in the publication section of my curriculum vitae—feelings that are the hallmark of the ritualist.

As Merton suggested, these strategies are probably adaptations by faculty members at industrial-scale schools (and elsewhere) used especially by those who have had some insights into the difficulties of being producers of knowledge as well as skilled disseminators of knowledge. These strategies are certainly not the only ones available, and there may be healthier alternatives. Vincente and Deborah Lechuga (2012) noted that the members of the professoriate are carefully enculturated to think of their research as a product to be used and consumed by others. This model of research comports well with what Ernest Boyer (1990) described as the scholarship of discovery, which involves the commitment to knowledge for its own sake, to the freedom of inquiry, and to following, in a disciplined fashion, an investigation wherever it may lead.

But Lechuga and Lechuga point out that professors can also think of themselves as learners in their fields of study as well. In that sense, conducting research helps maintain a sense of vibrancy, currency, and vitality, each of which might be an important contributor to a professor's self-esteem, regardless of whether his or her research products are being used or consumed by others. This perspective comes closest to matching another form of scholarship identified by Boyer (1990): the scholarship of teaching. As he states, "teaching is also a dynamic endeavor involving all the analogies, metaphors, and images that build bridges between the teacher's understanding and the student's learning" (Boyer, 1990, p. 23). Thus, those professors who are primarily teachers (that is, most professors) must continue to be well informed about developments in their field; read deeply; and remain engaged with all the issues—empirical, theoretical, and pedagogical—as they emerge.

CONCLUSION

This chapter has been a long slog, and one along a sinuous path. What conclusions might be offered now the end of this particular part of the trail is in view? First, just as the professoriate is involved in numerous different kinds of teaching, each of which requires its own set of skills and talents, so the professoriate is heavily involved in numerous forms of research and scholarship. Second, as the twentieth century closed, faculty members at industrial-scale universities were spending more time and effort than ever before on research and scholarship that was becoming increasingly expensive and consuming of time and other resources. My work as a scientific researcher illustrates those processes in play. Third, in this work, faculty at nonelite schools were not duplicating the success of the professors at elite research institutions. The research the former did seems to have been of lower quality and less influential than that carried out by the former, and, strictly on a quantitative basis, the professors at industrial-scale schools were not catching up to the professors at research institutions—rather, they were falling further behind. In rebuttal, a critic might claim that all I really showed in this chapter was that I was neither fecund in bringing forth research nor influential with the research that I did manage to birth. Doubtless there are faculty members at nonelite schools who are every bit as prolific and whose work is as highly regarded as their colleagues at research institutions—I certainly knew at least a few who were. But for every one of those, there were many, many more who struggled, straggled, and finally fell out of the marching formation altogether. And there were many more who advanced at a plodding pace, and with varying amounts of conviction in the cause.

5 · WHERE SERVICE LEADS

If we were to display a pie chart of the typical professor's workload, with the various sections of the chart representing the proportion of the professor's time and effort allocated to the task in question, then I suspect that most people who work outside of higher education would be surprised, or even shocked, at both the existence and size of the service segment, a phenomenon that itself creates a bit of a puzzle. Theoretically, a professor's service mission is the one that is most likely to take him or her outside the department and into the wider community of the university as a whole, the local community, and ultimately the whole world. All of this might suggest that, for a person outside the higher education community who knows a professor personally, the connection might be the result of that professor's service role. But I think this reasonable-sounding theory is nevertheless incorrect: I believe the service role is the one most likely to produce reactions from many readers along the lines of "I had no idea"—especially when they find out that professors were required to perform service, how much they did, how great the time and commitment was, how varied the service was, and how many forms of service expertise were required to enable a modern university to function effectively. In fact, as I show in this chapter, the service work of the professoriate was, in its own way, as complex as the professor's teaching or research efforts and, in some cases, could be nearly as time-consuming.

The chapter seems to naturally divide itself into two major parts. The first part establishes the definition and context of the professoriate's service work. It includes a discussion of the factors that help a professor define his or her service identity, a process that is sometimes more difficult than might be supposed. The members of the professoriate jump into their research work, and are thrown into their teaching work. But they must figure out what to do—or, more accurately, who they want to be—with regard to their service work, and doing so requires some time and thought. There are a number of institutional factors that contribute the professoriate's willingness to engage in certain types of service; in the first section of the chapter, I discuss some of the consequences of a particular governance model for the professoriate's willingness to be of service.

In the chapter's second major part, I discuss the service activities I carried out on behalf of my department, institution, profession, and community across my time in higher education, from the end of the golden age to the beginning of the technological era. What did this service work consist of? What went on in the seemingly innumerable meetings I attended? But my use of the term "seemingly" is misplaced. Those meetings really were innumerable; there is no possibility at this stage that even my corpus of collected materials with all its details would enable me to make even a crude estimate of the number of meetings I attended in the service of my department and institution. What was accomplished and not accomplished in all those meetings? I provide answers to those questions in this chapter.

Finally, I discuss the one of the models of faculty service that has replaced the previous attention to the public good—namely, the use of permanent faculty members in a kind of hybrid role as professors qua administrators. Various factors pulled me in that direction for much of my career. I discuss this phenomenon from the standpoint of role strain, or the difficulty some members of the professoriate might have in maintaining a faculty identity while serving their institution in ways that may seem relatively far outside the boundaries of the traditional faculty role.

DEFINING THE PROFESSORIATE'S SERVICE CONTRIBUTION

Those who have worked inside higher education in any capacity will almost certainly be familiar with the concept of the professoriate having a service obligation, or owing a service debt to many stakeholders and constituents both within and without the institution's boundaries. But others, even those who were once college students themselves, may be much less familiar with the amount and nature of the professoriate's service work. Furthermore, while other professions, such as medicine or law, sometimes acknowledge that physicians or lawyers may have a moral obligation to provide services in addition to those for which they are being compensated, the service obligation of the professoriate might be unique in the sense that professors provide services that are different from those for which they were trained. That is, the service requirement of the professoriate does not necessarily involve more teaching or more research and scholarship. Finally, as I suggested above, other professions may discuss their service contribution in moral terms: what their members ought to do, given that they have a choice about their service. For the professoriate, the element of choice is removed from their service contribution; instead, it is required and obligatory.

First, I am making a distinction here between the concepts of service and a narrower, related concept, that of academic citizenship. Just as our normal civic processes require an engaged citizenry, so does the academic community require certain forms of engagement and participation to function. Thus, attending departmental faculty meetings, including participating at them with thoughtful and respectful reflection, is a facet of academic citizenship, not service, as is voting in faculty-held elections or participating in group interviews of candidates for administrative positions such as deans. Similarly, attending holiday parties and other celebratory functions, including the commencement ceremony, are probably better understood as elements of citizenship, not service. Obligatory participation that could be reasonably expected from everyone, at least most of the time, is not service, although such participation may be an important element of citizenship. Service always involves going beyond whatever minima are required for citizenship (thus, paradoxically, it is possible that poor citizenship might be excused in a faculty member who was an excellent service provider).

Second, a distinction must be made between the service contribution expected of the permanent (tenured or tenure-track) faculty and the service contributions of contract or contingent (that is, not eligible for tenure) faculty, be they full- or part-time faculty members. Generally, contingent faculty members, who have made up the majority of faculty members hired in the past forty years, do not have an explicit service obligation to either their institutions or their professions. While not excluded from playing a service role (indeed, I have known many nontenured faculty members who were devoted institutional servants over the years I worked), their performance evaluations are almost exclusively based on their teaching. The fact that the service obligation falls on the permanent faculty has some interesting implications. Because the proportion of contract to permanent faculty members has increased since the end of the golden age (circa 1970), and because the professoriate's service contribution is vital to the institution (Massé & Hogan, 2010), this means that service efforts of the remaining permanent faculty members have necessarily become more diverse and onerous from the end of the golden age through the beginning of the technological era.

With these distinctions in mind, I will define "service" for my purposes here as an ongoing activity that falls outside the traditionally defined boundaries of teaching and research and that involves some measure of time and effort neither necessarily related to the professor's expertise nor necessarily benefiting the professor monetarily or professionally. This activity must have as its goal the advancement of some unit's specific agenda, and this unit could be the faculty member's department, institution, profession, or community. My definition is perhaps somewhat more general than that of Anna Neumann and Aimee Terosky (2007), who identify three types of service (disciplinary, community, and institutional) and define institutional service as an effort that supports a campus's "mission, operations, and cultural life (e.g., service on curriculum committee, graduation committee)" (p. 283). As I show later in this chapter, committee work carried out on campus on behalf of the institution might be the heart and soul of faculty service. However, I engaged in numerous other institutional activities that did not involve working on a committee. In addition, as categorical as my definition might sound, the parameters around those activities that might constitute a given professor's service contribution are nevertheless often squishy and specific to the culture of the institution. For example, for many professors, the activity of serving as an acknowledged expert reviewer of manuscripts that have been submitted to a scientific or other scholarly journal (that is, the activity known as peer review) constitutes a pure service activity. At my home institution, peer review was not seen in quite that light. As a nonelite institution, my university was willing to honor the peer-review process as a form of recognition in which one of its faculty members was perceived as being competent enough to serve as an expert reviewer. Although these sorts of examples abound, I believe that there is still enough precision in my definition to make the counting and categorizing of the service work I did meaningful and comparable to professors, at least those at other nonelite schools.

THE LEARNING CURVE IN ACADEMIC SERVICE

Of all the activities in which the members of the professoriate may find themselves engaged, it is safe to say that PhD holders who begin their work in academia need no further training in the conduct of research and scholarship—after all, that is the principal activity involved in earning a PhD. Newly minted PhD holders may have acquired some formal training in teaching along the way to their degree, but even the majority of them who have not done so have nevertheless taken enough college courses at the undergraduate level and beyond to give them at least some rudimentary ideas regarding the organization and conduct of a university course, and about practicing the art of classroom instruction. But neither of these conditions is typically true with regard to the service contribution. Thus, the brand-new professor must find his or her own way in the dark and must do so quickly, because the professor's suite of service activities is always part of the evaluation process, at least nominally. Furthermore, in addition to lacking knowledge about service, the new faculty member may also not realize that there is a certain danger associated with service—the danger of doing too much or too little. A quick review of guidance in books for new members of the professoriate shows that both of these realities are dealt with, in some cases with greater neutrality than in others. For example, Wendy Crone (2012) advises an active exploration of service requirements with a mentor, a process that is similar to the one she recommends for new faculty members with regard to teaching and research. Jeffrey Bakken and Cynthia Simpson (2011) outline a similar approach, in which each of the three main strands of the professor's role (teaching, research, and service) is treated more or less equally. In contrast, Robert Boice (2000) is somewhat more guarded about service, recommending that new faculty members resist the pressure to jump immediately into service until they can learn the service culture at their institution and therefore find a balance between true service (service for others) and self-service (service that produces visible and tangible credit for its providers). Mohamed Noor (2012) has an even starker admonishment, suggesting in one of his chapters that service can be a waste of time.

Like many new faculty members (Whitfield & Hickerson, 2012), I was not particularly knowledgeable about service when I began my career. As part of my exit interview from graduate school, my dissertation advisor told me that he thought I would be a good teacher and a "good departmental citizen." I am certain that he used this exact phrasing, but I had only the vaguest idea of his meaning. And given that I had successfully defended my dissertation, I was eager to be off to my first real teaching position, one that would start only a few days later. No doubt I should have raised some questions, but I am not certain that I was even paying full attention at the time to my advisor's sage guidance. The fact that I am bringing it all up here is an indication that I would see the wisdom of his comment much later.

Still, the lack of concern on my part and that of others may be somewhat justified. Even if new professors do not know much about their service obligation, they may know that service is almost always seen as the third, and therefore least important, of the professor's three braided roles of teaching, research, and service. Interestingly, it may be the case that service is valued more in universities where research productivity is not so highly prized—that is, the nonelite or industrial-scale schools. For example, at Eastern Illinois University, the institution where I spent the majority of my career, each department is required to specify in its evaluation criteria the weight that an individual's service contribution will be accorded, relative to his or her research productivity, when the person is being evaluated for retention, tenure, or promotion. Although it is scarcely imaginable that any of the elite schools would put more weight on a person's service contribution than on his or her research productivity when evaluating the person for tenure, that is the case in several departments at my former school.

In a more general sense, even when the aggregate service rendered by a faculty member is ranked only in the third place for purposes of a personnel action, the even bleaker reality is that service may not matter much at all. In one of the few empirical studies devoted to the professoriate's service work, Boice (2000) tracked over twenty years' worth of tenure and promotion cases from a number of universities. He found that the extent and quality of the applicant's service contribution was never the determining factor in making a negative overall recommendation for tenure and promotion. And if the quality and extent of a professor's service does not matter for retention, tenure, or promotion, then members of the professoriate might be correct if what they learn about service during their careers is how to say no to doing any more than the minimum. But it might be more correct to state that the professoriate has not learned how to properly gauge the importance of its service contribution at any sort of institution. This is essentially the position that Katie Hogan and Michelle Massé (2010) arrived at following their analysis of the professoriate's service work. They point out that the actual labor of service is rarely tabulated or analyzed as a key aspect of higher education's political economy. Yet this work of the professoriate, invisible though it might be, is nevertheless crucial and necessary. According to Hogan and Massé, without professors' service, which is performed mostly by the thinning ranks of the tenure-track and tenured professoriate, the university would be forced to close its doors because it probably could not afford to pay independent contractors to do that work. In other words, what might appear diversionary—or even useless—is actually essential and should therefore be valued rather than dismissed.

THE INVISIBLE THREAD

What does service, especially institutional service, do? I am deliberately not asking what service consists of. Instead, the question I wish to address here has more to do with what is accomplished by the professoriate's constant doing of service and less to do with service's contents. Even this question is still somewhat imprecise. At one level, the professoriate's service is productive, in all the usual ways that academics may use that term: reports are written, recommendations for policy are offered, decisions about the future are made, and all of these represent a form of accomplishment. At another level, though, I will argue that the professoriate's doing of service also may also produce changes in the way the members of the professoriate view and identify themselves, their colleagues, and their institution.

To understand how this might work, we must first appreciate a fact lurking in the background, one that may not have been fully apparent until this point, even though it has been on display in the previous three chapters. That fact in the background is the concept of the professor's autonomy and independence as a worker. For example, strictly speaking, a professor has no boss (if, by that term, we mean a person with the authority to order a professor to do anything in particular), and other forms of supervision are light to nonexistent as well. No one keeps track of a professor's whereabouts. No one asks the professor to account for his or her time, at least not in comparison with the way other workers must account for their time on the job.

All this freedom might lead professors to believe that they are their own agents, responsible only to and for themselves. It is this illusion that I believe works to undermine the professoriate's willingness to serve. All their autonomy does not mean that there are no ties among the members of the professoriate—far from it. I chose the metaphor of the invisible thread to express this idea of the connectivity that must exist among faculty members at a particular institution: though it does not attack the illusion of complete agency directly (which is why members of the professoriate may continue to believe in that agency), the doing of service nevertheless operates as an invisible thread[1] that, like a lasso around the professors at an institution who have worked together, binds them and pulls them together in the sense of reducing the psychological distance between them. This gives the members of the professoriate an opportunity to realize the necessary connections among themselves. And finally, through service and the operation of the invisible thread, faculty members have an opportunity to realize their subservience. That is, they are also given an opportunity to realize the role they may play in achieving the goals of the various units in which they operate.

The "I" and the "We" in Service

As almost all professors are, I was assigned to or "housed" within a particular academic unit, a department containing other professors whose training was similar to mine. It was when I began my position as a tenure-track assistant professor in such a department that my service career, and my learning about the nature of academic service, began in earnest. In my first year in that position, the department chairperson assigned me to serve on the Curriculum Committee, and I attended its first meeting on September 17, 1979. In my files, I found the handwritten notes that I made at the meeting. We discussed the current alignment of topics within our two Introductory Psychology courses. We agreed to survey the professors in the department who taught either or both of the courses on a regular basis to see if we could find some common ground concerning which topics in Introductory Psychology should be taught in which course. I duly conducted the survey and presented the results to the faculty at a department meeting—my debut in formally addressing my departmental colleagues—on Thursday, October 25, 1979. There were no problems with our proposal; only one very senior faculty member questioned the need for any changes, and the reorganization proposal passed at the next faculty meeting, on Tuesday, November 20, 1979. The previous sentence expresses a rather subtle transformation: once I wrote the survey, tabulated the results (which I still possess), wrote the reorganization proposal, and circulated it to the members of the curriculum committee for their approval, the document stopped belonging to me and instead belonged to a larger entity (the Curriculum Committee). And once the department voted to accept it, the document became the basis of a departmental policy. I would not have been able to articulate it at the time, but I had learned a few important things in this simple episode that would be repeated countless times over the course of my career. First, the entity known as the Psychology Department was not simply an administrative convenience; instead, like an autonomous organism itself, it had its own goals and needs. It could be that these goals and needs arose from the specific interactions of its members, or perhaps from some other source. I am agnostic about their origin. But I am certain of their reality, as I am about the fact that in some cases, these needs existed at a level that was not simply the average of the need level of the entity's constituent members. A second point concerns the fact that, as Massé and Hogan (2010) described them, my teaching work and my research work continued to belong to me for as long as I did them. But my service work did not behave in quite the same way. Instead, it seemed to depart from me rather quickly and belonged instead to another agent, a collective one of which I was simply a part, and usually only a small part at that.

The Locals and the Cosmopolitans

In 1949, Robert Merton published the now-classic work *Social Theory and Social Structure* In one example presented in the book, Merton sought to identify people of influence among a magazine's subscribers who lived in a town in Massachusetts After solving the practical problem of identifying a certain set of influential people in the town through an interview process, Merton noticed that some individuals responded to the interview questions strictly in terms of conditions that were relevant in the town. But others, no less influential, frequently incorporated references to events and matters far beyond the town in their responses to the interview questions. Merton dubbed the people in the former group locals and the people in the second group cosmopolitans. Within a decade of its publication, other researchers (for example, Gouldner, 1958) had begun to apply the local-cosmopolitan distinction to the service orientation of the professoriate's members. Locals were professors whose service orientation was allegiant to their institution; they had an internal service orientation. Cosmopolitans exhibited an external service allegiance, one that focused on service to the professor's academic discipline rather than to the institution.

This distinction is important for a number of reasons, not the least of which is the fact that, as a beginning faculty member develops his or her service orientation, it appears that this distinction is one of the first dimensions to emerge in his or her evolving service identity. Earle Reybold and Kirsten Corda (2011) have provided some evidence in support of this assertion. They conducted a longitudinal study of pretenure faculty at a striving public university. Comments in the interview process suggested that many of these junior faculty members realized early in their tenure-track years that they had only a finite amount of time and energy to devote to service, and that service at the local level would therefore necessarily require time that could otherwise be devoted to external service. A comment such as the following from one of their respondents illustrates this thought process at work: "I have done a lot of service, but at the college level, and division level, and department level; I don't have a national presence" (Reybold & Corda, 2011, p. 135).

There is an inference that is perhaps invited here: service work that does not establish a national presence does not add any luster to one's professional credentials. Later in the interview process, the same respondent seemed to indicate as much when she stated that she felt her service was helping to build the institution but was not contributing to her career. Reybold and Corda (2011) found that, in their admittedly small sample, this perception was universal: all of their participants came to believe that the institution's expectations for service were that it would be in the service of the institution's goals—not their own.

Institutional Service and Morale

Historically—certainly in the technological era, if not before—faculty members have frequently reported that service is simply a waste of time (Tierney & Bensimon, 1996; Ward, 2003). Rather than figuring out what service activities might be most meaningful for them, it appears that many or most faculty members learn instead that the institution's attention to service is in reality only lip service.

But just as there are many attendant costs of performing service, as the forthcoming analysis of my work will show, there may also be hidden and unrealized costs involved with neglecting it. With regard to institutional service at least, service work affords the professor the opportunity to work with colleagues outside one's own disciplinary boundaries. In addition to the perspective taking and information gathering that can result from these contacts, there is also an opportunity to build trust and cooperation among colleagues, as the service work is divided up and portions of it completed by different individuals. This in turn may have a beneficial effect on organizational commitment, defined in terms of an individual's identification with or level of involvement in a particular organization (Mowday, Porter, & Steers, 1982).

In addition to this type of commitment, doing institutional service may have beneficial effects on morale. There are numerous ways to understand morale in organizations; I am using the term here in something like its military sense. That is, good morale characterizes the resiliency of some academic units to continue with their mission in the face of real and recognized short- and long-term threats to their well-being and stability. One possible source of good morale might be the sense of participating in a community within the institution, and with that participation, the idea that processes or events that have a negative effect on one of the individuals in the community have the potential to negatively affect the other members as well. This line of thought might suggest that the participation in departmental or institutional service may have positive effects on a unit's sense of community, which in turn may foster positive effects on morale. Some research indicates this chain of events is at least plausible. For example, Susan Marston and Gerald Brunetti (2009) asked their respondents, who were professors with at least fifteen years of teaching experience, a number of questions dealing with job satisfaction. One of the questions was how important service on committees should be in the life of a professor. The following response is typical of these experienced professors: "I think it is critical. People who come to the office, teach, go home—that's enough for them but that doesn't help create a community" (Marston & Brunetti, 2009, p. 334).

INSTITUTIONAL SERVICE UNDER THE PRINCIPLES OF SHARED GOVERNANCE

Earlier in this chapter I suggested that the junior members of the professoriate had not been adequately prepared for their service role in the academy, and as a result, they began their careers by ascending a kind of learning curve for service—a curve whose trajectory could take those members of the professoriate in at least a couple of directions, with potential consequences for themselves and their institutions. Despite the almost all-encompassing autonomy of the professoriate, institutions of higher education are not helpless in shaping which service path their faculty members choose to take. In this section I discuss one institutional approach to service that may foster organizational commitment among faculty members—at least, it is thought to do so when it has been implemented correctly. As I show, however, even with this approach, which empowers faculty members to shape policy and participate in important institutional decisions, faculty participation may not always be enthusiastic.

My former institution, Eastern Illinois University, was administered under the principles of a model known as shared governance. The basic principles of this model have been in wide use in higher education since at least the early 1900s (Tierney & Lechuga, 2004). These features include the creation of, and granting of official status to, a number of boards, panels, committees, councils, and other bodies that are staffed by faculty members and other employees of the institution and charged with a number of responsibilities, which might include oversight of aspects of the institution's processes, crafting language that might be used in future policy, fact-finding, listening to various constituents, and reporting. Faculty members are encouraged to participate in governance, either through elected committees, such as the Faculty Senate, or appointed panels. Eastern currently recognizes approximately thirty elected committees and another thirty appointed ones.

There is widespread support among the professoriate for the principles of shared governance. In a study spanning 750 institutions and encompassing over

3,800 participants, William Tierney and James Minor (2003) found that more than 80 percent of faculty members believed that shared governance was an important part of their institution's values and identity. This level of approval, and with it a willingness to participate, was, however, strongly conditioned on which aspect of the institution's functioning was in question. Faculty members were most supportive of shared governance in matters of curriculum, curricular planning, setting standards for teaching, and setting standards for promotion and tenure (W. Jones, 2012). They were substantially less likely to approve of shared governance in matters that seemed purely budgetary. A shared governance model can be particularly effective when there is a level of trust among the various constituents that warrants cooperation.

The shared governance model is usually contrasted with an approach that is often referred to as the top-down model. One of the key ways in which these models differ is in the degree to which they offer faculty members and others a chance to articulate their interests. Under the principles of shared governance, faculty members are given opportunities to voice concerns, opinions, and suggestions concerning university policy and thus to potentially help shape the decisions that are being made to take the institution forward. At institutions where the top-down model is in place, authority is housed only at the highest levels and is often stingily delegated downward through a chain of command (such a chain of command could run from the president through the provost and dean to the unit chair or head). Faculty members find usually find themselves at the bottom of this rigid hierarchy (Jenkins & Jensen, 2010). Articulating their legitimate interests to those above them is challenging for faculty members when their input is not sought, and in general, faculty members at such institutions are less likely to show an organizational commitment to the institution.

As the twenty-first century wends its way forward, the shared governance model has come under scrutiny on a number of bases, not the least of which is the fact that one of its underlying assumptions is that most of the burden of shared governance must fall on permanent faculty members, the very group whose numbers are steadily—and probably irreversibly—dwindling. In the absence of a cadre of permanent faculty of sufficient critical mass, shared governance models may no longer continue to function at all (Eckel & Kezar, 2006), or such models may be required to change in ways big and small (Crellin, 2010; Gallos, 2009).

Symptomatic of these changes, my former institution has found it to be a challenge to identify faculty members who have the organizational commitment, or whatever else is required, to participate in shared governance at the institutional level. For, despite the findings I cited indicating that they say they want shared governance, members of the professoriate—including my former colleagues— can nevertheless be very casual in their commitment to it. For example, in spring

2014 (this example comes from the year after I retired, but the pattern is all too typical of the years when I taught there), the Faculty Senate at Eastern conducted elections for eleven boards or committees throughout the university, on which there were twenty-six open positions. Most of these positions had to be filled by a permanent faculty member, of whom there were approximately 430 at the time. When the nomination petitions were returned, it turned out that for twelve of those twenty-six positions, there was only one candidate. Even worse, for five positions, there were no candidates at all—not a single person had come forward—with the result that only nine of the twenty-six positions were contested. After the election was held, it was discovered in a few cases that the solitary candidate who ran was ineligible to serve on the committee, meaning that fully five of the twenty-six positions went unfilled after a fairly labor-intensive process by the Faculty Senate to conduct the election.

VARIETIES OF SERVICE

Just as a professor's roles in teaching and in research or scholarship have many facets and nuances, a professor's service work will require him or her to work with a number of different constituencies, stakeholders who are often understood as operating at different levels in their relation to the basic departmental unit that usually characterizes the most local and fundamental of all the groups to which the professor might owe allegiance. Although it would probably be more accurate to think of these stakeholders as operating at different radii or being in different orbits as they revolve around the department, as the department itself revolves around the university, I will nevertheless stick with the conventional language and detail my service at five levels: departmental; college; university; professional; and finally, and most tortuously, public service. In a separate section I will deal with the operation of a particular kind of committee, the search committee, which functioned as a kind of all-purpose engine for admitting new members of the professoriate, as well as other professionals, into the academy. My plan is to march through these varieties of service relatively briskly, first focusing on the nature of the work and its volume, or proportion of my overall service work, if possible. In a later section, I offer a summary of the service work that I did in terms of what I learned by doing it.

Departmental Service

Table 5.1 shows the Psychology departmental committees on which I served at Eastern, or similar roles I fulfilled. On the left side of the table, I have listed the name of the committee or role—I will explain some of them shortly—and on the right side, I have quantified my length of service, using the concept of a committee-year. That is, one year's service on a particular committee has been counted as one committee-year. Given that my career at Eastern spanned thirty-four years, and I have accounted for some eighty-three service years of activity at this level, it is valid to infer that I served on several departmental committees most years. From the perspective of the volume of the work, I have seventy-four files consisting of numerous forms of documentation (memos, notes, drafts of documents, guidance from the administration, and so on), or an estimated 4,919 pages collectively, that document my departmental committee work.

The fourteen committees or roles listed in the table probably includes all of the ones that my former department fielded, but the departmental unit expanded and collapsed some of the committees as the need arose, or as a threat to the department's integrity may have passed. For example, my two years of service as the departmental newsletter editor occurred in the 1980, prior to onslaught of technology. In the 2000s, I served on the External Relations Committee, which took over some of the functions of the newsletter and put the results on the department's website. Most of the committees listed are standard departmental level organizations; for example, almost all university departments ask some of their members to serve on a personnel committee that makes recommendations (or decisions) on the retention, tenure, and promotion of its faculty members.

Actually, this listing and discussion of committees and their purposes and methods does not exhaust all of the service activities on which I expended efforts at the departmental level. There were a number of other varied service activities, some of which were very transient and ad hoc. For example, a given day

TABLE 5.1. Service Contributions at the Departmental Level

Departmental committee or ad hoc role	Committee-years of service
Personnel	27
Curriculum	16
External Relations	9
Spencer-McGown-Wilson Award	5
Department assessment coordinator	4
Graduate	4
Library liaison	4
Assessment	3
Facilities Use and Planning	3
Awards	2
Enrollment Management	2
Newsletter editor	2
Budget	1
Retirement and Summer Teaching	1
Total departmental committee service	83
Total ad hoc departmental service	11
Total departmental service	94

might find me writing letters of recommendation for colleagues and students, giving a talk at the institutional level that included a history of the Psychology Department at the fiftieth anniversary of the graduate school's founding, or conducting the byzantine Personnel Committee election.[2] But there were also other activities that required a longer and sustained commitment of time and involved meetings. Among other things, these activities included organizing discussion groups, planning departmentwide retreats, setting up research colloquia, organizing dinner meetings for older faculty members (we used the term "veteran" faculty members), serving on a committee to study faculty replacement procedures, and serving as the designated deputy chair during the department chair's vacation days, which I did from 2001 to 2013. Taking this work into account in my departmental service portfolio adds another eleven committee-years, twelve files, and nearly 2,000 pages of documentation, for a total departmental service contribution of ninety-four committee-years, documented by eighty-six paper files whose total content I estimated to be 5,116 pages.

College of Sciences Service

Table 5.2 summarizes my service contributions at the college level. By any measure of workload that I have been using to compute service (such as committee-years, number of paper files, and numbers of pages in those files), there is much less here than at either the departmental level below it or the university level above it. But despite that fact, there are still several interesting features about this service. First, there was clearly a representational aspect in my service at the college level that was not so readily apparent in my departmental service. At the college level I might be expected to advocate for the goals of a particular constituency (the people in my department). Yet it was still incumbent on me to seek common ground with the other committee members and to be cooperative. The result of those pressures was that I learned to prioritize my advocacy concerns: if all the committee members on a college-level committee insisted on achieving all their goals, the result would be a gridlock in which nobody was served.

TABLE 5.2. Service Contributions at the College Level

Service	Years involved	Committee-years of service
Ringenberg Award Selection	2001–5	5
Baharlou Award Selection	2010–13	3
Cognitive Science Initiative	1994, 2000	2
Physical Sciences Space Allocation	1996, 2003	2
Priorities	1995–97	2
Special Investigation	2002–3	1
Total College of Science service	Not applicable	13

In writing about the *I* and the *we* in service earlier in the chapter, I noted that as a result of my service work, I came to learn that the Psychology Department had its own needs and goals that were in some ways independent of the needs of its members. That comment could apply to the College of Sciences as well. When I worked on the Priorities Committee, for example, it became very clear to me that the dean, who had organized the committee, had a number of goals that she wanted the college to achieve, including the awarding of scholarships and the carving out special funds for research travel, equipment, and internal grants awarded to a department for renovations that might be required for new curricular programming. But the dean was often thwarted from achieving any of these goals: the money required to pay for them usually seem to evaporate into the departmental budgets for overload pay—pay for faculty members who voluntarily agreed to teach courses beyond the contractual maximum required. Essentially, the dean wanted committee members (faculty members from various departments) to cooperate to find ways that this sort of overload pay could be minimized, even though, at the department level, getting the overload pay was something that some faculty members clearly wanted. Third and finally, it is important to see that there were continuities across the department and college levels as well: there was a college-level curriculum committee (on which I did not serve) and collegewide awards program for students and faculty. In both cases, departmental faculty members were charged with the responsibility of making recommendations for the various awards.

University Service

Table 5.3 shows the fifteen different university-level committees, boards, councils, or panels on which I served a total of seventy-one committee-years. Space considerations preclude a detailed discussion of the role and mission of each of these entities, although that information may be obvious for a few of them. For example, faculty senates are historically among the most important organs of a university operating under the principles of shared governance. Over 90 percent of the colleges and universities in the United States have an entity that performs functions typical of a faculty senate, though the entity may have a different name (Tierney & Minor, 2003). But the name is not always a reliable indicator of the work that the entity can do—some faculty senates are little more than a ceremonial body. However, in other institutions (including Eastern), the faculty senate may be a powerful body capable of helping craft policy language, when asked to do so; operating as a sounding board for the administration; engaging in fact-finding; and, finally, serving as the locus for the faculty's ability to speak truth to power. Other panels that I have listed may be less familiar to those who work outside higher education, and possibly even to those within it, if they work for an institution that does not engage in certain forms of research. For example, the

TABLE 5.3. Service Contributions at the University Level

Service	Years involved	Committee-years of service
Institutional Review Board	1987–2010	23
Faculty Senate	1996–2002, 2008–11	9
University Personnel Committee	1981–87, 1993–96	9
Sanctions and Termination Hearing Committee	1999–2002, 2011–13	5
Veteran Faculty Circles	2001–2, 2005–9	5
Council on University Planning and Budget	2005–8	3
Enrollment Management Advisory Board	1999–2002	3
Honors Council	2006–9	3
Judicial Board	1992–95	3
Assessment/Student Learning Committee	2011–13	2
Distinguished Faculty Award Committee	2006–8	2
Faculty Excellence Task Force	1985–987	2
Library Advisory Board	1992–94	2
McNair Grant reader	2006–7	1
Retention Task Force	2001–2	1
Total university service	Not applicable	71

Institutional Review Board—on which I served for twenty-three years, chairing it from 2003 to 2010—was responsible for reviewing all research at the institution that involved human participants, with the aim of making sure that the research was both sound and ethical.

Some of the committees seem to duplicate those at the level of the college or even the department. For example, as table 5.3 shows, I was involved once again with an awards committee, this time for a universitywide Distinguished Faculty Award. There was also a university-level Library Advisory Board, which duplicated a structure present at the departmental level. Even more important, the University Personnel Committee made recommendations directly to the provost regarding retention, tenure, and promotion of permanent faculty members. However, I also served the university in some roles that were unique to that level of organization. Veteran Faculty Circles is an example of this form of service. As my own career developed and matured, I became more convinced that my institution was somewhat unaware of the problems, issues, and concerns that affected veteran faculty members, as opposed to its awareness of the challenges facing junior faculty members. So, whereas the institution organized and maintained an explicit, high-profile program for mentoring junior faculty, as was appropriate, there was no formal attention devoted to the legion of issues that veteran faculty must face to continue to be successful. On my own initiative, later recognized and sanctioned by the institution, I established a program for such faculty based on my growing convictions that there were particular topics that veteran faculty members needed to discuss among themselves and that it was only veteran faculty members who could speak on those topics with any real authority or validity.

Professional or Disciplinary Service

Almost all of the permanent members of the professoriate are affiliated in varying degrees with supra-institutional professional or disciplinary organizations. Like the universities, which require faculty labor to thrive or even exist, these professional organizations encourage and require their members to perform any number of functions. In this section and the next one, I detail the service work I performed outside the boundaries of my institution (before coming back within its walls to discuss my doings in the final category of service work).

As is true of institutional service, professional service can be defined in terms of work carried out at any one of a number of levels. At the highest level, professional service consists of executing some recognized, recurring role with a professional organization or other professionally defined entity. Such work includes editing a scholarly journal, leading a national or international organization, and reviewing federal grants as a regular panel member. At a less engaged, ad hoc level, disciplinary service might consist of reviewing journal articles, books, or conference presentations on an as-needed or as-requested basis, as a part of the peer-review process. It might also consist of serving as an outside consultant in a tenure review, as I did on a couple of occasions. Tellingly, when I organized all of the paper records that I kept in the corpus, I found that I had no records of sustained professional or disciplinary service; the service that I carried out was very much in the latter, ad hoc, category. That conclusion is supported by an examination of my electronic records as well. I was able to locate electronic records of disciplinary service activity—for example, the text of a keynote address that I delivered at an undergraduate research conference in 1999. But I did not find any electronic records indicative of sustained, high-level professional service involvement—an outcome that I believe is very indicative of my status as a self-diagnosed member of my institution's localist contingent, rather than its cosmopolitans. My affiliation with national organizations of psychologists or cognitive scientists was limited to my membership in such organizations.

Public Service

Perhaps because academics work in settings that are, by definition, not open to everybody, they sometimes face criticism claiming them to be removed from everyday life. The enduring image of the ivory tower may be invoked to symbolize this remoteness. There is an irony in this particular symbol: many of this nation's greatest universities were created as a direct result of the Land-Grant College Act of 1862 (often referred to as the Morrill Act), which ceded to states federal lands with the explicit objective of erecting on them universities that would serve nation's interests in agriculture, industry, and its people.

In response, in the nineteenth century, uniquely American universities sprang up, weaving together some traditions of the British universities, with their emphasis on the humanities (a strand that is very much present in the undergraduate curriculum of many universities); models from the German universities, with their emphasis on science; and finally an American strand emphasizing the need for the institution to be in the service of the people for whom it was created.

But as a former president of the University of California, Clark Kerr (1963), pointed out over fifty years ago in a series of lectures delivered at Harvard University and shortly thereafter worked into a book, a number of forces unleashed in the twentieth century conspired to change the university into a different entity, with a different purpose than previously. And in Kerr's view, that purpose had become the production of knowledge—vast quantities of knowledge and information, scientific findings, and other discoveries that fueled the technological progress that gave the United States an insurmountable lead in every aspect of its national enterprise. Massive federal grants that were awarded to universities in the 1950s and later fostered the model of the research university with its emphasis on productivity, and that model became increasingly likely to eclipse the more balanced vision of the university inherent in the Morrill Act. Under these changed conditions, the research institutions, and soon other institutions as well, simply tied their professors closer to what seemed to be the most important one of their three historic roles: research.

All this might seem an arid and somewhat pedantic exhumation of the past were it not for the fact that these forces have had demonstrable and continual effects on the way the professoriate works and the ways in which its work is evaluated and rewarded. To show these effects on my career, I need to refer to some of the circumstances of my position at a public university whose faculty members were organized under the terms of a collective bargaining agreement. Because the collective bargaining process seemed to work best when expectations and obligations on both sides (the administration and the faculty) were clearly and precisely expressed, each academic unit was required to develop a document that would express, with the most precision the unit could muster, its requirements for retention, tenure, and promotion (in the case of the permanent faculty).

Each unit's document was also required to be aligned with the broad-based criteria promulgated in the agreement or contract that our union representatives negotiated, and that is why the resulting document had the rather grand title of Departmental Application of Criteria (DAC).

For this analysis I began by studying the DAC that was in use from 1992 to 1995. Until the end of that time period, the DAC did not attempt to break down the levels of service as I have done in this chapter. Instead, the 1992–95 DAC listed just six instances of suggested activities that would be clearly counted as service in a faculty member's portfolio. None of the six activities pertained to work outside the university or the disciplinary boundary. This began to change with a revision to the DAC dated April 1993. This revised version of the DAC was the first one in our department to show a breakdown of service activity into the different levels that I have used in this chapter, so it was the first version to include the heading "Community Service," thus legitimizing this level for inclusion in a portfolio. But the language defining "community service" restricted it to just two forms of activity. Faculty members could engage in community service by either offering "public lectures, etc." for "audiences other than professional peers" or by providing "consultative services involving faculty member's expertise" with "non-psychologists outside the university." And that language remained in our DAC until I retired.

Thus, the DAC in the Psychology Department at Eastern did show a limited form of evolution with regard to the inclusion and documentation of community service during the final twenty years I worked there, in the sense that service to Eastern's various publics was eventually recognized and credited. But this movement toward recognition of public or community service was conditioned on the kinds of changes Kerr noted in the concept of the multiversity. That is, even the professor's public service needed to be related to an exchange of information of some sort, and the information exchanged needed to be related to the professor's expertise somehow, although that term was never itself defined. But all of the other numerous valid forms of community service (such as service on a school board or city council, and coaching a Little League team, to name just a few) still could not be credited in a professor's portfolio, unless the applicant managed to show, through some rather convoluted language in the portfolio's narrative, that the activity was both consultative and somehow involved the faculty member's expertise. In this approach, one can see the attempt, probably not made at a conscious level, to align the faculty's public service mission with the public service mission of some other professions such as medicine or law—in which the service rendered pro bono might be identical to the service that was rendered professionally. That practice is all well and good, but such an approach nevertheless had a chilling effect the faculty's performance of certain types of public service, and they happened to be those that were most clearly alignable with the larger public service mission of the institution—that is, civic engagement for the public good.

SEARCH COMMITTEES

Until this point, I have found it convenient and useful to organize the chapter around the trope of levels of service, starting at what was for me and most academics the most intimate service level, the department, and radiating outward, ultimately beyond the walls of the institution into the wider world of the profession and the community. But that useful organizing scheme breaks down somewhat in attempts to discuss the work of that most unusual form of service-rendering committee, the search committee. For not only did the members of the professoriate provide needed service to other existing stakeholders within and without the institution, they often played a significant role in replicating themselves—that is, in admitting other people into the role that they played and, by doing so, creating new members of the professoriate. And the professoriate's role was not limited simply to faculty searches: as one of the most important constituencies on a university campus, faculty members were often chosen to serve on committees tasked with finding suitable administrative and staff people for the institution.

As was the case with virtually everything the professoriate did during the 2000s, changes in technology played a role in the operation of the search committee. In 2001, when I served as a member of the search committee for the provost's position at my institution, the applicants submitted paper copies of their materials. The committee's support person (usually the office manager in whatever department the search committee chairperson was from) was then responsible for receiving and collating those materials and for keeping them in an accessible but nevertheless secure location for the search committee members, who were obligated to review the materials in person, on their own schedule, during the normal business hours of the institution. Thus, it was commonplace for the committee members, who otherwise might not have any reason to communicate, to sometimes find themselves sharing the secure space and perhaps having a conversation about the files they had reviewed, sometimes with enthusiasm, sometimes otherwise.

But these practices fell by the wayside as the 2000s went forward. In the 2012–13 academic year, when I chaired a search committee for the position of dean of the Honors College at my institution, there was no more paper submission of application materials—everything consisted of an electronic file, stored on a secure website accessible only by the search committee members and by personnel in the Provost's Office. As the chair of the search committee, I used the e-mail channel to communicate with the committee members; the support staff who placed the position announcement in various locations on the World Wide Web; the technical support person at the institution who was responsible for setting up and keeping secure the information stored there; the administration;

the applicants themselves, whose questions about the position were directed to me; and perhaps other people as well. These facts have some implications for the nature of this important work for the professoriate of the future. During the time I chaired the search committee I described—whose work began in the middle of October and lasted for five months, until the middle of the following March, when my involvement in the process concluded—or a period of perhaps 100 workdays, I sent and received (and read and processed) some hundreds of e-mails dealing with the search, and each one of them was an opportunity to fumble rather than carry the ball. The number of e-mails in my case seems to comport pretty well with the number reported by Phoenix Lam (2013), who recorded 2,063 e-mail messages received in one year, from 292 different senders. But the majority of them, 1,659 (80.4 percent) messages, were sent from 156 different internal colleagues, similar to what I noted in my e-mail box with regard to the search.

Turning to the body of work itself, my corpus of paper records shows that I chaired or served on twenty-seven search committees in my thirty-four years of service at my former school, thus establishing this form of service as accounting for a sizable proportion of my total institutional service commitment, given that each search committee required the better part of an academic year to complete its work. (However, I have not added these committee-years to any of tables that I presented above, although doing so would certainly be valid.) Of those twenty-seven search committees, eight were concerned with the hiring of an individual whose work was primarily at the institutional level, either as a staff person (such as the director of admissions or director of research), or as an academic person (such as provost or dean). The nineteen remaining search committees dealt with hiring an individual who would work at the departmental level. These nineteen committees represent a substantial percentage of all the search committees that were formed during the time when I worked at my former institution, from 1979 to 2013. In that period, my former department added seventy-three new faculty members (according to a spreadsheet that I maintained to track such things) who were employed on at least a half-time basis, for at least one year. Significantly, at my former institution, forty-three (59 percent) of those new faculty members were hired as tenured or tenure-track professors—a figure that bucks the national trend of only 33 percent of all new faculty positions being awarded to tenured or tenure-track people. All forty-three of those positions would have required a national-level search, coordinated by a designated search committee. My estimate is that for approximately 25 percent of the contingent faculty members hired during the same period, the hiring process was aided by an ad hoc committee of permanent faculty members who functioned in ways similar to a full-blown search committee. If the addition of that number boosts the total number of search committees formed in the department to fifty or thereabouts, which I think is a reasonable estimate, then it appears that I served on slightly less than 40 percent of the faculty search committees in our department during the time I worked for my former institution. Given that a typical departmental search committee consisted of four to five faculty members, and given that we had a baseline number of approximately twenty faculty members in our department, then it would appear that a faculty member might legitimately expect to be asked to serve on 25 percent of the departmental search committees.

WHAT WAS THE WORK IN SERVICE?

A Professor at the End of Time is a book about work—my work and, as I have extended it, the work of the professoriate at large, especially the work of those at nonelite schools, at the beginning of the technological era in higher education. So, after discussing all the varieties of service and their sundry levels, it is fair to ask what the work in service actually consisted of.

The answer is that the work depended somewhat on the variety of service, particularly with regard to what proportion of the work involved real-time meetings and their number, frequency, duration, and location. For example, public service work may have required participation in an activity that did not necessarily involve attendance at meetings, at least in the sense of the meetings that I discuss in depth later in this section. Professional service, in the way that the term is usually understood, may have required serving as an editor or other reviewer, and that work could be done during unscheduled times. Serving as an officer in a professional organization, another form of professional service, may have involved a mixture of meetings and individual activity. In some cases of institutional service, the work might involve listening and speaking, in an effort to get people involved or bring people together. For example, some of the fund-raising that I carried out for my former institution in the 1980s and 1990s involved making phone calls to alumni, but at that time I was not involved in any meetings with alumni or other interested donors. Similarly, in the case of the Veteran Circles that I organized in the early- to mid-2000s, most of the work involved making phone calls and writing letters to those older faculty members who might be interested in the program. The actual meetings of the veteran faculty, which consisted of my hosting dinners at off-campus restaurants where our often spirited and wide-ranging discussions could occur, were painless and fun, certainly in comparison to some other meetings I have endured. On some occasions, travel became part of the service work. An example of this was my participation on the institutional-level Retention Task Force in the early 2000s that involved attendance at a distant conference that provided institutional representatives with knowledge they could use to help increase the likelihood that their first-year students would return for their second year of higher education.

But most institutional service was rendered on a face-to-face basis, in real time, in the form of a meeting—an event that was packaged with a set of activities related to preparing for such a meeting and another set of activities for dealing with the consequences of having attended one. Over their careers, academics develop a concept, or a cognitive scheme, which is something like a mental blueprint, for the structure and operation of the committee meetings they attend. The existence of this scheme does not mean that professors enter meetings already knowing what will happen, only that they enter them having expectations about the meeting's likely direction and plans for particular eventualities in the meeting itself. This cognitive scheme probably arises from the number of regularities that almost omnipresent in the meetings professors attend. For example, almost all of the meetings that professors attend as part of their institutional service are presided over by a recognized chair who has set the agenda and has promulgated it in advance of the meeting. Thus, when my faculty colleagues complained that the agenda for a regular departmental faculty meeting sometimes did not appear until merely hours before the meeting, the complaint can be understood as a schematic violation—that is, the delay was a threat to their planning capabilities. As this suggests, when professors enter a meeting, they generally know where they intend to stand on the agenda items. Sometimes their positions are well known to their colleagues inside (and beyond) the academic unit, sometimes less so.

At the meeting, the professors' work is focused on analyzing information or data that might be presented. There is almost always a discussion on which attention must be focused. Although not every point is crucial to every professor in a given meeting, each professor may hope to construct arguments or make points that he or she hopes are cogent and relevant. Finally, the meeting may include the formulation of policy, and those policies may be supported by voting. Each one of these putative actions or events at a meeting—analysis, discussion, and voting—may require the professor to work.

In addition to these elements of the professor's service work—which are organized by the professor's cognitive scheme for meetings—there is also the work involved in conduct or behavior at the meeting. These work elements may include listening, speaking, and, for some professors, taking notes.

There is a brief coda to this section. After I retired I agreed to serve with a group whose members were interested in forming an arts council in the small town in which I lived. Doing so required my attendance at a number of meetings. It was in those meetings that I realized how much I had learned about meetings in my academic life, such as how to conduct myself, listen, determine other committee members' agendas, unify the contributions of others with a bridging or connecting comment, keep the meeting on track with my contribution, and get my contributions heard (and those are just some of the "how to" questions I could answer; there would be another long list of "when to" questions to which I could also respond). The upshot of this episode is that I did not realize until after I retired how skillful professors are at making meetings progress to some objective, nor did I realize how much of this competence I had acquired through my own institutional service.

FACULTY IN ADMINISTRATIVE ROLES

The professor standing in my office doorway was in the midst of arguing for his position on some issue, and the urgency and strength of his conviction was apparent. When it became my turn to speak, I happened to use the phrase "as faculty members, we"—whereupon he broke in: "You're a faculty member? You seem more like an administrator to me." At the time of this conversation, his office and mine were in the same department, on the same corridor. My office, identical to his in almost every particular, was two doors down from his.

What would make me "seem more like an administrator," despite all the similarities in our external trappings, and despite the fact that we had worked together as departmental colleagues for nearly twenty years at that point? After all, for a faculty member like me to serve in an administrative role seems like just one more example of institutional service by a professor. But my colleague was on to something, although in the heat of the moment, he may not have expressed it very clearly: when members of the professoriate serve in administrative roles, there are some differences, subtle and otherwise, between that service and the normal institutional service associated with the Faculty Senate and similar groups. First, there is the notion of the source of authority. The authority of professors' voices on almost any topic resides in their expertise and knowledge level in their professional role as teachers and scholars. So when they attend a meeting, they bring their authority in the door with them. This is much less true in the case of many administrators, not that they lack knowledge or expertise. But rather the authority in the administrator's voice may be more narrowly defined by his or her place in a hierarchical organization chart: it is imbued in his or her position. Second, there may be questions of value systems and identities. Values, value systems, and the identities that arise from them are highly important in higher education. Peter Scott (2004) has gone so far to assert that public universities may be "the most value-laden institutions in modern society" (p. 439). As Richard Winter and Wayne O'Donohue (2012) have expressed it, the academic identity can be localized in the liberal values of truth and critical inquiry, its appreciation of learning and scholarship, and finally its passion for intellectual freedom for its own sake. But those values all weigh something, too, and lugging around any one of them, let alone all of them, might be a burden too heavy to fit in any administrator's briefcase.

Concretizing this theoretical discourse somewhat, my former institution simply used one of its available mechanisms to borrow (actually, it was a form of buying) its permanent faculty members to fulfill some administrative roles, while nevertheless leaving them located primarily within their departments to serve all the normal functions of the professoriate. Previously, I explained the Credit Unit (CU) model and its use in assigning faculty members their teaching loads. Under the provisions of this model, all teaching work could be broken down into its essential elements and converted to a kind of currency called the CU that could then be used to equate teaching assignments. The tasks of the administrative role and the teaching assignments could then be swapped out for whatever the equivalent number of CUs happened to be.

Table 5.4 shows, in chronological order at the time of appointment, the five administrative roles that I played in the department and in the institution. Actually, I came out of the faculty ranks to serve as the Psychology Department acting chair. In the parlance of our institution, "I left the unit" (that is, the bargaining unit), because department chairs were not considered faculty members, although they all held faculty rank and taught regularly, and carried out research in many cases.

Although I was comfortable serving in these roles most of the time, there were definitely occasions in which I experienced a phenomenon known as role strain. According to sociological theory, people tend to organize their behavior in terms of the structurally defined expectations assigned to each role (Merton, 1949). In modern society, when people occupy more than one role—and indeed many people in modern society are multiselved—role strain can occur when people are confronted with expectations that are incompatible with particular roles. For example, numbers (as in the number of students in a class, or the number of students enrolled in a program) are not necessarily that important to the professoriate, because numbers do not have any real bearing on the values of critical inquiry, scholarship, or intellectual freedom that make up the academic identity. But a frank acknowledgment of the importance of numbers is crucial to many administrators. So as a professor teaching in the Honors College, I did not feel any urgency about the relatively small size of the classes I taught—in fact, those small sizes only seemed to help me with an important part of my identity as a professor, that of fostering learning. But as the coordinator of our department's Honors Program, I realized that it would be best if I maintained a particular number of students in the program for it to help pay for itself or to enable it to deliver the biggest bang for the buck. The emphasis on money in both phrases is telling. Neither public nor private universities are run according to the logic of profit, but neither can they afford to go broke, and that factor was always particularly important in admitting students to the Honors Program or the General Master's Degree program that I coordinated

TABLE 5.4. Administrative Roles

Administrative role	Years involved	Credit Unit equivalency per year
General master's degree coordinator	1981–84	3
Departmental honors coordinator	1984–2013	3
Psychology Department acting chair	1997–98	24
Institutional Review Board chair	2003–10	6
Assistant department chair	2009–13	6

for a few years, or in managing the resources of the entire Psychology Department as I did for one year. Returning to my colleague standing in the doorway, if I seemed like an administrator to him, it may have been because I was not showing the effects of role strain strongly enough to suit him. I should have been more uncomfortable with my administrative duties than he apparently thought I was.

CONCLUSION

As was seen in the performance of teaching duties and the conduct of research and scholarship, in service the professoriate also engages in many forms of the work. My career certainly bears the markings of a professor who did so. These service forms can be understood hierarchically, as beginning within the institution and radiating outward, and as activities that either enhance a professor's status in the community of academics or that have nothing to do with that pursuit.

Where service leads—I designed the chapter title to have at least two meanings. It might be part of a question about the direction of service: Where does service lead? What seems to happen when a professor takes a particular direction in discharging his or her service obligations? When faculty gravitate toward departmental, college, and university service (all in the category of institutional service as delineated by Neumann & Terosky, 2007), that may result ultimately in the creation of a local professor—a loyal and knowledgeable servant of the institution whose perspective is almost necessarily limited. On a more positive note, such a localist may be more capable of institutional thinking than other professors are, and as the professoriate may be forced to reinvent itself in future decades, those professors who can think that way may find themselves more useful to their institutions than their more cosmopolitan colleagues are, at least at industrial-scale schools. However, while less likely than the localist to think institutionally, the cosmopolitan may be might be more likely than the localist to develop the big picture as a result of his or her greater involvement at the national level. In addition, he or she may be more able than the localist to bring useful knowledge from other campuses back to the home campus.

But I intended the phrase "where service leads", to be the basis of another question as well: at which institutions, if any, does service lead in contrast to the other two traditional roles of the faculty? Given that the most fundamental priority of higher education involves teaching, there are probably no institutions of higher education where service by the professoriate is more valued than its capability for research and teaching. But there may be schools where the professoriate's complex and multifaceted service to all its numerous constituents and stakeholders appropriately occupies a more central role in the evaluation of faculty members, in their advancement, and in the continued vitality of the institution than does the professoriate's ability to create knowledge in research and scholarship. And it seems that if such institutions exist, they are more likely to be found among the ranks of the schools that I have categorized as industrial scale, where more flexibility exists concerning the role of research and scholarship. It is still unclear what advantages, if any, those institutions might enjoy in the revolutionary times that have begun and are sure to continue as the drumbeat of change in the twenty-first century reaches a crescendo.

PART 2 THE PROFESSORIATE'S IMPERILED FUTURE

In the book's final two chapters, I revisit some of the themes described in chapter 1 and extrapolate, or project their movement or their force onto a possibly bleak future for the professoriate. In chapter 6, I describe these forces as vectors—quantities with a direction and a velocity that imparts a momentum to them. The professoriate will find itself dealing with forces possessing terrific momentum, resulting from changes whose origins they had nothing to do with, but whose effects might be devastating nevertheless. Then in chapter 7, I construct a possible scenario, unfolding in what might possibly be the near future, in which these vectors are resolved or allowed to merge or collide with their potentially obliterating effects on the professoriate as that term is construed today.

6 · WHAT HAPPENS AFTER THE END OF TIME?

Vectors on a Collision Course

In twenty-first-century America, the words "change" and "time" are virtually synonyms. So a study of change implies a temporal perspective and a temporal analysis. Until this point in the book, that temporal analysis has all been in one direction: looking back into the past to analyze change there in order to identify the forces that brought us to our current position—from "then" until "now." In this final part of the book, the temporal analysis is extended in the other direction. From the ground-level, ant's-eye view of one professor's work from the past to the present, we change viewpoint and turn our perspective to the future. The focus remains change, but not simply on the changes that occurred in my working life. Rather, in this chapter we fix our gaze on the possible future to show the direction those forces might take—from "now" until "then." And if we can discern those directions and the state of affairs that could result, then we can address other questions: What might happen to higher education? As it has in the past, higher education will probably find ways to continue to meet its challenges, though not without some turbulence. The magnitude and number of challenges ahead seem greater than those encountered previously, which suggests that the face of higher education may look radically different, and its fate may be perilous in the future.

If that future is less than rosy for higher education, then it may be downright grim for higher education's perennial partners, the members of the professoriate. To explain why that is so, I reach back into chapter 1 to start this projection process with a discussion of the two systems of higher education whose roles were described there. As the roles of these two systems were already asymmetrical at the end of time, they will remain that way, perhaps to an even greater extent, in the future. That asymmetry has already begun to show itself in some new ways that a number of industrial-scale institutions of higher education are using to try to solve some of the financial problems that beset them now. I also discuss that quest for financial stability and sustainability (one of the most important terms in use in the early part of the twenty-first century). As it turns out, higher education may have some fundamental and unique problems in controlling costs, problems that were simply masked for decades during the time that higher education was a growth industry, but that have now returned with a vengeance. In recent years a number of possible technological solutions have emerged that may help institutions control the costs they incur. But it seems doubtful that any of these fixes will help the members of the professoriate survive at the industrial-scale schools, and they seem to know that. In part as a response to the dramatically increasing cost of higher education, there has also been a scrutiny of higher education by a number of its stakeholders, including its potential clients—that is, potential students and their families. To the extent that higher education may not always have delivered on its implied promise of a better life, or at least a life blessed with a higher income, institutions of higher education may be populated with fewer rather than more students in the future. And that has clear implications for the future of the professoriate, especially its permanent, or tenured, members.

This chapter concludes with an analysis of what might happen to the personnel. As the old guard—the baby boomers of my birth cohort—who oversaw this technological revolution move into retirement, who will take their place, and what will be the replacements' characteristics?

THE SERVICE BECAME A PRODUCT

The story of being a professor is a story of doing a number of activities. That is, what I was as a professor can be understood, and I think should be understood, as what I did during the time I occupied my role. My supervisors and others may have used terms that implied I was making something in my job. For example, every year there was a computation based on the number of students I served and the number of courses in which I served them, to create a numerical index called "student credit hour productivity"—and a higher number in that category was always better. However, despite the fact that terms suggesting that fabrication and construction took place throughout my career, I never believed that any of them were more than a metaphor: there was no useful thing that existed after I taught, only events that had occurred. In the pretechnological era, what the members of the professoriate did (as a suite of activities) was to render a number of different services to a number of people, including the stakeholders of the institution, and a number of external constituencies.

What happened to this model of professor as service provider as the technological era progressed is one of the themes of this chapter. A number of factors came together to change the concept of teaching (at least) from a service rendered to a product delivered. Prior to the technological era such a state of affairs may have been an impossibility. For teaching to become a product, it would have first needed to become a commodity, something that could be picked up, moved, and translated into profit, like any piece of merchandise. The service-rendered model was not compatible with that idea. After the technological era began, however, it was quite possible for teaching (and other services) to become commodified, with potentially corrosive effects on the professoriate. Some researchers of higher education (for example, Tuchman, 2009) have detailed the processes by which this form of commodification occurs in the academy. But despite this literature, the rank-and-file members of the professoriate may not have seen it coming at all. I know I did not, even though with the historical presentism that hindsight provides, the commodification of teaching now seems to have been inevitable to me. As an aside, I wonder what the reactions of other stakeholders of higher education, including members of the professoriate, will be to my use of the expression "educational services and products" in chapter 1? My intuition tells me that most people, both those inside higher education and those outside, will simply read that phrase without pausing to consider what an educational product might be. If so, that may reveal the extent to which the process has already been completed. In any case, the current reality and proliferation of higher educational products is one of the outcomes that resulted when the vectors of the chapter's title crashed together.

THE TWO SYSTEMS IN THE FUTURE

To begin the story of what might happen to the professoriate as its services continue to become commodified, we need to return to a concept that was introduced in chapter 1 and has been present throughout the book—the idea that there are at least two systems (Heller, 2013) of higher education in the United States, an elite system and a second system that I have labeled the industrial-scale system.

I briefly sketched some of the characteristics of the two sets of schools in chapter 1. This will be a somewhat more detailed rendering, establishing some potential differences between the schools of the two systems in the future, compared to the points that I was driving at in chapter 1. Attendance at any institution of higher education has become more costly than ever before over the past forty years or more, and this might be more true for the schools of the elite system than for those of the industrial system and might be even more true when the elite institution is also a private rather than a public school. On the other hand, the institutions of the elite system, especially those in the private sector, may manage and husband tremendous wealth. The institutions of the elite system do not admit the majority of the students who apply, and the students who are accepted and who attend are usually highly academically talented. For example, it would not be unusual to find an elite institution publicizing the fact that the median score of its incoming freshman class on a standardized entrance test (such as the ACT or SAT) was at the 95th or even the 98th percentile. The institutions of the elite system are almost always categorized as research institutions, of which there were 283 in the United States by 2009 (Leahey & Montgomery, 2011). With regard to this research component, most of the pathfinding research projects, the studies resulting in breakthrough scientific findings, and the most influential scholarship and artistic creations that occur in the United States are accomplished at the elite institutions.

It is probably not the case that the industrial-scale schools can be defined in terms of an absence on each of the dimensions that characterize the elite institutions, although that may well be true for some of the four-year institutions of higher education in the United States. Still, just as we saw for the schools of the elite system, the features that characterize the industrial-scale schools tend to be positively correlated. The industrial-scale schools usually admit most—perhaps 60-80 percent—of their applicants. Such institutions do have admissions criteria, so they are selective. But the admissions criteria are usually nowhere near as stringent as those of the elite schools. For the industrial-scale schools, the median score of a given incoming class on the standardized entrance exam is much more likely to be closer to the median (50th percentile) of all the high school students who took the test than it is to the 95th percentile. Such schools are almost always less costly to attend than the schools of the elite system, and in some case, they are far less costly. Probably as a result, it is unlikely that the industrial-scale schools have large endowments or other wealth that they can use to initiate and pursue expensive new programs. Moreover, the public university, even the flagship campus of its state system of higher education, has probably had its financial appropriation from the state government held flat, or even cut, for most of the closing years of the twentieth century and the opening years of the twenty-first. To take just one example of an elite institution, at the University of Wisconsin–Madison, state appropriations covered 43.1 percent of the tuition costs in 1975 but only 19.5 percent by 2006 (Wiley, 2006). This downward trend was noted as essentially universal (Wiley, 2006), and it is likely to be even more pronounced at the other, nonelite, campuses of state public university systems. The industrial-scale schools may have a research mission, as the institutions of the elite system certainly do. But the research mission is always second to the teaching mission in the industrial-scale schools, and it may be absent altogether. Probably as a result of this lower emphasis on research and scholarship, the faculty members at the industrial-scale schools publish less research and scholarship than do the faculty members at the elite institutions. This gap in publication rates between the faculty members at the two categories of institutions has been steadily increasing since at least the 1970s (Henderson, 2011).

I established in chapter 1 that there are two broad systems of higher education, and I also stated that the factors that make now the end of time may have wholly different impacts on the institutions that make up these two systems. So what are the reasons for the recapitulation and expansion of this concept of the two systems here? One reason has to do with the asymmetry of the two systems' roles as they are currently construed. The systems balance each other: even if the cost at the elite schools were not an obstacle, students who would not be a good fit for the experience there now have many choices of schools at which they will get a quality education. But in many other ways, the asymmetry is indicative of an imbalance, and not just with regard to the ways in which the schools of the two systems are already imbalanced (resources, recognition, wealth, and possibly the academic talent of their students). The two systems will remain imbalanced and become more so in the future, as the brand-name institutions, and only they, become increasingly able to export their knowledge and competence over the Internet, in a way that the industrial-scale schools cannot aspire to do.

THE VECTORS THAT ARE ON A COLLISION COURSE

As a mathematical term, a vector refers to a quantity, such as velocity, that can be completely specified by its magnitude and direction. There is also a less formal and less precise way of thinking about vectors, as simply forces, pressures, or influences. But the first sense has some attractions that I cannot deny. For example, some of the vectors affecting higher education do seem to have a direction, in the sense that they can be plotted on a graph as a functional relationship of some other variable. For example, when I discuss the graying of the professoriate, I will be able to demonstrate that the median age of the professoriate increased steadily during the closing decades of the twentieth century as a function of the decade in which it was measured, reaching fifty-five years of age by 2000 (Bland & Bergquist, 1997). This trend has some implications: even though the members of the professoriate no longer face mandatory retirement ages, and even though they tend to work until they are somewhat older in life compared to people in other professions, nevertheless, there is going to be a need in the short term to replace the members of my birth cohort with the next generation of professors.

Again, in a mathematical sense, quantities that have a magnitude and a direction also require certain proportional force to bring them to rest, with the amount of time needed to do that corresponding to the force's momentum. Some of the forces that I will discuss here seem to have a property that corresponds to this notion of momentum: the vector in question is going somewhere with a sort of inexorable power that will not be easily arrested, if it can be at all. The aging property of the faculty that I described above is one such vector. The effect of the increasing age of the professoriate is a variable that is simply going to have an effect on the entire system of higher education and, by extension, American society as a whole. The analysis of higher education's cost that I undertake in this chapter reveals some similar properties. That cost has been increasing over and above the effects of inflation for some decades, so the cost of an education is a vector with a computable magnitude and a direction that can be plotted. The two vectors that we have mentioned have directions that would be trending up if plotted, but not all of the vectors that I will discuss in this chapter are moving that way. For example, there is evidence to suggest that the satisfaction of students and recent alumni of institutions of higher education with their education and their degrees is moving down in some cases, not up. And this brings us to a third sense in which the forces to be described here seem like mathematical vectors. If graphed, they are capable of converging on each other or diverging from each other. When vectors converge and collide in a mathematical sense, their impact can be described as the creation of a resultant force, one whose magnitude and direction are derivable from the characteristics of the forces that came to together to create it. In the next chapter, I present a model—verbal, not mathematical—that shows one possible resolution of the vectors that I discuss here. In real mathematical terms, the resolution of the vectors would be strictly determined by the magnitude and direction of the component forces, and therefore the resolution would be predicable and knowable. The mathematical analogy breaks down somewhat at this point: what I offer in the next chapter is one possible resolution of the vectors described here, but not necessarily the only one.

There is one final point in this section. Like the vectors, which I have necessarily presented as impersonal, impartial forces, the academy can be seen as an immense, distributed machine—one designed to create, promulgate, and disseminate knowledge of the human condition in all its forms. But I do not think of the professoriate as having any of these mechanical characteristics. Rather, I choose to describe the professoriate in the ways that I think about its members: focusing on aspects that are organic, anatomical, and utterly human. The concept of higher education may be analogized as a machine, but the members of the professoriate are not the ghosts in the machine—far from it. So if I lapse into describing the vectors themselves as brutal, massive, tidal forces of indeterminate and relentless power, possessing a bone-crushing effect on the professoriate or stretching its ligaments and sinews beyond recognition, I hope the vivid and perhaps overheated comparisons are seen for what they are: an effort to reduce the abstraction to emphasize the magnitude of what is at stake.

VECTOR NO. 1: SUSTAINABILITY AND THE COST DISEASE

Almost all studies of the cost of college can trace their roots back to the pioneering work of William Bowen (1968), who was among the first to study the economics of higher education. To do so, Bowen considered the "direct expenditures on instruction and departmental research" (p. 6) based on a budgetary analysis of three well-known private universities that were, and are, part of the elite system: the University of Chicago, Princeton University, and Vanderbilt University. In the period between the academic years 1951–52 and 1965–66, these costs increased by an average of 11.1 percent per year for the three institutions. It is true that these figures represent total direct expenditures. If enrollments were growing during that time period, then it would be expected that such expenditures would go up as well. But in continuing his analysis, Bowen demonstrated that increases in enrollment accounted for a relatively small proportion of the increase in expenditures, and that this phenomenon was not limited to the three institutions of his initial study. Bowen subsequently compared the direct cost per student of the three institutions in his original case study with the average direct cost of all private research universities and then compared both of these indices to an economywide cost index based on the gross national product, to control for the fact that all costs may have been rising at the same rate as those of higher education. During the period between the academic years 1955–56 and 1965–66, the direct instructional cost per student increased about 8 percent per year at private research institutions, while the economy-wide cost index which rose at a leisurely 2 percent per year.

What accounted for the bigger cost increase in higher education during that time period, relative to costs in general? Bowen went on to explain that universities were expanding their programming and taking on some new responsibilities. But the bigger part of the problem stemmed from what Bowen (1968) referred to as the "technology of education" (p. 12)—specifically, the productivity problem. Simply put, universities were seemingly incapable of finding ways to use improvements in technology to increase their productivity or efficiency in making their unique product (educated people), while the costs of making that product continued to increase. Bowen contrasted the situation in education with that in the automobile industry. If productivity increased by 4 percent because various technologies had been brought to bear, and wages to workers increased by 4 percent, then the cost of producing a car remained basically unchanged. But this was just what was not happening in higher education. During the period from 1948 to 1966, faculty salaries increased at a rate of 4.8 percent per year, compared to a rate of 4.2 percent per year in the manufacturing sector of the economy. Productivity had increased by approximately 2.5 percent per year in the manufacturing sector, partially offsetting the cost of the increased wages. However, in the higher education sector, productivity had not increased. As Bowen concluded, if faculty salaries go up and faculty output stays constant, then it follows that the labor cost per educational output must rise at the same rate as faculty salaries.

There are a number of reasons why technological improvements cannot always be brought to bear on some life's enterprises to increase productivity. One reason is simply that some processes or outputs cannot be hurried along too much, no matter how much technology is applied. For example, I know from my time in higher education that there are some concepts or ideas that it is possible for a college student who is a senior (age twenty-one or twenty-two) to learn that are difficult or impossible for a first-year student (age eighteen) to learn—a statement that comports very well with recent findings in the cognitive neuroscience literature about the maturation rate of the human brain.

The productivity problem is the basis for what has come to be called, following Bowen's work, the cost disease. Bowen (2013) has more recently formulated the cost disease in the following way: "In labor-intensive *industries* [italics mine] such as the performing arts and education, there is less opportunity than in other sectors to increase productivity by, for example, substituting capital for labor. Yet markets dictate that, over time, wages for comparably qualified individuals have to increase at roughly the same rate in all industries. As a result unit labor costs must be expected to rise faster in the performing arts and education than in the economy overall" (pp. 16–17).

The cost disease is not just a historical problem, and the increases that Bowen noted are still with us. For example, one study (Baum, Kurose, & McPherson, 2012) showed that educational expenditures per student at all types of public institutions had increased by about 1 percent per year over and above inflation during the time period 2002-8. As Bowen has pointed out in several contexts, the cost disease is not just the result of salary increases of faculty and other people. In very significant ways, the institutions undermine their own productivity. Even in areas like the construction of new residence halls, for example, some institutions feel the need to include amenities that 99 percent of the US population does not currently enjoy at home or anywhere else (Bowen, 2013).

Even though salary increases for the professoriate and others are not the sole cause of the cost disease, it is nevertheless true that higher education, at least as it has traditionally been organized, remains a labor-intensive industry, as Bowen has characterized it. And even though the varieties of that labor have proliferated over the years as the universities require increasingly specialized services in support of their educational programming, it is also true that the members of the professoriate, along with the members of a few other professions such as physicians, are certainly among the most highly trained, highly skilled, and expensive workforces in the United States today. So, from the standpoint of sustainability, at least one question that emerges is, could higher education die from the cost disease?

If it is possible that the answer to that question is yes, then the next question is, what might happen to the professoriate to stave off that demise, given that the institutions of higher education themselves will not succumb if they can avoid it?

The Cost Disease and Its Effect on Sustainability: A Case Study (Myself)

The cost disease is something that institutions suffer from. But the general problem—that is, the problem of trying to produce more in a way that is equivalent to increasing costs—necessarily involves the work of the professoriate. Thus, while the effects of the cost disease are borne by the institutions of higher education, it should be possible to see those effects emerge in the day-to-day work of the professors. To examine this possibility, I computed my salary by looking at my pay stubs and my official printed salary verifications, both in actual dollars and in 1979 dollars[1] (the year I began at Eastern Illinois University). I next computed two plausible and generally useful measures of measures of productivity. Graphing all three measures against the same time line will be the final step in the analysis. The basic effect of the cost disease will make itself visible if there is a generally rising trend line on the salary graph, compared with any other result (either a flat or descending trend) for the two productivity measures. Figure 6.1 shows my monthly salary amount in actual and in 1979 dollars from 1979 to 2013. My monthly income, in both actual and constant dollars, trended up during the period. This is not particularly surprising: during my career, I was promoted from assistant to associate professor and, ultimately, to full professor.

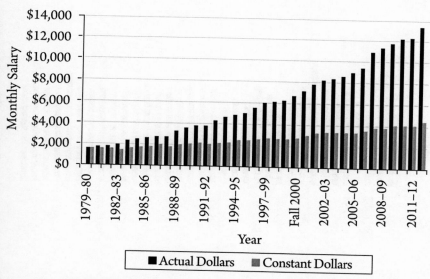

FIGURE 6.1. Monthly Salary at Eastern Illinois University as a Function of Employment Year

My salary increased during the period from 1979 to 2013, but what about my productivity? The first measure of productivity I computed is the credit unit (CU) index, which—as explained above—is a calibration of each type of academic work that we might carry out and was negotiated by our union representatives for us. According to our contract, each faculty member was required to carry at least eighteen CUs across the academic year, and he or she could not be assigned work whose total CU equivalency was greater than twenty-four, unless the department chairperson first obtained the faculty member's written consent. Figure 6.2 shows the CUs that I had in each of the academic years that I worked at Eastern. Overlooking the variability within the mandatory CU range, the general trend in the graph shows only the slightest rate of increase across my entire career, certainly much slower than the salary increases in actual or constant dollars. My average number of CUs was 22.4, a figure that represents 93.4 percent of my contractual full capacity of 24 CUs. At least if my productivity did not increase very much as a function of time, it was relatively high during my entire career.

The second productivity measure is a better-known and standardized measure of teaching effort known as student credit hour (SCH) production. SCHs are computed by multiplying the number of students enrolled in a particular course by the amount of course credit each student earns by passing the course. My SCH productivity is shown in figure 6.3. Perhaps most important with regard to the cost disease, in my case, the trend line is clearly declining, a phenomenon that deserves some comment.

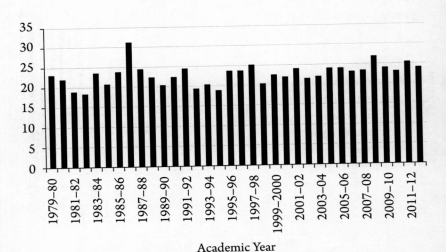

Academic Year

FIGURE 6.2. Credit Unit Production as a Function of Employment Year

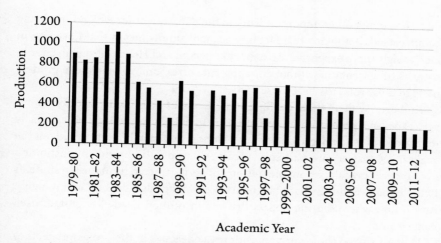

FIGURE 6.3. Student Credit Hour Production as a Function of Employment Year

For the first six or seven years that I worked at EIU, Introductory Psychology made up 40-50 percent of my assigned courses. Introductory Psychology tends to be taught in fairly large sections throughout the United States. During that time period at Eastern, a large section might have close to a hundred students (by no means big when compared to the size of such classes at the national level), thus generating nearly 300 SCHs. But I stopped teaching Introductory Psychology after the fall semester of 1990. As the 1990s wore on, I spent more and more of my teaching effort in smaller and smaller classes, including the department's Honors Seminar (which usually enrolled only ten students), or our Research Methods class, whose enrollment was deliberately capped at twenty students. Finally, in the twenty-first century, I seldom taught courses whose enrollment was even as large as fifty students. The last such course I taught, Cognitive Psychology, I relinquished in 2006. The course that eventually replaced it in my typical teaching rotation, Cognitive Neuroscience, never had more than twelve students enrolled. The second major reason for the decline in my SCH production was the increasingly large role that I played in administration. My activity in that role did not generate any SCHs, even though the CUs for those tasks appeared on my workload document. For example, in the final years of my career, I served as the assistant chairperson in the department (6 CUs), the coordinator of our department's Honors Program (3 CUs), and as a faculty advisor (1 CU). Those 10 CUs on my workload made up 43 percent of all my contractual effort that year. The administrative work I took on helps explain why the average of my CUs for the final ten years of my career was 23.34 (97 percent of full capacity), even while my SCH production fell below 200 SCHs per academic year.

Thus, while the dollar cost for me to generate a single SCH increased fairly dramatically, it might be argued that at least part of that cost was offset by the fact that I was doing other important work in the department for which I was being compensated. But taking that fact into account simply means that I became an increasingly more expensive assistant chairperson and Honors Program coordinator as time went on, without any apparent corresponding increase in productivity in those roles to offset those costs.

And even with all these qualifications, it cannot be gainsaid that I became a very expensive professor for my institution to field in any course, but especially for a group of ten undergraduates in an Honors Seminar. I never carried out the analysis to answer one particularly compelling question: Did my institution even recover my salary from the tuition dollars it gathered from the ten students in the Honors Seminar that I taught every spring for decades? I doubt it highly. And if not, where did the dollars that the institution needed to sustain itself come from?

When I shared these analyses with my colleagues in the professoriate, they immediately began to challenge me with objections. For example, the people in every other profession make more money as they gain more qualifications, so why shouldn't we? Although I think this objection actually misses the point of the analyses, there are nevertheless at least two responses. First, other labor-intensive industries might be better able to demonstrate that the most qualified and most senior people in the profession are actually doing something better than the less-qualified junior people are, and that something, whatever it might be, could be translated into greater productivity. But there is only sketchy evidence of something like that occurring within the professoriate. Second, it is important to realize that the effects of the cost disease are in no way restricted to the most senior members of the professoriate. Rather, the entire average cost of the professoriate—that is, the cost of fielding a professor in a class, regardless of his or her rank—is increasing faster than is the consumer price index.

Finally, in discussing the cost disease, neither I nor Bowen are trying to suggest that it is unique to the professoriate. The operation of the cost disease is a principle that apparently applies to any labor-intensive industry that does not increase its productivity corresponding to its costs. As a putative example, although I have not documented the following assertion empirically, it would not surprise me to find that if I wished to hire a boat builder to make a wooden sailboat for me by hand, it probably would have been much more affordable (that is, as a percentage of income, had I been working) in 1956 than it would be in 2016. Still, there is a crucial difference between boat builders and professors: The fate of the sailboat-building industry might not have national implications. But the fate of the higher education industry clearly does.

Faculty Attitudes toward Sustainability

Tarah Wright and Naomi Horst (2013) surveyed faculty knowledge of, and suggestions about, sustainability in general, and they found that faculty members were generally unaware of the problem of financial sustainability until it was explicitly brought to their attention. Once that was done, faculty members demonstrated that they were able to think creatively about the issues involved, at least in the context of completing the study. It is not clear how long that awareness remains once faculty members return to their daily routines of teaching and research. More generally, faculty members do not appear to be aware of how dramatically the cost disease and other factors have altered higher education's financial prospects and that the golden age has long since come to a conclusion (Altbach, 1998). In a blog post, the political scientist Phil Schrodt (2013), announcing his apparently somewhat reluctant retirement, evinces what I fear is the professoriate's prototypical response, one that shows how little cognizance there is on the part of the professoriate about the role that they themselves have played, despite their good intentions, in their institutions' financial difficulties: "Academic institutions have changed little since the post-WWII expansions of the 1950s, while the world around them has changed dramatically. What little change has occurred appears focused on the proliferation of pointless administrative positions whose sole purpose is to make the institution more expensive and less efficient. An imitation of the United States auto industry in the 1960s. We know how that turned out" (Schrodt, 2013).

Sustainability and Technology: The MOOC Is Here

Although the cost disease appears to have exerted its inexorable pressure for several decades, the revolution in technology that occurred at the close of the twentieth century, especially the creation and development of the Internet, may provide the necessary platform for a longed-for solution. MOOC is an acronym for massive open online course. Each word is operative: MOOCs are massive in their enrollment capacity, with several of them enrolling over 100,000 students. The reality of educating such a gigantic number with, technically, only a single professor staffing the course, is probably the main reason for thinking that MOOCs could be the answer to the issues that Bowen identified with the professoriate's output side, the productivity part of the equation in the cost disease. MOOCs are also open: although each MOOC is associated with an institution of origin, a person enrolling in the MOOC does not go through any application process to become accepted at that institution. MOOCs are not the first academic courses to be offered completely in the online environment, but they may be the first courses to be offered to potential students who are free agents in the educational marketplace, being untethered to any specific institution. Finally, like other academic courses, taking and completing a MOOC may produce academic credit for the student who does so. That means that a MOOC can operate like any other course on a given student's transcript of courses: the academic credit is portable and transferrable to any institutions with which the student might have a formal (admitted) relationship, including those institutions that the student attends in the future. The MOOC is indeed a radical concept in higher education, and although it is far too early to evaluate all the claims made for it, it must be granted that the MOOC concept could potentially remake the higher education landscape.

And that remaking could take place very quickly, as the MOOC concept has proved viral in both its contagion and mutability. The acronym was coined in 2008 by Dave Cormier to describe an online course called Connectivism and Connective Knowledge offered at the University of Manitoba and led by George Siemens and Stephen Downes (De Millo, 2015). The course enrolled 25 Manitoba students, who were accompanied by 2,200 other students who had access to all the course content materials and the discussion elements, which were provided via a number of outlets, including social media. The Manitoba students were, however, the only tuition-paying students in that venture. This initial offering was followed by a brief period in which entrepreneurial professors operating outside a corporate environment began to develop their own MOOCs, which could then be sold to and hosted by a number of institutions. At that stage, faculty members at several research institutions began to develop the MOOC concept in earnest. For example, at Stanford University in the fall of 2011, three MOOCs were rolled out, including the immediately popular Introduction to AI (artificial intelligence), which enrolled 160,000 students from around the globe. At that time, I can clearly recall several retired and former professors in my circle of e-mail friends who were having an animated online discussion about how much fun it would be to take the course. I was so busy teaching the students who were enrolled in my "SOOCs" (small oval [because we rearranged the chairs to form a circle] oral courses) and so buried beneath the blizzard of e-mail that came my way every day that I had no idea what they were talking about. In the next stage of the MOOCs' development, the faculty members involved in those initial courses partnered with Stanford to create for-profit corporate entities such as Coursera and Udacity, intended, essentially, to work as distributors for the wave of MOOCs believed to be coming. Such beliefs seemed to have been justified. By March 2013, after being in operation for only thirteen months, Coursera was already offering 325 MOOCs in partnership with a number of research institutions—including at least two universities in the Ivy League, Princeton University and the University of Pennsylvania.

In January 2013, Udacity began a large-scale partnership with San Jose State University (a campus of the California State University system) to offer MOOCs for credit, following a test run that showed the students were able to actually pass the courses, suggesting they were learning at least as much in the MOOC as they had been in the face-to-face equivalent (Heller, 2013). The results of the test run also impressed other stakeholders in higher education: in the winter of 2013, a bill was introduced in the California State Senate that would require the state's public universities to give academic credit for online courses that had been created and provided by approved vendors.

MOOCs offer the possibility of several apparently positive outcomes. First, their source, which is invariably from professors at schools of the elite system, suggests that the educational value offered by those schools may become available for everyone who takes a MOOC. For a student who took enough of them, it might be like getting an education from an Ivy League school for a fraction of the price. Second, through their interaction in developing and purchasing the MOOCs, the elite and industrial-scale schools may begin to work together, which might result in reducing the considerable distance that currently exists between them. Finally, the bête noire of the cost disease may finally be tamed as all the institutions using MOOCs succeed in increasing their productivity, while presumably holding their costs constant.

Instructional Costs in MOOC Delivery

Although there are quite a few stakeholders in higher education who are intrigued and optimistic about the possibilities that MOOCs afford for redressing higher education's sustainability issues (for example, Bowen, 2013), there is still an important question: is the enthusiasm for the MOOC concept justified? If the effort that the members of the professoriate expend in creating, developing, and teaching their MOOCs is not substantially greater than that expended in a conventionally taught course, then the answer to that question could be yes, provided the large enrollments that have been seen continue to be observed as the number of MOOCs in existence increases, and as competition among the MOOCs intensifies. In attempting to answer such questions about the professors' role and effort in their own MOOC development, in 2013 the *Chronicle of Higher Education* surveyed over a hundred professors who had taught at least one MOOC (Kolowich, 2013a). Prior to the rollout of a given MOOC, the professors reported spending an average of more than a hundred hours on its preparation, much of which included time for recording the video presentations that would have been called lectures at one time. In comparing that figure to my own experience, having developed at least four or more courses from the ground up in my teaching career, I can report that it is very easy to spend at least a hundred hours developing the materials that will be used in the face-to-face presentations in a conventionally taught course. Many of the MOOCs in existence have adapted from preexisting face-to-face courses, and the materials— including tests or whatever mechanism is going to be used to assess student learning and performance—that may have been developed for that format, need to be changed for the online presentation. Once under way, the professors reported spending an average of eight to ten hours per week on their MOOC, a figure that is close to the number of contact hours plus preparation time that I allocated in teaching a conventional course. The number of students enrolled in a typical MOOC (over 30,000) almost necessitates some form of automatic grading, a process I eschewed as my own career developed. There are a number of programs in the works that may eventually be able to coherently grade a student's written work. But none of that software was in everyday use at the industrial-scale schools during my career. So the professors in my department who assigned written academic work in the form of essay tests or term papers or who required real-time computation to be done on a test, such as a statistics test, were generally responsible for the timely grading of the assignments.

Thus, on the input side the cost of creating and teaching the MOOC, in terms of the professor's and other people's time, seems comparable to that of a face-to-face course, even after allowing for the possible exception of time and effort involved in grading. But it is the output side where the MOOC concept could really change the productivity equation in higher education. Although most of the students who begin a typical MOOC do not complete the course with a passing grade, the average number who manage to finish and pass (which the *Chronicle* survey found to be about 2,600 out of the 30,000 or so who started out) is so vast compared to students who pass a face-to-face course, or even compared to a typical Internet-offered course, that the institution which offered a substantial number of MOOCs could be in a position to use the excess (if that would be the correct term) income dollars generated by the MOOC to subsidize a number of conventionally taught courses and thus possibly redeem their situation with regard to sustainability issues I discussed above.

The MOOC's Unintended Consequence: The Fungible Professoriate

The institution where I worked for thirty-four years is located in a rural area in the Midwest, and my family and I lived in a farming community located some miles from the institution. As my career wore on, driving to work and back home again, I learned how to maneuver around the lumbering combines on the road at harvest time, and I learned how to dodge their companions, the heavily laden grain trucks that barreled up and down the country roads to get the harvest to the elevator in the quickest possible time. Once the crop (the grain was invariably corn or soybeans in that part of the Midwest) was safely stored in the elevator, all the farmers played a waiting game to see what the grain futures looked like. Given that the grain was completely fungible—any grain in the elevator could be substituted on unit-by-unit basis for the farmer's grain—the decision about what to do with the crop was usually based on how the storage costs stacked up against the future commodity prices.

Grain is a fungible commodity. But for most of their existence, professors have not been. Rather, their relationship with their institutions has been based (unintentionally, no doubt) on a business model that resembled the movie industry's star system of the 1930s. Using such a model, individual movie companies such as RKO or Warner Bros. would sign an actor to work for them almost exclusively, in that way owning the actors' performances but also investing in the actors by providing them with the movie vehicles and visibility needed to maintain their star status. And those stars then constituted the movie company's stable of talent that could be counted on to generate viewership and profits. Similarly, during higher education's golden age and beyond, a given professor worked for one school at a time. And the school made a deal with him or her as well, in a sense owning the professor's teaching efforts at least, but also providing and guaranteeing, through the twin mechanisms of academic freedom and tenure, a secure place for the members of the professoriate to practice their work. The MOOC concept may undermine this relationship because the underlying business model of the MOOC implies that the professor who is acquired via the product offered by Coursera, Udacity, edX, or any of the other for-profit companies sure to be seen in the future is the same or just as good as the one that the institution already has in its stable and can therefore be substituted in kind.

The Professoriate May Be Pushing Back

I noted that some of higher education's numerous stakeholders may be enthusiastic about the MOOC concept, but not all the members of the professoriate are. If the reluctance that the professoriate may begin to feel about being made fungible erupts into a more direct confrontation, then a recent development that occurred at San Jose State University (SJSU) might indicate how some of those skirmishes could play out (Kolowich, 2013b). After officials at SJSU made a deal with edX to offer a MOOC of the popular course Justice, taught by Michael Sandel at Harvard University, professors in the Philosophy Department at SJSU wrote an open letter directed to the administration and others, stating that they did not wish to cooperate with the administration in what they saw as an effort to "replace professors, dismantle departments, and provide a diminished education for students in public universities" (quoted in Kolowich, 2013b). Moreover, they suggested that individuals like Sandel, a professor at a wealthy elite private institution, might be complicit in the fate of the professoriate at the public institutions where such MOOCs are routinely used. Ellen Junn, the provost and vice president of academic affairs at SJSU, stated that how much or how little of the edX materials (that is, the MOOC "JusticeX," as it was renamed for consumption outside Harvard) that faculty members incorporated into their blended courses was each faculty member's responsibility. And Sandel acknowledged that faculty members who worry about the consequences of using MOOCs in public universities have a legitimate concern, one that merits debate throughout higher education. Moreover, he stated that he did not want his *online lectures* [italics mine] to be used to undermine faculty colleagues at other institutions" (Sandel, 2013).

In summary, the MOOC concept may become an increasingly powerful tool that many institutions of higher education use in the future to address the problems with sustainability brought about by the cost disease. And the issue of sustainability seems to be a problem on which higher education could founder if it is not solved. But, however the MOOC concept might play out in that future, it remains to be seen whether the professoriate as a whole will prosper under its terms of use.

VECTOR NO. 2: AFFORDABILITY

The terms "sustainability" and "affordability" are clearly related to each other, but the focus of each term is different, and thus so is the direction of its vector. Although they may have similar long-term consequences for the professoriate, the mechanism by which the effect is achieved is different for each of the terms. If by "sustainability" we mean the ability of institutions themselves to provide the best quality services (or, as we have seen, products) at the lowest cost per unit they can, then that puts the focus of that term on the institutions of higher education. Seen from that perspective, the threat to the professoriate comes about as institutions wrestle with possible solutions to the cost disease—solutions that may leave the professoriate out in the cold if the institutions determine that they can no longer afford the professoriate. However, if by "affordability" we mean the wherewithal, financial and otherwise, possessed by the prototypical clients of higher education—the students and their families—who must make a decision about whether the value of a college education is justified, then the focus shifts from the institution, over which the professoriate has some control, to the family as a consumer, over which the professoriate has usually no say. Sustainability is a concern of the seller. Affordability is a concern of the purchaser. Both may threaten the professoriate, but from different directions, within or without. As long as families and students view higher education as worth its cost, then it may not matter how quickly the institutions solve the problem of the cost disease—the consumers may continue to find a way to fund the cost. But if affordability somehow fails, either because the cost of higher education is no longer justifiable by families in some empirical, outcome-oriented way or because it appears that college is no longer worth the cost (that is, the consumers are no longer satisfied with the outcome), then professoriate faces a different kind of threat.

Rather than being outsourced, as might happen if the sustainability vector is not eventually controlled, the professoriate may simply become a professional class whose services will no longer be required in that particular sector of the future economy.

The acts of attending and completing college have long been regarded as investments in the future of the student. As is the case with every other investment, the underlying idea is that some quantity of something is divested on the front end, and then, following some particular events over time, some greater quantity of something is harvested on the back end. When applied to higher education, the term is inevitably freighted with several meanings, in part depending on who is doing the talking. The professoriate has often made the case that the investment and repayment should be understood using intangibles, such as time and effort on the input side being repaid with other intangibles such as critical thinking ability, values, or the ability to live the life of the mind on the output side. For example, Frank Donoghue (2008) discusses the history of this kind of repayment as a response to the relentless attacks made by business leaders on the humanities throughout the twentieth century. For parents and students, the investment is often understood in the more concrete terms of monetary cost on the input side and higher income as the benefit being harvested.

The data from innumerable studies seem to support the idea that college is a valuable financial investment in the future. For example, the Department of Education's National Center for Education Statistics has found that in 2015 a degree holder earned an average of $48,500 whereas a diploma holder earned $23,900 (Study.com, n.d.), suggesting that college degree holders might expect to make more than $1 million more than high-school graduates across their working lives. But this $1 million differential has been disputed, and even other governmental studies have produced conflicting results. For example, the National Center for Education Studies (2015b) has analyzed workers' incomes since the 1980s and found the bachelor's degree holder took home an average of 38 percent more than the person with no more than a high school diploma—a big difference, but far less than the one reported in other studies. And more recent research puts the absolute dollar figure far lower than the $1 million that is often quoted. Kim Clark (2008) discusses the work of Sandy Baum, an economist who carried out an analysis of the financial returns of higher education for the College Board in 2007. Baum found that college graduates earn, on average, $20,000 more per working year than those with no more than a high school diploma. When multiplied by the forty years that a person might expect to work, the difference becomes $800,000—close to the $1 million differential cited above. But, as Baum notes, most of that money is going to be paid in future dollars, and therefore the amount needs to be adjusted for erosive effects of inflation.

After that adjustment, the difference is more like $450,000 in current dollars. But when the cost of earning the four-year degree is factored in, plus the lost income (what the person could have made during the four or more years spent earning the degree), the actual differential is closer to $300,000, according to Baum.

While that is still a substantial figure, it is important to keep in mind that it is an average. If there is a great deal of variability around that average, the picture could change a great deal. Indeed, when John Schmitt and Heather Boushey (2012) analyzed the variability in incomes between college and high school graduates, they found that for those college graduates who were at the high end of the income spectrum, the differential amount between their income and that earned by the average high school graduate was in fact much, much greater than it was forty years ago—the bachelor's degree was apparently having a polarizing effect, as the income disparity between these high-income college graduates and the typical high-school graduate was growing. However, Schmitt and Boushey also found that those who were at the bottom of the income spectrum for college graduates earned less than people who had not gone to college. Other studies have explored the factors that place a given college graduate on the high or low end of this income spectrum. One factor seems to be the college student's major. One study (Carnevale, Strohl, & Melton, 2011) found that there were several college majors whose median incomes differed by a factor of two: that is, some college graduates had majors that resulted in their earning twice as much per year as students who had majored in another subject. In one extreme case, the researchers found that the median income for those who majored in early childhood education was $36,000, while the median for those who majored in petroleum engineering was $120,000, a differential factor of 3.33.

VECTOR NO. 3: THE GRAND EXPERIMENT MAY BE OVER

In 1944, Congress passed the Servicemen's Readjustment Act, more popularly known as the GI Bill, with little debate or controversy. Among its sweeping provisions, the act promised cash payments for living expenses and tuition at a college or university for active-duty service personnel returning from World War II. By 1956, when the original program came to an end, approximately 2.2 million returning service personnel had availed themselves of these benefits, making them the first large influx of college students in twentieth-century American academic life (Bound & Turner, 2002) and launching a process that would democratize American higher education. I am not sure that this influx was really the source of the now deeply entrenched thought that everyone should go to college. But in the seventy years after passage of the GI Bill, college enrollments rose dramatically. When the bill was passed, approximately 15 percent of high school graduates went directly on to college, a percentage that rose to 40 percent by 1970 and now hovers at 60-70 percent. But wherever and however the idea of universal higher education was hatched, it seems that there was little reflection at the time about whether it was a good idea or not.

I used the term "grand experiment" with my colleagues to refer to the notion that, whether anyone at the time thought so or did not, the basic concept of universal higher education was both truly radical and experimental. It was radical in the sense that it represented a departure from the way American universities had operated for at least a century before the GI Bill was passed. And it was experimental in the sense that there was no preexisting model or body of evidence to suggest that universal higher education was either workable or attainable. But now, at the beginning of the twenty-first century, after running the experiment for seventy years or so, there may be evidence that the concept of universal higher education, however egalitarian and American it might be, may be impossible to realize without thorough changes in our concepts of the university and the professoriate.

When universities represent the benefits of attendance to their clientele and other stakeholders, including legislators and businesspeople who might hire their graduates, they often assume the achievement of a number of cognitive skills by their graduates, including reasoning and other critical thinking skills, problem-solving skills, and communication skills. But when students' learning is assessed objectively, the results typically indicate that many students who are making good academic progress toward their degrees are not acquiring these or other skills in college. One of the most well-known recent studies was conducted by Richard Arum and Josipa Roksa (2011). The researchers gathered data from survey responses, academic transcripts, and results from the Collegiate Learning Assessment (CLA), a well-known standardized test that asks participants to write coherent passages analyzing and criticizing a variety of arguments by evaluating the evidence for and against them. The sample consisted of some 2,300 students from twenty-nine institutions spanning the spectrum of higher education. Among the more widely reported results, Arum and Roksa found that at least 45 percent of the students did not demonstrate any significant improvement in performance on the CLA during the first two years of college. Although the rate of improvement did pick up across the final two or more years, still some 36 percent of the students in the sample did not show any statistically significant improvement on the CLA at the end of four years in college. While 64 percent of the students did show statistically significant gains on a number of cognitive skills, when the size of the improvement was expressed as an effect size measure (that is, in terms of the number of standard deviation units that a typical student had advanced), the overall effect of college was not particularly large. Students typically gained about 0.5 standard deviations on most of the measures of cognitive skill, an effect equivalent to gaining about 7 points on a typical IQ test. That is not a small effect by any means. But given the size of the effort needed to produce that amount of change—years of time, sustained and strenuous effort by the student and dozens of highly trained professionals, and tens of thousands of dollars—then it seems that there is not a lot of bang for the buck.

In the twenty-first century, there are rumblings that the grand experiment—the desirability and usefulness of universal higher education—may indeed be over. Many commentators (to single out just one, Murray, 2008) are now wondering publicly if college is the right course for many young Americans.[2] If the grand experiment ends, then it is obvious that there will be an effect on the professoriate, certainly in its numbers: fewer students means less need, and thus fewer professors will be required. The conclusion of the grand experiment could therefore have a similar effect that the affordability vector might have. But the mechanism by which college becomes perceived as less affordable could be very different from the mechanism underlying the grand experiment's conclusion. In this case, it might be the members of body politic at the national level who are no longer eager to use federal money to support the notion of higher education for everyone (via federally subsidized loans), especially given a college education's increasing cost and seemingly diminishing payoff. It is this latter scenario that I explore in the next chapter. And for the members of the professoriate, that outcome would be bitter as well as being definitive—since they might be forced to conclude that despite all their dedication, seriousness of purpose, and high-minded ideals, the concept of mass higher education turned out to be an illusory and impossible dream.

VECTOR NO. 4: DIMINISHING STATE SUPPORT FOR THE PUBLIC UNIVERSITIES

I was in the audience for a university-wide meeting to discuss the results of a strategic planning initiative in the late 1980s. The overall mood was upbeat: enrollments at other state universities had declined, but ours had held steady. The final speaker was Thomas Layzell, then chancellor of the Illinois Board of Governors of State Colleges and Universities, which was the official name for the system of five public comprehensive universities, including EIU, that the board governed. Layzell complimented our university for its fine planning work but then also noted, "EIU, you are facing some challenges; your enrollments are flat."

As the comment reveals, officials of the political apparatus erected by state governments to approve budgets and appropriations for public higher education may have been among the first to recognize an important truth about the cost disease. As long as a public institution was growing in enrollment, and therefore taking in a greater number of tuition dollars, the effects of the cost disease may have been masked by enrollment growth. That is, simple growth may have been misperceived as an increase in productivity, even if real productivity (cost per student) was not increasing. But simple growth equated to happy times for everyone, to be sure. As long as the state economy was growing and absorbing a greater number of college graduates who were earning more money, paying more in taxes, and therefore contributing more to the state's economy than high school graduates did, the situation was win-win for the state government and public universities. But when enrollments stopped growing, the effects of the cost disease truly began to bite, and states found themselves in the unenviable position of having to make up the shortfall between the revenue produced by tuition and the lost dollars eaten up by the cost disease.

In many states, making up that shortfall became increasingly difficult as other financial needs, including Medicaid and other health costs, infrastructure demands, and the adequate funding of pension systems, grew. For example, writing early in the twenty-first century, Thomas Kane and Peter Orszag (2004) noted that Medicaid funding was "the biggest challenge casting a shadow on public education's future." No doubt each state took its own pathway to continued solvency, and there might not be very many common elements across states' stories. But the pathway often included cutting back on state support for public institutions of higher education. For example, in Illinois, King Alexander and Daniel Layzell (2006) have shown that in the period from fiscal year (FY) 1990 to FY 2005, general revenue funds' support for the state's higher education declined by 1.8 percent per year, after adjusting for inflation. Most of the loss occurred in a three-year period, from FY 2002 to FY 2005. This cutback was particularly debilitating for the public universities, where state funding in FY 2005 was 14.7 percent less than it had been in FY 1990, again after adjusting for inflation (Alexander & Layzell, 2006, p. 145). That trend continued across the next several fiscal years, as Illinois was forced by circumstances to divert an increasing percentage of its general revenue funds to help shore up its public pension systems, which by 2013 were the most underfunded such systems in the nation, to the tune of nearly $100 billion.

This is a brief sketch of just one state's financial issues affecting higher education. But Illinois's problems are not unusual. Ronald Ehrenberg (2006) noted that over the past thirty years—that is, since the end of the golden age—the share of state funding going to higher education has declined by more than 33 percent. What effects have this large and widespread cutback had on the professoriate? One response to the problem that public universities might adopt on a state-by-state basis could involve finding the right size for themselves with regard to diminishing state appropriations. If the universities were able to cooperate with each other, this kind of rightsizing might lead to a centralization or consolidation of some departments and faculty at particular public universities, almost certainly involving programs in the arts or humanities that have small enrollments relative to other programs. Arts and humanities would not be the only types of program that would incur this treatment: programs with small enrollments and big expenses in the sciences could also be affected. Thus, instead of having the entire state public university system run ten small programs at each of its campuses, the future might see each of the universities (with the state flagship campus exempted) maintain just one or two of the small programs. By amalgamating such programs, the university could be rightsized, sloughing off some programs that are historically known for not attracting large numbers of students. Thus, in the future, a given state university system might offer a French major on two of its campuses, rather than the ten or twelve where it can be found now. But while the university would be rightsized by such an action, the faculty would be downsized, because not all of its members would be needed once the amalgamation process achieved the economy of scale that it would be designed to do. If this approach is actually undertaken anywhere (if it is currently being done, I am not aware of it), there will be intense criticism from those who point out, rightly, that such an approach diminishes student choices. But that is precisely what this book is about: the central notion is that the universities, under pressure from within and without, will look to their own needs and devise ways to ensure that they survive, regardless of whether or not that survival includes the professoriate, as we know it today.

VECTOR NO. 5: THE GRAYING OF THE FACULTY

In addition to the possible effects of the cost disease on sustainability, affordability, and value, there is an inescapable vector whose force must be acknowledged: the professoriate has gotten older. A not-so-gradual shift in the age distribution of the professoriate began in the 1980s and continued apace through the 1990s and 2000s. In one study of a large public state system, the percentage of tenured and tenure-track faculty ages fifty-five and older increased from 27 percent to 32 percent in the decade between 1985 and 1995, while the percentage under age forty fell from 22 percent to 16 percent (University of Wisconsin System, 1996). These percentages shifted at the national level as well: 32.8 percent of all instructional faculty were fifty or older in 1992, while 18 percent were forty-five to forty-nine. By 2000, 50 percent of the members of the professoriate were over fifty-five, and 68 percent were over fifty (Bland & Bergquist, 1997). One of the somewhat ironic subthemes of this book is that the technological era in higher education was ushered in largely by faculty members who were considerably older than the tech-savvy young people shown in the TV commercials for the electronic technology of the 2000s.

For most of the faculty who were baby boomers at the end of time, their future will include retirement—a retirement that now seems imminent for many of them. This raises some questions: What are the characteristics of the retiring faculty, the boomers who participated in the end of the golden age and the beginning of the technological era? And what are the characteristics of those who will replace them?

As others have noted (for example, Hermanowicz, 1998; Shils, 1983), senior faculty members have described their work as much more than a job, even more than a career. Members of the professoriate who are baby boomers often describe their work as a calling. The idea that a line of work or business could become one's calling or vocation harkens back to the Reformation and the writings of Martin Luther, who expanded the term's original meaning. The idea of a calling was once restricted to ministers, who were thought to be called directly by God to preach the gospel, but Luther felt that any the work of any station in life could be considered by those who did it as an offering to God. There are several aspects of the notion that to be member of the professoriate was to acknowledge a calling that I find important. First, there is the idea that if one is called, then one's work is one's life, and the expression "life's work" becomes relevant. Second, there is the concept of identity: if one's life is one's work, then one's identity, or how one defines oneself, becomes bound up with that work. In this regard, it is interesting at least that when I asked my boomer colleagues how they identified themselves, their initial response was the phrase "college professor" (or just "teacher"), instead of "spouse," "parent," or "grandparent."

Quite a few positive aspects accrue to those who feel that they are called to do their work. For example, one study (Duffy, Bott, Allan, Torrey, & Dik, 2012) has shown that individuals who perceive themselves as having a calling and succeed in living out that calling report greater work satisfaction and meaning in their work, compared to those who do not perceive their work as a calling. It seems worth noting in this context that the job "college professor" is almost always rated among the highest in job satisfaction in poll after poll. But the calling comes with a cost as well. Stuart Bunderson and Jeffrey Thompson (2009) found that those who perceived their work as a calling were also more likely than those who did not to conceptualize the work as a moral duty: there was an ethical component to the work, and that included making personal sacrifices so the work could continue. The authors found that, in their sample of zookeepers, those who thought of themselves as called to that job were willing to sacrifice their pay, personal time, and comfort for the sake of the animals in their charge. The researchers referred to this as the "double-edged sword" of perceiving a calling: On the one hand, those who are called report more satisfaction, meaning, and purpose in their work than those who are not called. On the other hand, those who are called are willing to make sacrifices of themselves that go far beyond what a mere worker or employee would be willing to make. I saw both edges of this sword—or maybe both the yin and the yang of this concept—in myself and my colleagues during my years as a professor. I felt, and I know that many of my colleagues also felt, that in being the best that we could be, we were doing the work that we were meant to do, and that gave us a sense of meaning and purpose that most other people I knew did not seem to possess. But the sacrificial aspects to the profession were never far beneath the surface for me. My colleagues and I might use the expression "it takes a lot out of you" to describe the fact that when we finally left the workplace at the end of a day, we were usually exhausted and numb, especially as we aged. And that statement does not begin to address the circumstances that may have arisen when we arrived at our homes to greet our families in that condition.

Before discussing the characteristics of the professors who will replace the retiring baby boomers, there are at least two important facts that should be borne in mind: the replacements will be drawn from the ranks of Generation X in the near term, and many or most of them will probably serve as contingent faculty rather than tenure-track faculty. Both facts are important in contextualizing the vector that has been created by the aging and retirement-bound boomer cohort of professors. Ehrenberg (2011) has carefully documented the changes in staffing patterns in higher education over the past forty to fifty years. Using data originally collected by the US Department of Education, Ehrenberg showed that the percentage of current full-time faculty members who were neither tenured nor employed in a tenure-earning position increased from 18.6 percent of all faculty in 1975, as the golden age was coming to an end, to 37.5 percent by 2007. Statistics drawn from my institution definitely showed this shift in hiring patterns. For example, in 1992 (Eastern Illinois University, 1992), 527 of 676 total faculty members (78.0 percent) were tenured or held tenure-track positions. But by fall 2012, only 414 out of 720 of faculty members (57.5 percent) were tenured or held tenure-track positions, a drop of about 20 percentage points in twenty years (Eastern Illinois University, 2012). And even full-time jobs not on the tenure track became harder to secure as the twentieth century closed. Ehrenberg (2011) also found that the percentage of all faculty who were employed on a full-time basis fell from 77.9 percent in 1970 to a scant majority—51.3 percent—by 2007. William Doyle (2008) has shown that the trend toward the graying of the faculty that was first identified in the 1980s and 1990s has not abated in the 2000s. In other words, the median age of those holding a tenured position is continuing to rise. As Doyle points out, this disparity creates the possibility of a very different working environment for those junior academics who are entering the professoriate now, as well as for those senior faculty members who are holding onto the possibly coveted tenure-track positions. But the coveting might be a little misplaced, in the sense that it is difficult to covet something that occurred in the past. For if the trends identified by Doyle and Ehrenberg continue, the tenure-track academic jobs are not going to be passed on to the members of the next birth cohort. Rather, many or most of those jobs will vanish into the past.

SUMMARY: WHERE ARE THE VECTORS PUSHING THE PROFESSORIATE?

The forces that have manifested themselves at the end of time are pressuring most institutions of higher education to remake themselves, and those changes necessarily have a strong impact on the professoriate. As we have seen, the professoriate is either being stretched or squeezed by a number of diverging or converging vectors over which its members seem to have little direct control. For example, as institutions have come to realize their predicament with regard to financial sustainability produced by the cost disease, they have availed themselves of a technological fix: the online course, perhaps in the format of a MOOC. In doing so, the institutions converted perhaps the most important service the professoriate provided (teaching in higher education) into a commodity or product whose creation simply bypassed the overwhelming majority of the professoriate. While such an invention may—repeat, may—solve the problem of sustainability based on a front-end analysis, there are also lingering and unanswered questions on the back end of the sustainability problem related to affordability and satisfaction.

Although quite a bit has been learned over the past thirty years about the institutional factors that enhance retention rates and progress toward graduation (one of the strongest factors is the learning alliance that a student might form with a dedicated professor), much less is known about graduates' satisfaction. Given the apparently shrinking college differential—the difference in earning potential between graduates and nongraduates—students have become increasingly oriented toward the bottom line for them at the end of time. When graduates ask themselves, "Would I do it again [go to college], given how much I make, and the nature of the job I have?" the institutions know that answer had better be, "Yes, certainly." And the professoriate must in turn be ready to do its part to make sure that the answer is affirmative for the majority of potential graduates.

Even with their technological fixes, institutions must continue to hustle to build incoming classes of sufficient size, although our culture's mantra of "everyone should go to college" should seemingly encourage sufficient numbers to attend. As institutions dive deeper and deeper into the pool of available traditionally aged people for their prospective students, those institutions are finding that fewer and fewer of the prospective students they locate are adequately prepared for the college experience that the professoriate has been trained to provide.

Finally, there is an issue for the professoriate involving the finality of the aging process. At the end of the twentieth century and the beginning of the twenty-first, the ranks of the tenured faculty were populated by baby boomers who are now retiring in large numbers. There is some evidence to suggest that boomers who became professors may have felt called to do that work, with this concept implying a kind of moral imperative or duty. Whether or not the Generation X professors share that concept with the boomers remains to be seen. But forming the kind of professor-student learning alliance that institutions want to enhance their retention and satisfaction rates could be more difficult if the motivation for those kinds of relationships is found much more often in professors who feel that they have been called. Regardless of how that part of the issue plays out, Generation X professors face an additional structural problem. In their efforts to address the problems created by the cost disease, institutions have already replaced many of their tenure-track faculty with contingent faculty, who are often paid dramatically less than tenure-track professors for doing essentially the same work. It is possible to see a negative feedback loop in this solution: the institution's productivity is down as a result of the grand experiment of having everyone go to college, so the institutions have hired less expensive professors who may in turn be less invested in their institution's outcomes and, therefore, less likely to promote the kind of relationships that lead to retention, graduation, and satisfaction. The solution has exacerbated the problem: there will be fewer students, not more, and they will be less, not more, satisfied with their outcomes. And as the professoriate is diminished in numbers, resulting from the reduced need to have as many of them, it will also be diminished in role, resulting from the reduction in some of the functions at which it is already known to excel.

7 · SOME TIME TRAVELING FOR ME

Even at the end of time, as my career in the professoriate was reaching its conclusion, the campus of my institution seemed safe and secure, somehow buffered from all the changes that were about to befall it and perhaps all of the institutions of higher education in the United States. On a typical October morning, as my final fall semester progressed, my senses would be brimming with all of the sights, sounds and even smells of the campus just as they had always been: the brightly colored leaves glistening in the emerging sunlight after a brief shower had moved on, the breeze blowing the raindrops onto the ground and creating a light tattoo calling the students to class, the petrichor. On such days, it was easy for me to think that all this would go on forever. But if I am correct in my reasoning about the future of higher education and the professoriate, then those feelings of permanence that my senses created for me were just an illusion: all I experienced on those mornings would be swept away, perhaps far more quickly than my future projection in this chapter would have it.

In chapter 6, I described in detail the forces (or vectors) that had emerged by the end of time to wreak wholesale changes on institutions of higher education and the professoriate. In this chapter, I show what might happen to the institutions of higher education and the professoriate as a result of these forces. To do so, I have used an approach here that differs somewhat from the objective and data-based narrative that I have used thus far in the book. Rather, I have created a more concrete visualization, or scenario, written from a future point of view to depict the result. I also introduce a new species of knowledge worker whose ranks are predominant in the professoriate in that future. I go on to examine the vastly diminished and changed role of the relatively few remaining professors at the industrial-scale schools. I intend this scenario to serve as a response to the overarching question of the entire book: what will happen to the professoriate—not simply as a profession or career, but as a concept—once all the forces now in play have resolved themselves?

Later in the chapter, I align the scenario with some of the specific vectors I described in chapter 6 to show how the job done by those individuals in the future who will be responsible for college teaching represents an answer to the challenges posed by the vectors.

I am far from the only person to envision wholesale changes in the operation of the higher education industry in the future. So while I am out there in the future, following the alignment discussion, I describe a few of the other possible models that have been proposed as either likely outcomes or possibly desirable solutions to the challenges facing higher education. After discussing them, I hop back into my time machine and return to now, the end of time, to consider those variables that my scenario has not addressed specifically, as well as some of its other limitations. Finally, there is just enough time in the chapter for me to say good-bye.

Before launching on this agenda, I need to restate an essential caveat. I do not intend the vision of higher education in the future that I have constructed here as a forecast per se about the future. As Nate Silver (2012) has explained, although we use the terms "prediction" and "forecast" somewhat interchangeably, there remain subtle differences between them as descendants from their original Latin and German, roots respectively. A prediction is simply a comment about the future, something said ahead of the time that it might occur. Forecasting, on the other hand, involves reading precursors accurately, and by doing so harvesting knowledge that in turn enables statements about the likelihood of something occurring. Unlike some of the people who are successful in using this sort of prognostication now (such as weather forecasters), I cannot claim to know what is going to happen in the future—in this case, for higher education and the professoriate. What I am offering here is something more like a possible outcome, or perhaps a plausible outcome, depending on whatever one's judgment might be about the identification and operation of the vectors as I have described them in the book.

SCENARIO IN 2215: EASTERN ILLINOIS REGIONAL EDUCATION CENTER (EIREC)

Probably the first element of the heading above that draws attention is the date: Why is the scenario set 200 years in the future, a time that seems impossibly distant? First, I wanted to set a date that was so far into the future that it would be inconceivable to believe that any of the forces that I believe are in play now, and that are changing the work and the position of the professoriate, would not have been resolved. Thus, while the vision of higher education that I present here might look radically different to those of us reading it now—that is, at the end of time—this visualization of higher education will not look new to any readers from beyond the end of time. It is also the case, I am sure, that different issues will have arisen 200 years from now whose form and force I cannot possibly imagine from my perspective in the early twenty-first century.

Second, I wanted readers to imagine a time in which today's concept of a professor would be as distant and perhaps seem as quaint to readers of that time as the concept of an infantry soldier at Waterloo does to contemporary readers. As I stated in chapter 1, it was this idea that the actual, but unknown, behavior of the soldiers at Waterloo might still be just barely recoverable from the extant data that prompted the military historian John Keegan (1976) to launch his epochal and field-changing work. I harbor no illusions that *A Professor at the End of Time* will accomplish a similar feat. Nevertheless, a similar animating idea can be seen throughout this book. In that unknowable future, the apparatus and work of the professoriate in the late twentieth and early twenty-first centuries will seem as primitive and ineffective as a smoothbore musket might seem to those of us looking at one in a museum now.

But I also admit the date is somewhat irrelevant. That is, I believe the resolution of forces that I have described will occur much sooner than the date mentioned in the subheading of the chapter. How much sooner I cannot know. But I can say that the members of the professoriate with whom I discussed the scenario believed, initially at least, that many decades would elapse before any of the changes described in the scenario would occur, and they often expressed amusement and perhaps derision in response to the prospects that I have outlined here. Generally, it was not until they thought about the scenario for a little while that the amusement began to subside.

EIU beyond the End of Time

Following a round of gracious introductions, the governor of the state of Illinois advanced to the lectern on the stage of a packed auditorium on the campus of Eastern Illinois University (EIU) one brisk morning in October 2215. A brief shower had already moved on, and now brilliant sunlight streamed into the room, although even that seemed to have none of its usual cheering effects. Most of the faces were glum; everyone present knew what the governor had come to say, but there were some who hoped that, by some miracle, the fate about to befall them could be averted. The governor began with a careful exposition of her administration's attempts to solve the state's university problems less drastically. Beginning with a period of retrenchment and some consolidation among the state's twelve public campuses that had taken place a few years earlier, there had been a substantial savings in the delivery of higher education. But despite everyone's best efforts, the reduction in student and taxpayer cost had been insufficient. The governor reminded everyone of the state's "moral and necessary" obligation to provide quality higher education in this part of the state at an affordable price. So, she then stated, "we arrive at a new place, a place of possibilities for an exciting and innovative model of higher education." The plan called for two of the twelve public university campuses, one in the Chicago metropolitan area (where fifteen million of Illinois's twenty million people resided) and one institution outside the metropolitan area, to be redesignated as Regional Education Centers.

The governor's address referred to a new beginning, but her talk also came at the end of a lengthy period of political wrangling. Some years earlier, there had been something of a revolution by taxpayers who had seemingly awakened from a long slumber with the realization that the state of Illinois could no longer afford to support, even minimally, the twelve public university campuses their forebears had erected so willingly three centuries earlier. For the politicians, the acceptance of the idea that a university could be demoted (although nobody used that term), while leaving open the possibility of demoting several others as need arose, was a deal consummated only after an intense and lengthy squabble. The politicians' fervent hopes, and their political futures, rested on the notion that, having failed to contain the increasing costs of the universities, the state could remove itself completely from the business of owning universities, one school at a time if need be.

There would be some physical changes for the Regional Education Centers (RECs). The athletic teams (EIU had fielded twenty-one distinct men's and women's squads) were eliminated, as was the need for their stadiums, field houses, playing fields, and so on. Most of the residence halls had already been torn down and the land sold to private developers.

There would be other changes in how the students' education was programmed at an REC. For a baccalaureate degree, students admitted to the former university would be charged a one-time degree payment[1] that essentially functioned as a voucher covering a virtually unlimited number of online courses, as well as room, board, and tuition for their single residency year. The voucher remained in effect for a specific number of years, usually seven, after its purchase. If, for whatever reason, the students had not completed their degree by then, they could buy individual services or courses for an à la carte fee. The vast majority of each student's course work was administered remotely (that is, what was called online in the twenty-first century). After reaching a certain number of credits (usually 75 percent of the total number of credits needed for graduation), students were eligible to sign up for their residency year to complete their degree.

Here is how that residency year unfolds for the students. When they arrive on campus, they are greeted by a division head and by the relatively few quasi-permanent faculty members of their major academic department. The division head, who may or may not have an academic background, supervises these faculty members, who staff the face-to-face courses taken by students in what they still refer to as their senior year. The division head also supervises the small army of contingent workers who staff the online courses. (The term that I use to describe the role of such an online teacher, "docent," is already becoming increasingly common in higher education.)

College Teaching in That Epoch: The Role of the Docent

Although the term "docent" is not new, the role, as I envision it here, would be filled by a new species of academic professional, a species that would largely replace the members of the professoriate as that term is conventionally understood in the twenty-first century. For that reason, it makes sense to provide some details of the docents' training, their capabilities, and their differences from the traditional professoriate here. First, the docents would hold a new sort of degree, a Professional Degree (PD), that represents a streamlining of the conventional academic process. Those who aspire to be docents hold a PD in college teaching, and they maintain a license that permits them to be employed in that way. The PD degree is usually offered by the relatively few universities that have retained that term in their names, following the conversion of an increasing number of former universities to RECs. The PD requires about one academic year of full-time study following the baccalaureate degree. During that academic year, individuals studying for a PD in college teaching take a few courses that bolster their background knowledge in several related academic areas. But their main focus of study consists of acquiring the technical know-how needed to administer college courses online. This degree and license credential would, therefore, have largely replaced the traditional PhD degree as the entry-level academic qualification for college teaching. Consequently, it would no longer be the case that American universities churn out 100,000 new PhD holders every year. Instead that number would have been reduced to something closer to 10,000, the number of people who would still be needed as faculty members in colleges and universities for so-called senior year students and as trainers for those individuals who continue to seek the PhD. That is, a person holding the PhD would still be required to train a person seeking to earn that degree.

Docents are not professors as that term is understood now, at the end of time. The docents have not been trained to do research or scholarship, and hence they lack the capability to do so. That is not a limitation, because their role in no way entails research or scholarly productivity. The docents possess a certain amount of disciplinary content knowledge above and beyond what the typical undergraduate who majored in that discipline would have. But the amount or depth of that disciplinary knowledge in no way approaches what a typical PhD-level

professor would have today. Furthermore, unlike the role of the college professor of today, which is made more expensive by its adherence to a research model
whether such involvement is warranted or not, the docent does not work on
independent research or scholarship: there is no expectation that a docent will
inhabit a research area, think deeply (and long) about a research topic, or even
study a research area. In the broad literature on higher education, there have
been a number of studies documenting the means by which members of the
professoriate today have continued to grow and advance as scholars and teachers, even in the academic climate of the industrial-scale institutions that are not
always hospitable to such growth (for example, Eddy, 2007; O'Meara, Terosky,
& Neumann, 2008; Terosky, Phifer, & Neumann, 2008). As I have conceived
of them here, the docents will not face those problems: academic or scholarly
growth will simply not be part of their job.

Concepts such as academic freedom and tenure that once were the hallmarks of
the professoriate's status as a very special sort of workforce are mainly gone, and neither the docents, who never enjoyed those benefits, nor the remaining professors,
whose memory of having them is now lost in the mists of time, seem to miss them
overly much. It is probably not crucial to my story of the professoriate to attempt
to explain how these characteristics of the academic workplace eventually disappeared, and I will not lengthen my account unnecessarily with an excursus about
what may have happened. But the short form of that story would probably have to
do with market forces being brought to bear. That is, the universities of the future
came to realize that they were no longer required to offer tenure or wide degrees of
academic freedom to retain a skilled professoriate in the numbers needed. The institutions found out that there were enough people who had been trained and were
willing to become professors even without those protections. In the absence of the
academic freedom and tenure principles, the remaining members of the professoriate and all of the docents are governed by employee regulations.

So my analysis suggests that the appearance of the docents is not simply a
continuation of the current tendency to deprofessionalize and unbundle (or
separate) the teaching, research, and service roles of the professoriate (Kezar,
2012). There is a resemblance between the docents and the current contingent
faculty members. But the current contingent faculty members have a disciplinary status, having been trained in an academic discipline and identifying with it.
The docents will not be like that. Furthermore, in some universities today even
the contingent faculty members enjoy some of the prerogatives of the permanent faculty members, such as multiyear contracts and possible financial rewards
based on merit. These would be unlikely to be available to the docents, as I have
envisioned them here, even if only because such practices cost money now. And
one of the objectives of creating the docent role is to achieve a nearly permanent
reduction in the personnel costs of keeping the university open.

Enacting the Scenario in a Typical Psychology Department

I am sure that even as forces in the future will homogenize and unify the college experience for students, especially for those who study at an industrial-scale school, each department and academic discipline will nevertheless retain something of its own ancestral cultural identity. Because I worked in a psychology department and am familiar with that culture, I will use psychology as the disciplinary location for the operational details of the scenario I am providing. Those operational details involve not only administering a bipartite curriculum (that is, a curriculum that has been delivered online for the most part, but with a substantial face-to-face component occurring at the tail end of the student's undergraduate life), but also using a starkly segmented faculty to do so (that is, with the few remaining members of the professoriate handling the face-to-face courses, while the docents staff the online component). My familiarity with psychology notwithstanding, with the necessary modifications, I am virtually positive the model could be adjusted to fit any of the typical undergraduate majors of the current time.

To establish the size of this particular enterprise as it might occur at my former school, we need to turn to some statistics about the commonality of the psychology degree in the United States at the end of time. Of the 1,791,000 bachelor's degrees conferred in the United States in 2011-12, there were 109,000 awarded in psychology, which is over 6 percent of the total—making psychology one of the most popular of undergraduate majors (National Center for Education Statistics, 2015a). And the number of psychology majors at EIU has historically run very close to that percentage; approximately 5 percent of all undergraduates at EIU choose psychology as their major. For purposes of this exercise, if we were to hold EIU's undergraduate enrollment constant at about 10,000 students—which has historically been a good overall estimate—then it is conceivable that 500 of them could be psychology majors in this projected future, with most of the numbers concentrated in the upper division (junior and senior years). Thus, in my vision of the future as outlined above, there are good reasons to believe that some 125 students might descend on EIU's campus yearly to complete their senior year as a psychology major.

Their needs are met by the five quasi-permanent professors remaining in the department (down from over twenty when the technological era began, sometime around 2000). Each of these five professors teaches five classes each semester, with about twenty-five students in each class. The professors do not necessarily offer every course in the psychology curriculum (perhaps thirty-five to forty undergraduate courses for a typical department) each year. Rather, the professors staff only those courses whose content has been judged to be more amenable to face-to-face teaching, as opposed to online education. At the procedural level, the students' face-to-face course work focuses on cognitive skills, such as critical thinking, and on other skills, such as team building and team working. The students' course work is still evaluated and graded by the professors, as was true in the past. In the Psychology Department, as in most of the science departments, the face-to-face course work generally consists of performance-based activities such as conducting, reporting, and presenting research. While students are still tested, in the sense of taking quizzes and examinations, these activities account for a much smaller percentage of the student's overall grade than they did in the past. Testing plays a smaller role than it once did because it focuses on content knowledge, and content knowledge plays a smaller role in the suite of skills, characteristics, and attributes that college graduates are expected to have.

What Might the Work of the Professoriate Look Like?

For any reader who has plowed through chapters 2-5 of *A Professor at the End of Time*, in which I dissect my work as a professor in great detail, this section's brevity may be a shock (or a relief). But before I preview the work of the future professoriate, I need to hedge a bit. In discussing the work and role of the professoriate, I will note that while that work and the concept underlying it may all but disappear from some venues, the two systems of higher education that I sketched in chapter 1 and detailed in the last chapter will continue to exist. And the lines between those two systems, which are sometimes blurry today, may be much sharper in the future. Thus, those individuals working as professors in the schools of the elite system may not see the upheaval I predict as wrenching as those laboring as the remaining few academicians in the schools of the industrial-scale system. The schools in the elite system will remain the centers of scholarship and research, and so they will remain the primary location for training the nation's scientists and scholars. Their academic units may grow smaller with time, as relatively fewer people seek a PhD. But it is the industrial-scale institutions that I believe will bear the brunt of the forces imposing themselves on higher education, and it is the emaciated professoriate of such institutions whose work and fate I wish to describe here.

In the academic units of the industrial-scale institutions, the work of the remaining professors will be evaluated on different criteria than those used for of the typical professor in the golden age or the technological era. I used the schema of the three traditional roles (teaching, research, and service) to discuss the current work of the professoriate, and it is on the activities in these areas that almost all professors are evaluated. In my future scenario, the members of the professoriate at the nonelite schools will retain a teaching role, but they will jettison, or will have had extracted from them, their research and service roles. At the industrial-scale universities and the RECs, assuming for now that such a model could take hold, the professors have no research agenda other than the collaborative research projects in which they engage with their students. These projects are not intended to be contributions to a scientific literature or advances in scholarship, so there is no intentional pathway to publication for them. Consequently, the professor's research or scholarly productivity is no longer taken into account when the administration makes decisions about retaining or promoting him or her.

We might expect to see substantial changes in the professor's behavior in teaching, too. There could be an emphasis on the principles of the so-called flipped classroom (Berrett, 2012). That is, the regularly scheduled class time is used a place for discussion and other forms of interaction, rather than being used for lectures or other forms of straightforward, verbal knowledge dissemination. Thus, the classroom becomes more like a workshop focused on discovery products, such as the findings of student research projects and the reports that students write and present to the class, instead of a site where students play the more passive roles of listener and note taker that often predominate now.

With the retraction of the research mission, the time previously devoted to it would be allocated to other tasks. Many of these would be service tasks, although the nature of the service being rendered would also undergo a transformative shift from the way the professoriate typically thinks of service currently. For example, the public service mission that almost all professors today acknowledge would no longer be focused on service for the public good; instead, it would be focused on the university good, which is tantamount to saying the corporate good. Along these lines, it might be expected that there would be more vertical integration of the professor's role. One way that might be achieved would be to have professors work more overtly and directly with lower-level students such as high-school students. That is, the remaining cadre of professors would be used by their institutions as agents in a well-thought-out and deliberate student-recruiting effort. There might also be more public speaking for purposes of outreach, rather than for sharing information among peers. So instead of holding a departmental colloquium aimed at faculty and presented by a visiting researcher in the afternoon, the department might host a public lecture for community members by a local faculty professor in the evening. The professor's outreach role might include more regularly scheduled visits with working alumni in their place of business. The purpose of such visits might consist of information gathering by the professor to see which courses turned out to be most helpful for working alumni. Such visits could become opportunities for fund-raising with successful alumni. Finally, the professors of the future might expect that their service work to carry them into more explicit and defined relationships with corporate entities that work as partners with higher education. In the future, such partnerships would not necessarily be the underpinnings of grants and other research-based incentives, as they are now. Rather, it may be the case that, along with their tangible support, the corporate partners play a far larger role than they currently do in the design of the curriculum, targeting characteristics like communication skills, team work, problem solving, and critical thinking in place of the content knowledge whose provision has been the professor's stock in trade.

RESOLUTION OF VECTORS

If the vectors that I discussed in chapter 6 represent powerful forces clashing together with titanic momentum, then the resolution of those vectors should be understood as the pathway along which higher education will be sent careening, once those vectors have had their impact. In this section, I bring most of the vectors on stage one more time in an effort to show how the future scenario I have presented may be understood as an outcome of their operation.

To be clear, the scenario I am presenting does not foresee the death of either higher education or of the university: Both of these concepts will continue to thrive, although in radically different forms than they have today. Furthermore, there will continue to be personnel within the university who can look forward to having a certain career trajectory, and some of these individuals may refer to themselves as professors. Thus, the concept of the professor may not be abolished, in the same sense that many people in my cohort witnessed the real end of certain once-common jobs such as elevator operator or TV repair person. Still, when the work that I and thousands of other professors carried out at the beginning of the technological era is compared to the tasks of those future workers in the university, the similarity in our titles will indicate only a superficial resemblance. Although my scenario postulates a future containing a radically different, but nevertheless prosperous, higher education apparatus, there are a couple of sober realities to consider. First, the apparatus will consist of two rather starkly distinct subsystems, the schools of industrial-scale system having given up on an aspirational model that involved chasing the same objectives as the schools of the elite system. And second, for the schools of the industrial-scale system, their survival, let alone their prosperity, is predicated on a decision to discard their professoriate.

Other commentators who have examined the same facts I have are much less sanguine than I am about higher education's ability to thrive under any circumstances. For example, Bill Readings (1996) has suggested that the professoriate is already operating in institutions that have lost their way and are in ruins. According to him, "the University no longer inhabits a continuous history of progress, of the progressive revelation of a unifying idea" (Readings, 1996, p. 129). Jeffrey Selingo (2013) calls the academy is a "risk-averse, self-satisfied industry" (p. x) and asserts that American higher education is broken. Finally, Nathan Harden (2013) hypothesizes that half of the 4,000 or more institutions of higher education (counting the two-year schools) in the United States will be closed in a matter of a few years.

Moreover, I am not the first author writing at the end of time who has suggested that the professoriate might somehow disappear in the future (for example, Donoghue, 2008; Schuster, 2011). Jack Schuster (2011) wonders if "the forces now reshaping the academy and its faculty portend a *withering* away of the traditional faculty" (p. 1). But despite all these elements of the story that have been mentioned by other people on the scene who have been sifting through the evidence, I think that I am the first one to document how the forces impinging on the faculty today have fundamentally changed, commodified, and ultimately diminished its work. And I think I am the first to document how those forces, operating together as a kind of device, could make the disappearance of the professoriate at least a plausible outcome of its machinations.

Resolving the Cost Disease

How does the vision I situated in the future resolve the cost disease? In the schools in the industrial-scale system, the vast majority of the teaching, as measured by a productivity indicator such as student credit hours, will be provided by the docents. And they will be compensated on a scale that will be much lower than that on which professors are paid now. Further, the MOOC concept, still something of an experiment at the end of time, may take root in the future. For example, if there comes a time when there are MOOCs available for all the courses that typically constitute the general education portion of the curriculum, and if there are some choices to be made among those MOOCs, then the institution will simply decide which MOOC they wish to rent for each course in their curriculum, paying a relatively small per student fee to the school in the elite system whose professor authored and developed that MOOC's content. For the first three years of the student's undergraduate education (assuming that the entire experience is designed to be completed in four years), the students are then simply directed to go to the portal of the MOOC the institution has rented. Assuming the docents are provided with the technology to handle ever larger class sizes in the MOOCs they administer, the pressure that creates the cost disease now—the pressure to raise teacher salaries while productivity remains nearly constant—will be eased. Docents' salaries may increase, but that increase will be offset by the increases in class sizes in the MOOC. And the institutions will no doubt be clever enough to make sure that the increase in class size that pays for the docents' salary increase will also be large enough to pay for salary increases for the skeleton crew of professors who remain. It is true that this model assumes that there is some elasticity in the number of potential students available: class sizes cannot be increased if there are no additional eligible students who wish to enroll. As this part of the analysis suggests, to the extent that my scenario is accurate, there would probably be some reduction in the number of institutions of higher education in the future. Whether that reduction would be equal to the 50 percent reduction predicted by Harden (2013) obviously remains to be seen.

Affordability and Satisfaction

Higher education's survival may be dependent on its solution to the problem of the cost disease. But solving this problem—essentially a problem of affordability—will not be sufficient to guarantee higher education's future. To do that, potential students and their families will have to perceive an added-value benefit in the experience of going to college, regardless of the cost. Even if the bachelor's degree actually is an added-value benefit, the reality is that as many as 20 percent of recent recipients of bachelor's degrees do not perceive it as such (Godofsky, Zukin, & Van Horn, 2011), and they claim they would not have attended college had they known in advance how it was going to turn out for them. It is this category of dissatisfied degree holders whose numbers must be reduced if higher education is to survive.

What happens in the first job entered after college can play a huge role in the satisfaction or lack of it among recent graduates. When the salary for that job barely offsets the cost of having gone to college once student loans are factored in, when the opportunities for advancement in it appear limited, and when the skills it calls for are not the ones acquired in college, it should hardly come as a surprise that so many recent graduates claim their degree is not valuable to them. However, they might be more likely to get a job with the attributes they desire under the assumptions I postulated in the future scenario. First, their final year would offer them more opportunities to use and master elements of the skill set that employers often claim they want—skills involving communication, critical thinking, and problem solving.

Second, in the future that I have sketched, institutions of higher education will pivot from the principles that currently animate them, principles that are largely derived from the goals and values of the professoriate, and toward what I describe as a mission-centered focus. That focus will be squarely on the needs of students as expressed by them and their families. What might the needs be? Actually, the institutions and the professoriate already know what the needs are, especially for families of students who attend the industrial-scale schools. Their needs include the provision of an accurate, data-based, forecast from the institution regarding the job and career prospects for students who major in various disciplines, including information such as median salary earned, the possibilities for advancement in that career and expectations for increases in compensation, and the extent of linearity or alignment between the completion of a degree in that major and the credentials or entry qualifications needed for a specific career.

State Support and Economies of Scale

One of the harshest realities facing the public four-year schools now is the retrenchment of state financial support that began in the 1980s, if not earlier. Although legislature-approved reductions in state funding are generally made on a percentage basis, seemingly affecting all the state schools equally, the fact that the nonflagship campuses in the state system are generally smaller than the flagship campuses means that the regional comprehensive universities do not have the flexibility in their budgets that the flagship institution enjoys, so budget cutbacks affect them to a greater degree. In the scenario of the future I envisioned, a state government had decided to get out of the higher education business altogether, thus creating obviously profound consequences for the members of the professoriate as their numbers were inexorably diminished through the closures of their institutions. But even if states take much less drastic approaches to cost containment, these may still produce devastating consequences for the members of the professoriate.

One of these approaches that state governments might use has to do with what I call economy of scale. From the standpoint of the professoriate, this approach has the putative advantage of maintaining the existing departmental and college structure. However, as I show, there are other, much less happy outcomes for the professoriate associated with an economy-of-scale approach. The first step of such an approach would involve bifurcating the entire state public higher education into two streams, each serving its own cohort of students. The student cohort bound for the flagship campus would see little change from the way such campuses look today: within very broad restrictions, each student would continue to be free to choose a major or program from a seemingly innumerable list of available options. For the students whose application materials indicate they might be a better fit at a regional, comprehensive campus, a different picture emerges. The regional campuses would continue to offer a number of programmatic options, or choices of majors. But prospective students would see that certain majors or programs, those with historically low enrollments, had been bundled together on one or another of the regional campuses. To provide a concrete example, there are twelve public campuses in Illinois, including the elite flagship campus. At my former institution there are thirty students majoring in philosophy, and that department houses nine faculty members. There may be more or fewer philosophy majors on the other ten regional campuses, but an extrapolation of the numbers from my former school suggests there might be 300–400 students majoring in philosophy at all the public campuses combined. These students are taught by perhaps 125 professors of philosophy (counting the twenty-four faculty members at the flagship campus, a number that includes their visiting and affiliated faculty). If enacted, the consolidation model described in this section would result in the continuation of the existing department at the flagship campus, with its twenty-five or so faculty members and 100 student majors, and the creation of a second department at a regional campus, consisting of twenty faculty members and 200–300 student majors. The space for the single, larger philosophy department at the regional campus would be created by the bundling together of other smaller departments at that institution that had been sent to other regional campuses. It would be up to the institutions themselves to engage in the necessary, but nevertheless colossal, free-for-all horse trading that must occur to determine which institution would house which programs and majors.

There would be obvious financial savings at the level of the state government, resulting from the severely lowered number of philosophy professors needed to staff the public higher education system. And there is at least one powerful benefit to the professoriate. Unlike the future scenario in which most of the course work is delivered online by docents, at least in the consolidation model, the traditional departmental and collegiate structure of the university is maintained.

Resolving the Gray Vector

The gray vector refers to the relentless and irreversible aging of the professoriate, a group whose median age has been thought to be fifty-five for at least the past fifteen years (Bland & Bergquist, 1997). As I discussed in chapter 6, the concept of moral obligation or duty played important roles—both beneficial and sacrificial—in the work and the identity of this cohort of the professoriate, and now that the members of this group may have felt some need to relinquish their places, it becomes imperative to see who has succeeded them (and who might in the future) and to assess the extent to which the concept of duty might play a part in their assumption of a role in the professoriate. If the work of a number of authors (for example, Ernst, 2013) has provided us with a weathervane indicating the characteristics of those younger people who have already entered the ranks of the professoriate, and of those who might be following them, it seems clear that the culture of the academy at the end of time no longer has the power to create members of the professoriate who feel a sense of duty to its mission.

For example, Zachary Ernst (2013), who resigned his position as a newly tenured associate professor in the Philosophy Department of the University of Missouri—a position I can only assume many hundreds of PhD holders in philosophy would love to have—cited several factors in his decision. Ernst wrote that he believed that the academy's perverse incentive structure maintained the status quo, rewarded mediocrity, and discouraged interdisciplinary scholarship and research. Significantly, he also cited the corporatization of the American university—the tendency to hire private-sector business leaders or CEOs of corporations as presidents of large multicampus universities, even when those individuals lacked any experience as professors or administrators in higher education. In his essay—which led to a firestorm of comments, showing how combustible this issue had become—Ernst stated that while he enjoyed teaching, the roadblocks he experienced in attempting to do the kind of interdisciplinary scholarship in which he was most interested turned out to be too much to overcome.

To the extent that the experiences of Ernst are telling, what are the implications of the gray vector for the professoriate as a whole? It may be the case that the cohort of the professors who, like me, were the last and the first—the last ones to operate under the principles of the golden age, and the first ones to make our way in brave new world of the technological era—and who are now (at the end of time) the grayest of the gray will simply not be replaced. That is, they will leave, and many of the people who may have been once willing to take their places are now broadcasting their findings that the academy, as it is operated at the end of time, is not nearly so appealing a location to spend one's career as it was heretofore. Even without the pressures of the cost disease, and even without the force exerted by the issues of affordability and satisfaction, it may be the case that the inexorable wearing action of the gray vector alone will prove to have been enough on its own to bring about the end of the professoriate as we have known it for most of the decades of the twentieth century.

Certainly, the combination of the cost disease, the aging out of its current inhabitants, and the speculative reluctance of a succeeding generation to assume their places has created dramatic changes in hiring practices in the American professoriate. Ronald Ehrenberg (2011) has summarized some of these changes: "The stereotypical model of undergraduate instruction in the American higher education is outdated. The image of a full-time faculty member with a doctoral degree, who has tenure or who is on a tenure-track and will eventually be evaluated for tenure, lecturing to, or leading discussions with undergraduate students could not be further from the truth at most colleges and universities in the US" (pp. 101–102). With regard to the future of the professoriate portended by these changes, Ehrenberg's forecast is not all that different from mine: "The leading private liberal arts colleges and the wealthy private, and flagship public research universities are in a world of their own. There we are most likely to see the full-time tenured and tenure-track faculty maintained" (Ehrenberg, 2011, p. 125). But at the other colleges and universities, the vast majority that I have labeled the industrial-scale universities, Ehrenberg foresees a deskilling of the professoriate, by which he means the emergence of a new class of faculty members who do not hold a PhD and who do not work in the university on a full-time basis.

OTHER MODELS

There is an anecdote that has existed for centuries, beloved by academicians, policy makers, economists, and others who have used it in any number of contexts. The anecdote concerns the behavior of a frog immersed in a container of water from which it can easily escape. According to the anecdote, if the water is heated up very gradually, the frog will eventually be boiled alive because its nervous system is too primitive to register the cumulative effect of a long series of minute changes. I will note that there is no contemporary scientific evidence in support of the anecdote—although there are findings from what seem to be carefully done experiments in the nineteenth century (for example, by William Sedgwick [as cited in Scripture, 1897] reporting that, indeed, the frog never budges until it is too late).

Regardless of the degree of empirical truth in the anecdote, and regardless of whether it is apt or fair for me to do so, my scenario from the future casts the professoriate in the role of the frog. That is, although the forces that have fallen on the professoriate are anything but gradual or subtle, professors have nevertheless displayed a persistent behavioral inertia. If, as the scenario postulates, this pattern continues, then at some point it will be too late for the professoriate to save itself.

But it need not be that way. In this section, I will describe several other visions of the future in which the universities and their professors focus on change from within to meet the challenges of the present and future, instead of waiting for changes to be imposed on them from without. For example, Clayton Christensen and Henry Eyring (2011) have presented case studies from two universities, each of which is almost certainly located squarely in one of the two systems of higher education that I have used as an organizing rubric throughout the book. Each case offers possibilities for the professoriate's survival, although the path forward is very different in each case, and whether the survivors of such transformations can truly be considered members of the professoriate is somewhat debatable.

Elite Emulation

One way in which the industrial-scale universities might survive while maintaining an intact professoriate is to successfully imitate the places where that is likely to be the case anyway, such as the schools of the elite system. Christensen and Eyring identify what I have labeled a Harvard emulation model, in which the institution would systematically recruit what is admittedly a *rara avis*: a world-class scholar, or possibly a junior professor with the capability to become a world-class scholar, who is also willing to commit the time to mentor the institution's brightest students. Such students might be grouped together in all-encompassing environment in which academics and extracurricular activities are deliberately braided together to create a sort of academic house, in which the synergy created by grouping the brightest students together would enable more of them to reach their full potential. Speaking as a former professor, I think it could be very intellectually exciting to teach in this kind of environment. However, Christensen and Eyring concede that scaling up the program to operate across an entire university requires a great deal of institutional wealth; Harvard certainly possesses the necessary resources, but probably few other institutions do. The elite emulation model is also predicated on an assumption that the industrial-scale universities wish to emulate the elites—or, perhaps more accurately, that the professors at such institutions wish to emulate their colleagues' success at the elite schools. There is certainly some evidence to support assumption. As I detailed in chapter 5, institutions that wish to elbow their way forward (and upward, in any number of national ranking schemas) may provide incentives to motivate professors to engage in higher (that is, more original, more copious, more impactful) levels of research and scholarship. The fact that such tactics can succeed is prima facie evidence that nonelite institutions may become somewhat more like elite ones if a sustained and agreed-on effort is made to achieve a greater resemblance. But for the schools that are not jostling for prestige, the nonstriving institutions, this approach may not be feasible or even desirable.

Disruption Model

According to the model of disruptive innovation (Christensen, 2003), there are two categories of companies or firms that operate in many varied areas of enterprise. Firms in the leading category often do business as usual, by building additional features or services into their products based on feedback from their customers and by matching the products of their known competitors as they do the same thing. Firms in the leading category are often oblivious to the work of the firms or companies in the disruptive category below them. These disruptive firms forge an entry into the same market occupied by the leading firms by selling simpler products to less demanding clients (who may have become closed out of the leading firms' products as their prices rise). Once the disruptive firm has achieved a solid footing in its niche, it may begin to move upscale from that point, disrupting and possibly even bringing about the demise of the former leaders in the market. The personal computers produced by Apple and others are one example of disruptive innovation. Initially, these computers were no rivals either to the mainframe computers used in business or to the expensive minicomputers used in many academic settings in the early 1980s. Eventually, however, personal computers became powerful enough to eclipse the minicomputer altogether, basically putting its manufacturers out of business in the process.

But Christensen and Eyring (2011) found something of an anomaly when they applied the disruptive innovation model to higher education. They detected disruptive entrants, such as community colleges (I am using this expression to refer to the nation's vast system of public two-year institutions that offer an associate's degree) who may try to move upward in the market by offering bachelor's degrees after they achieve a firm footing with their traditional base of students. But such entrants had not generally succeeded in driving very many of the institutions of higher education in the leading category (that is, the established four-year schools) out of business. Christensen and Eyring went on to identify three possible reasons why that had not happened very often. First, college teaching had been hard to disrupt because, in the past, its intangible human qualities could not be replicated cheaply, by which Christensen and Eyring meant that the qualities of face-to-face teaching could not be offered remotely. Second, they noted that many universities have students representing two very different categories, one of which is not particularly disruptable. Most of the students in the traditional age range of college students are probably seeking an immersive and transformative experience in college. Indeed, going to college has been described as a rite of passage or liminal experience by sociologists and anthropologists (for example, Turner, 1967). Providing all the infrastructure, including the physical plant, capable of sustaining that immersive experience is expensive and not easily replaced by cheaper alternatives. Finally, Christensen and Eyring (2011) noted that there is often a network of other customers (I would use the term "stakeholders" here), including alumni and possibly legislators, who buffer or otherwise protect the institutions from the effects of disruptive innovation.

Whereas such buffering factors existed in the past to protect an institution, Christensen and Eyring argued persuasively that such factors are no longer operative, at least for two of the protective factors. For example, the existence of the Internet, with its capability for streaming college courses and for the provision of content remotely and cheaply, means that college teaching can now be provided at a distance. Second, the growing category of students who are not in the traditional age range—who might be simply trying to acquire a professional credential and not a complete personal identity that might be result from the liminal experience—represents a market that could be sold a different quality of higher education.

Christensen and Eyring document in detail the case of one such institution that has been able to exploit these changes, thus offering a model of how leadership at a particular institution may enable its survival and the survival of its professoriate. Ricks College had been a private two-year college in Rexburg, Idaho, since the early part of the twentieth century, with roots as a normal school or normal academy (that is, a school devoted to training primary and secondary school teachers) going back even further, into the nineteenth century. In 2000, the administration of the Church of Latter-Day Saints, with whom the school had always been affiliated, announced that the school would immediately begin a process whose objective would be the emergence of a four-year institution, to be named Brigham Young University–Idaho, or BYU-Idaho. This switch would be accomplished by 2005. There are a number of noteworthy aspects to this emergence of a new four-year school that suggest its disruptive potential. BYU-Idaho has no research mission. Although the institution still grants tenure to its professors, a professor's publication record, or lack of it, has no bearing on the decision to grant tenure. Second, the institution makes full use of its physical infrastructure through the elimination of a general, summer-long recess. Likewise, there is no institutional participation in intercollegiate athletics, which may also lower the cost of attendance. Finally, unlike the Harvard emulation model offered above, there is no selectivity in admissions, enabling the institution to offer its services to those students who might have otherwise been excluded by selective admissions criteria.

This approach has been successful in quite a few respects. By 2010, BYU-Idaho was serving the needs of approximately 80 percent more students than it had been a decade earlier. Faculty numbers had grown too, although by a significantly smaller percentage—closer to 50 percent. By cutting back on some aspects of the traditional college experience, the institution had become more efficient as well. For example, as a two-year school, Ricks College required 153 square feet of space per student to carry out its mission. Even though some buildings had been added, BYU-Idaho was able to accomplish the more complicated mission of a four-year school using only 126 square feet of space per student. Although the particulars are different, BYU-Idaho seems to operate in the same sort of space that my future scenario envisions for Eastern Illinois Regional Education Center, but it does so in a way that enables the retention of considerable numbers of its professoriate. From the standpoint of its professoriate, there may be another advantage of using a disruptive innovation model that upgrades a two-year school to achieve this objective, compared to the downgrade model that I speculatively advanced for EIU. The faculty members at an existing two-year school will probably not have invested years of their lives in pursuit of what would become an irrelevant degree such as a PhD, and if they already have a PhD they may not have invested years of their lives engaged in research for the sake of enhancing institutional or personal prestige or career advancement.

Instructional Productivity Models

In the future scenario posed by Ehrenberg (2011), the widespread use of MOOCs is accompanied by the influx of a deskilled professoriate. In one future scenario developed by Christensen and Eyring (2011), disruptive innovation from purposefully led two-year schools results in more efficient forms of higher education, possibly leading to the closure of at least some four-year schools that are no longer competitive in the marketplace for students. These scenarios have some common features. They resolve the cost disease vector by lowering the cost of running an institution of higher education, and almost certainly the largest single cost for such an institution is salary. Although faculty members everywhere are relentlessly vocal in their complaints about the salaries of the administrative, staff, and support personnel of their institution, the reality is that the professoriate, as it has operated traditionally, is probably among the most costly workforces in America. For example, as I demonstrated in chapter 6, the cost borne by my institution in having me produce a single credit hour of instruction increased at a pace far greater than inflation during the years I worked in the professoriate. Furthermore, both the approaches of Ehrenberg and of Christensen and Eyring posit the departure of the professoriate as it is known now. For Ehrenberg, minus their PhD degrees, the teachers in higher education are deskilled, in the sense that they no longer interested in, or qualified for, research and scholarship.

Other theorists have devised alternative models that might not involve cost-cutting, and which, therefore, might not involve a wholesale reduction in the numbers of professors in the future. For example, William Massy (2011) envisions a future professoriate from which more instructional value is extracted than is currently done by focusing on the faculty's instructional productivity, rather than on its research or scholarly productivity. From the standpoint of economic theory, instructional productivity involves measuring "output quantity and quality per unit of input—producing the most, or the highest quality output possible given the resources on hand" (Massy, 2011, p. 74). In other words, given that the professoriate is already in place, legitimate questions can be raised concerning what can be done to get more and better teaching from its members. Like the cost-cutting measures I have already described, the instructional productivity approach could be part of the solution to the problems generated by the cost disease. Rather than provide powerful incentives that reduce the professoriate's teaching effort (such as the provision of paid sabbatical leaves), institutions might provide more powerful incentives for faculty to increase their teaching effort and their skills. Or institutions might provide financial incentives for professors whose students are able to demonstrate authentic, durable learning independent of the grade distribution in the class, although such incentives have proved to be very controversial when introduced at the level of primary or secondary school teachers. Raising expectations for the quality of college teaching being provided might also help to produce a more favorable resolution of the afford-ability and satisfaction vector if students and their families begin to perceive that the students who graduate from institutions with such a focus are more successful in getting and keeping high-quality jobs, compared to students from institutions that pay only lip service to the importance of the quality of teach-ing taking place within their walls.

But as was the case for the other scenarios, there are high hurdles on this path to the future. Massy (2011) recognizes several issues that would need to be dealt with. First, to raise the quality and quantity of teaching relative to its cost, there must be reliable methods available to count costs. It might come as a surprise to those not involved in higher education to learn that there are no completely agreed-on standard methods for doing so. And the conventions that universities have adopted are often opaque, sometimes mixing costs that are clearly instruc-tional with other costs that may or may not pertain to instruction. For example, most universities do not distinguish between classroom-related costs, which are clearly instructional, and the costs associated with departmental research—non-grant-supported research that may involve students or may not. Even in the cases where those calculations are done, institutions may fear making the results of the analysis known. In the case of public institutions, exposing those numbers to external constituents, such as lawmakers or members of a higher education supervisory board, could be a risky strategy if it appears that the instructional costs of some program in an institution are somehow too high, especially when the institutions have no a priori standard to use to determine when instructional costs are too high.

Second, if measuring the quantity of instruction is difficult, measuring its qual-ity has proved to be even more daunting. As Massy notes, "the lack of good mea-sures [of instructional quality] has severely limited the degree to which market forces can discipline the provision of educational quality" (2011, p. 76). I would add that the absence of good measures of instructional quality may be a result of the fact that there are profound differences of opinion among the stakeholders in higher education about the elements of educational quality. According to one viewpoint, educational quality might be inherent in the competence and perfor-mance of the professor. This viewpoint has led to the nearly ubiquitous practice of student evaluation of college instruction, in which the students' ratings of an instructor's performance become an important component in retention, tenure, and promotion decisions. But such uses do not sit well with a number of faculty members who question the validity of student-rated items such as "the instruc-tor seems knowledgeable about the material" or even "the instructor generally begins the class on time" for purposes of retention or tenure decisions. In the view of many in the professoriate, students, by virtue of their very status as students, cannot assess the quality of their instruction, only the extent to which they liked it or not—a very different thing.

AND BACK FROM THE FUTURE TO THE PRESENT

Unanswered Questions

Earlier in this chapter I presented a scenario for the future of the industrial-scale four-year universities that involved their shedding a proportion of the professoriate they currently have and adopting in its place a new class of knowledge workers who no longer shared many characteristics of the professors who were present as the golden age of higher education ended and the technological era began. I claimed that such a scenario would resolve the vectors I described in chapters 1 and 6, in the sense that the scenario depicts what might happen when the massive and inescapable collision of forces whose beginnings are already rumbling the foundation of higher education in the United States has ended. But, try though I might to produce a vision of the future in which all the elements in play in the current day were neatly tied up and secured, like the final chapter of a mystery novel, I found there were at least a couple of elements of the current situation that resisted my efforts to tie a bow on them. In this section, I describe those elements—namely, the role of community colleges in the future, and the fate of that magnificent piece of social engineering I called the grand experiment.

One of the models advanced by Christensen and Eyring (2011) posits a future of disruptive innovation in higher education, with community colleges possibly poised to be the disruptive agents that provide needed higher education services to those clients who might have been priced out of the market for a four-year school. Once their base is secured, community colleges might then move nimbly to a more upscale market in which they commanded the resources needed to offer a somewhat stripped down, but still serviceable, baccalaureate degree—ultimately putting the squeeze on those four-year schools that failed to adapt. Now, as the twenty-first century begins, community colleges have probably already become the most likely venue to attract those students who need affordable face-to-face instruction. For that reason alone, an up-gunned community college could conceivably take business away from the four-year schools, as perhaps such colleges already do—at least, the business of those students and their families who share a popular perception that the first two years of study at a four-year school are not as important as the final two years.

But whether the community colleges of the future could attract even more students to their four-year programs is debatable. First, they would have to secure the resources, including physical space and human capital, that offering a baccalaureate degree requires, and that would be a very daunting task for any sector of public higher education to achieve at the end of time. Second, the community colleges, like the four-year schools, have already suffered from their own version of mission creep. Those of us who are (or, in my case, were) in the professoriate tend to look at the two-year schools as primarily doing one thing, which is preparing students to transfer to the four-year schools. This perception is probably not very accurate. The reality is that the community colleges already cover a number of educational bases in their communities, stretching their resources to the maximum. For example, Paul Osterman (2011) lists seven additional distinct missions (including vocational training and adult basic education) that the community colleges already carry out beyond what some might see as their primary mission, preparing students to transfer to a four-year school. To take on the additional demands of baccalaureate programs, the community colleges would surely have to relinquish one of these other missions, and that would not be easily done.

What I called the grand experiment—the radical and untested idea that everyone could and perhaps should go to college based on the benefits that historically had accrued to those who earned a bachelor's degree—may have run its course. Given the rising tide of commentators who question the idea that college is a good financial investment for everyone (for example, Reynolds, 2013); and given the dissatisfaction with their experience reported by a substantial proportion of recent graduates, as shown by Jessica Godofsky, Cliff Zukin, and Carl Van Horn (2011), there may be far fewer students in college in the future, and that factor alone would have consequences for the professoriate.

But even if the grand experiment has concluded, having finally supplied us with an answer that should have been anticipated—namely, that not everyone could go to college, not without dramatically changing the meaning of what it was to have earned a degree—there are lingering consequences of its ending that go beyond the immediate and unhappy fallout for the professoriate.

The grand experiment was certainly perceived as a great contributor to upward mobility in the United States during the experiment's sixty-five-year span, from approximately the end of World War II until the end of the first decade of the twenty-first century. Even as America becomes one of the more economically imbalanced nations among the Western democracies (Organisation for Economic Co-Operation and Development, 2011) over 70 percent of Americans (contrasted with only 40 percent of Europeans) still cherish the notion that the economically disadvantaged among us have a reasonable chance of escaping the effects of poverty (Alesina, Di Tella, & MacCulloch, 2004). Along with "hard work and discipline" (Davidai & Gilovich, 2015, p. 61), education has long been regarded as one of the routes that people in the United States could take to improve their financial standing. And all the statistics showing that a college degree is a great investment in future income potential reveal a willingness on the part of universities to play their part in fulfilling that promise of upward mobility.

However, some commentators at the end of time (for example, Ikenberry, 2006) have begun to wonder if the social compact between higher education and the American people is still in place. Stanley Ikenberry (2006) notes that 75 percent of the children from families in the top quartile of income in the United States go to college, but only 10 percent of the children from families in the bottom quartile do so. Assuming for a moment that a college degree is still a good financial investment in future income for most people, these statistics show that, even with all the governmental support enjoyed by the universities over the past several decades, it may not be the case that higher education is quite the equalizer or leveler in American society that some believe it to be. In fact, that may never have been the case. But even if higher education's power to confer upward mobility might be largely illusory in the twenty-first century and beyond, what replacement for it can be imagined?

Time for Me to Say Goodbye

On the first note to chapter 1, I offered an anecdote about Isidore Rabi of Columbia University, who allegedly asserted to Dwight Eisenhower, then president of the university, that its faculty in fact *was* Columbia University. As I hope I have shown, at the end of time, a similar statement asserting the equivalence of Columbia—or any other university, elite or otherwise—with its faculty could hardly be less true.

What happened? Although the United States has probably always had something like two systems of higher education, broadly defined, their trajectories nevertheless diverged considerably across the second half of the twentieth century. In the elite universities, with their brand recognition and their supported research and scholarship, the professoriate has been so far able to endure. But for the other 90 percent of the colleges and universities in the United States, the continued existence of the professoriate was challenged as a result of a confluence and clash of a set of titanic sociological, financial, technological, and demographic trends that I called vectors. Each vector represented a force or trend having directionality and momentum that has pushed higher education onto its particular pathway.

The technological vector represents the now-ubiquitous phenomenon of the cheap and widely available personal computer, but there is more to it than that. All those interconnected computers and the residing content knowledge that is easily available on the web afforded by such interconnectivity helped commodify the teaching that professors did in the industrial-scale schools. When that occurred, the professoriate's deep knowledge became packageable and thus capable of existing independently of the individual professor's mind and work. And under those circumstances, professors likewise became fungible.

I presented this sequence of events as something that simply befell the professoriate. But to the extent that professors were quick to accept all the technological changes that occurred as laborsaving with regard to teaching, thus enabling them to emulate the faculty members of the elite universities with their focus on research and scholarship, the professoriate of the industrial-scale schools was somewhat complicit in its own demise. And complicit or not, that professoriate and the universities they inhabited seemed very slow to realize the forces gathering against them. In fact, they persisted in emulating the practices of the elite institutions long after the disadvantages of doing so were apparent.

The theme of discontinuity with the past that I used to describe the technological era will be even more apparent in the future: universities, especially those of the industrial-scale system, will not look like the universities of today. As I showed, it is possible to concoct a number of plausible scenarios in which the forces that are in play today are permitted to operate at different strengths and interact in different ways. In each of the several scenarios that are thus created, the outcome for universities may vary somewhat. The outcome for the professoriate, though, is almost always disastrous.

Certainly by the time the golden age ended, and the technological era began, there were critics of the modern professoriate and the operation of the higher education industry more generally (for example, Anderson, 1996). There may well be some professors who merit the criticism, and certainly higher education will continue to face some heretofore unimaginable challenges that will require change. But there is a point that I want to assert in the face of that criticism, amid all the heat that this book and the numerous others written about higher education will generate: the vast majority of the professors that I encountered at the industrial-scale university where I worked were skillful, hardworking, and concerned primarily with student outcomes. And whether they were the university or just its employees, they represented a uniquely positive force all their own.

CODA

I have concluded the telling of my story from an academic standpoint, using the scholarly language of academia. But as I finished I felt the need to cap the story in a more concrete and earthy way. And so, this brief coda—in music, a term that describes a concluding section that, while not essential to the entire work, nevertheless presents a conclusion that has not been previously heard.

Throughout the book I have used a writing technique that I borrowed from the diarist Isaac Babel (1990) who, as what we might call an embedded journalist today, rode with the feared and ferocious Cossacks of the *Konarmiia* (Communist Cavalry Army) during its advance on Warsaw in the Russo-Polish War of 1920–21. In his diary, Babel attempted to incorporate all the sensory aspects of his experiences. The objective was to enable the reader to see the events depicted from the details in the writing, but the descriptions were not limited to visual details. Indeed, aspects of sounds, tastes, and even smells were included to create a lapel-grabbing immediacy in the writing that would not be present if the description were restricted to the information available in only one sensory channel. Babel (2003) also used his diary technique to create a series of short stories, and I borrowed it to create a verbal documentary of my work and times and the larger work of the professoriate *in toto*. If I have succeeded, the reader will see what I and the members of the professoriate did at the end of time, and they will see it with a heightened immediacy animated by the unearthing of the several hundred pounds of contemporaneous documentation that I have safeguarded for decades.

To play the final few notes of the coda, I now apply this technique to an already rather visceral scene from Thomas Mann's epic bildungsroman, *The Magic Mountain* (Mann, 1969). Mann's work tells the story of Hans Castorp, a recently graduated engineer, who pays a visit to a cousin in a tuberculosis sanatorium in the early years of the twentieth century. Hans is diagnosed with tuberculosis himself and remains at the mountain-top retreat for seven years. At the book's conclusion Hans, now cured, leaves the sanatorium and joins the army to fight in the tumultuous campaigns of 1914. In the novel's final pages, he is seen on the battlefield: "Like all the others, he is wet through and glowing. He is running, his feet heavy with mould, the bayonet swinging in his hand. Look! He treads on the hand of a fallen comrade; with his hobnailed boot he treads the hand deep into the slimy, branch-strewn ground" (Mann, 1969, p. 715).

With heartfelt gratitude to Mann for having created this brooding scene, I inserted myself and tens of thousands of other professors into it to show the presumed fate of my cohort in the professoriate: The camera first sees me loping as quickly as I can through the squishy mud, laden with my pack, weapon, and ammunition. I run through the various screamings, rumbles, and mysterious hootings produced by the flight and detonation of the almost infinite volume and variety of shells hurled down on us. As the camera pivots into position at my back, we see, ahead of me, the artificial lightning on the horizon created by the muzzle flashes of the heavy weapons. Closer, there is the stench of carbide and blood in the nostrils. And then, seemingly aware of an audience, I suddenly turn, the scene now at my back. One gesture: a jaunty salute to those who remain in this present, as if to say good luck, and thank you. And with that I return to the action. My unit is moving forward.

APPENDIX: THE MATERIALS
AND THE METHOD

Those who read the appendix must have some special agenda for doing so. My hypothesis is that the readers who pursue it are interested not only in the narrative I created about my time in the ranks of the professoriate, but also in how I came to know all those details of my career with such apparent precision. Or perhaps they wish to know how confident they can be in the results of the various analyses that I have embedded throughout the book. In other words, those readers want to know about the raw materials and the method that underlies the narrative.

Accordingly, I discuss those details here, elaborating on them to a greater extent than would be possible or prudent in the main body of the book. I describe the materials and records, paper and electronic, that I collected, saved, created, owned, and used during my time in the professoriate. My second objective in the appendix is to illustrate the analyses and the various methods to which these materials were subjected to create the findings that are on view throughout *A Professor at the End of Time*.

The corpus of materials consists of objects that are largely textual and physical in nature, some handwritten, some produced on a typewriter, and others created using a personal computer's keyboard. Other objects in the corpus exist only in electronic format (although they are still textual and could be printed); still other materials are not textual, but rather artifactual. I have used all the materials of the corpus to describe and analyze my work in the professoriate, although my process seems much more paleontological than the term "analyze" implies. In the case of some of the paper materials, I used documents that I had not closely examined or even glanced at since I filed them ten, twenty, or even thirty years ago. A given document considered alone might tell a bit of the whole story. But, as a fragment of bone might yield a clue as to the size and shape of the beast from whence it came eons ago, a document or file from one of my cabinets cannot tell the whole story by itself. Each artifact must be fitted together with other related materials for a coherent picture to emerge. For the paleontologist, the related bones to be assembled are usually found in the same stratum and more or less adjacent to each other. But in my case, the other materials needed to create the complete mosaic of my work may be stored distantly, in a sense, because so much of the documentation is organized thematically, rather than simply chronologically.

My principal method consisted of organizing the individual pages of the corpus by content and then counting those pages, or estimating their number, to provide numerical answers to various questions about my work and that of the professoriate more generally, as it moved from the golden age, through the pretechnological transition period, and finally to the technological era in which it is currently entrenched. I hope to show how I assembled those raw materials—that is, juxtaposed disparate kinds of files to create a story that is more than the sum of its parts, and by doing so, to demonstrate just how that work was carried out during those epochs. I have concluded the appendix with an example of my method in action that I hope provides an answer to a question that vexes many in the professoriate: Why is it that the work of the college professor seems to be so poorly understood by those outside academia? The answer may have to do with how much of a professor's daily work remains interior, fixed only in the professor's mind, and therefore invisible to others.

DELINEATING THE CORPUS

As I began to sketch this outline of the materials in the corpus, I became aware that I could not reduce its contents to a single word without at least some loss of meaning. Earlier, I used the word "records" as a summary expression for the objects in the corpus, and while that term is not quite as accurate or as rich as I would like, there is an essential correctness about it: throughout my career, I was interested in making a record of, or keeping track of, my activities, and the easiest way to do that seemed to be create a file, in the most basic sense of that term. The files were usually housed in a labeled manila folder, and they consisted of paper. I did not require luxurious paper. I wrote on and retained just about any sort: the pads with blue lines on yellow paper that are known as legal pads, Post-it notes, pages torn from spiral-bound notebooks, and loose-leaf pages, to name just a few varieties. In addition to pages containing longhand writing or printing, I created and retained pages of copy paper or typing paper consisting of genuine typescript produced with my electric typewriter that dated from the 1960s (I bought it secondhand circa 1977). When I prepared to write *A Professor at the End of Time*, preparation that involved a substantial amount of unearthing and organizing, I fully expected to find my typewriter, forlorn and secreted in a closet either in my lab at school or at home. I briefly entertained the notion of composing at least a few pages for this book at the typewriter keyboard. But I never did find it. And so this manuscript—like all manuscripts today, I assume, and like many of the printed pages in the corpus—was written to the accompaniment of the faster, but much less satisfying, clicking of the computer keyboard's keys rather than to the solid thwack of a key's metal head on the typewriter's rubber platen.

These paper records—a term that I am using to describe coherent textual objects of a certain length—have all been inscribed or written. But I retained and produced other paper objects, too, in which either the textual emphasis or the length was reduced. For example, my scientific research produced voluminous observations of certain forms of human cognition that were transformed into numerical indices and stored on paper, and which I then referred to as data.

None of these paper materials were ever published in any conventional sense; their widest distribution may have consisted of promulgation to a highly selective local audience. But there are published paper materials in the corpus, mostly books and scientific journals to which I subscribed.

If the term "records" is not an exactly or completely accurate way to describe these materials, what term might be better suited? Perhaps I should turn to one of the functional uses of the corpus, or at least, the use to which I put big chunks of it, which was to create a body of documents—a term that is extraordinarily laden with meaning: "The word 'document' descends from the Latin root *docer*, to teach or show, which suggests that the document exists in order to document. Sidestepping this circularity of terms, one might say instead that documents help define and are mutually defined by the know-show function, since documenting is an epistemic practice: the kind of knowing that is all wrapped up with showing, and showing wrapped with knowing" (Gitelman, 2014, p. 1).

The word "document" had a technical meaning at my former institution as well: just as Lisa Gitelman used the term as a predicate ("to document") in the quotation above, faculty members at my institution were required to document many of their numerous activities. That is, the existence of a document served as a proof that a certain form of activity had occurred, typically an activity whose performance might be required for a faculty member seeking retention, tenure, or promotion. In this sense, to document an activity meant to retain a piece of paper whose existence would be impossible, or nearly so, if the required performance had not occurred.

THE PAPER FILES

There are more than 630 paper files in the corpus, occupying four file cabinets and consisting of an estimated 65,000 pages. That does not include another 15,000 pages that I discarded immediately prior to my retirement, which suggests that the total contents of the paper files may have reached some 80,000 pages at the close of my career.

Unpacking them—literally or figuratively, in the sense of decoding them—reconstitutes and reinvigorates each record for me. For example, in reading a memo from Paul Panek, chairperson of the Psychology Department at Eastern Illinois University in 1987, I was impressed with the ease with which I recalled some of his more pronounced characteristics, such as his often justifiable wariness about every budgetary matter, his insecurity about his leadership (which turned every question asked, no matter how legitimate, into an attack to be repelled), and his gruff persona that hid the genuine warmth he felt for his colleagues and students. Even though the issues Paul was writing about in the memo are long since resolved, I am now retired, and Paul has been dead for years, the memo retains all its pungent vitality for me, although that characteristic will not generally be apparent in the rugged accounting I do here.

The size or volume of any particular file is expressed as a page count, perhaps giving the impression of a greater level of precision than I really have. For the vast majority of the files, the page count I present in this book is an estimate. But because in the book I made several inferences about the volume, or size and scope, of the work based on the extent of the paper products or documentation that the work generated, I need to describe the estimation methods I used and establish the accuracy of those page counts. The technique that I relied on most frequently consisted of counting a portion of the pages in a given file and then using the height of the resulting counted stack to estimate the remaining number of pages. For example, I might count what looked to me like a fifth of all the pages in a given file and then multiply that number by five to get an estimated total. In some cases, I counted the portion of pages that seemed to weigh a certain proportion of the whole, such as half of the total. Sometimes I compared counted stacks side by side with stacks whose number I was estimating. At irregular intervals, I checked on the accuracy of these estimation techniques by first using them to arrive at an estimate of a file's volume and then counting the number of pages in the file. In those relatively few cases where I calibrated the count that way, even those based on my very roughest hefting and visual inspection estimates, I was surprised with my own accuracy when I compared the estimates with actual counts. As a result, I believe the majority of the estimates are off by no more than 10 percent.

The Teaching Files

Table A.1 shows the total number of files and their estimated page counts for the materials I used in my teaching duties. Fully an estimated 11,180 pages (almost 84 percent of the total number of pages in the paper files devoted to teaching, and 134 of the 185 paper teaching files) consist of what I would call courseware that I created over the decades that I taught. Courseware can in turn be divided into two subcategories: course notes and course materials. Discussing the contents of the course notes files requires some understanding of how face-to-face college courses are scheduled. Given a fifteen-week class schedule with three meetings per week, I expected to prepare up to forty-five activities for each course I taught, be they lectures (I used that term, though I seldom actually lectured in the classic sense), other forms of presentation, class exercises, quizzes, or tests. The course notes were a concrete manifestation of that preparation. Once the content of the class was broken down into subunits and smaller topics within each of those subunits, then each topic could be allocated an appropriate portion of time: a part of a day, a whole day, multiple days, or whatever portion seemed right. The planned discussion or coverage, to use the quasi-technical term, of the topic itself could be expressed in an outline form, consisting of both content statements (factual elements that were to be spoken and elaborated on in class) and (in my case) elements that were something like stage directions (statements about sequencing or timing, or reminders to the students). The process of outlining was repeated for each topic, and when aggregated across the entire semester, these outlines became the basis for the course notes. Thus the course notes became the spine of the course, its main structural element. As my discussion suggests, the notes had a modular organization, permitting the rearrangement of topics within a course, or the deletion of some topics for the sake of adding others. Given that, a given set of course notes might undergo a kind of organic growth across the time period in which they were used. But any given set of notes had a finite life expectancy, too (contrary to the popular but largely incorrect image of a professor seen lecturing from a set of sere notes yellowed to the point of crumbling). So this image of organic or incremental change in the notes must be contrasted with the fact that sometimes they were just as likely to be completely redone

TABLE A.1. Teaching Files

File category	Number of files	Page count
Old notes	19	2,784
Notes or binders	11	1,587
Course materials	104	6,809
Supervision of graduate students	10	450
Supervision of undergraduate students	18	596
Class schedules	3	353
Course proposals	4	178
Honors Program		
Scheduling	10	249
Programming	5	134
Data	1	200
Total teaching files	185	13,340

from scratch as they were to be partially remade. In the corpus, I have evidence of both practices: I retained nineteen files labeled "old notes" for courses that I taught over the years, consisting of more or less complete sets of notes that were later supplanted by a totally new set. I also have eleven sets of "current" notes— the set of notes for a given course that I used the last time I taught the course in question, which may have been in the last year of my career or earlier.

By volume, the largest subcomponent of the teaching files consists of a category I call course materials, accounting for 104 files that total some 6,809 estimated or counted pages. The course materials consisted of all those documents that the course notes generated for each class: the tests or quizzes, the make-up tests for students who missed the original administration (which inevitably occurred), the course schedule, the syllabus, the grades (stored in a paper grade book all through the 1980s), and sometimes the student evaluations and comments. In general, in each academic term I created one such file for all the courses that I taught in that period.

The Research Files

My research files consist of the documentation of all the writing I did that was devoted to scientific discovery. But these files also contain all my remaining documentation of the other, numerous, forms of scholarly writing in which I engaged over the course of my career. Consequently, as shown in table A.2, it seems sensible that even though a large plurality of the files (121 of 331 files, or 37 percent), and their corresponding page counts (10,103 of 24,925, or 41 percent) have to do with creating manuscripts for publication in scientific journals, those files do not nevertheless make up a majority of my work.

In my role as a cognitive scientist, I was the leading or contributing author on thirty-seven research projects. The goal of each of these research projects, realized or otherwise, was its publication in a scientific journal. Some of those projects consisted of a single study or experiment, while other projects were made up of several experiments, which were then stitched together in published paper to make a coherent story. Thus, the records of the thirty-seven research projects can be further broken down into records for a total of fifty-six experiments with human or animal participants. Each experiment or study consisted of several elements or pieces, which may have been housed in its own individual file. Those elements could consist of the original printed materials that were used, sheets on which the participants' responses were coded for analysis, or printouts of the statistical analysis of the data. Probably the most important element of each project was the file containing the research log, a daybook or journal I used to make dated notes about the progress of the study, sketch out the write-up, or make suggestions to myself about the next study. It is the materials supporting

TABLE A.2. Research Files

File category	Number of files	Page count
Programmatic research		
Published: 13 projects, 28 experiments	76	6,428
Unpublished: 6 projects, 10 experiments	29	2,071
Nonprogrammatic research		
Published: 14 projects, 14 experiments	13	1,334
Unpublished: 4 projects, 4 experiments	3	270
Grants		
Internal: 3 projects	3	202
External: 10 projects	18	2,606
Cognitive psychology textbook	56	4,500
Conference presentations	26	917
Colloquia and invited presentations	4	34
Textbook reviews	57	1,425
Prospective journal article reviews	24	1,221
Prospective conference presentation reviews	2	13
Laboratory groups	5	180
Research in graduate school	3	229
Data files	12	3,495
Total research files	331	24,925

the creation and execution of these fifty-six experiments that occupy the 121 individual files and some 10,103 pages in the corpus mentioned above. Simply enumerating these pieces does not begin to reveal the effort—at times exhilarating or discouraging, but always exhausting—that scientific research required at the industrial-scale school where I worked.

Although the main objective of my empirical research was publication in scientific journals, my scholarship assumed many other forms, too. For example, I wrote a textbook in my disciplinary area that was published in five editions throughout the 1980s and 1990s. In addition, I wrote grant applications to provide funding for my research, and I wrote reviews of scholarly writing, which themselves required scholarship on my part. Many of the books that I reviewed, especially in the 1980s, were textbooks for courses that I taught. But I also reviewed other scholarly books, as well as reviewing manuscripts that were being considered for publication in scientific journals. In every case, I provided what was referred to as an expert review. I cannot verify that I created a file for every textbook or prospective journal article that I reviewed, but I still have fifty-seven paper files dealing with the former, and twenty-four paper files for the latter. I had largely given up the textbook review process by the end of the 1980s, so the number of paper files is likely to be a fairly accurate estimate of the number of those reviews. On the other hand, I did not seriously begin to review prospective journal articles for publication until the 1990s, and I kept reviewing them until the end of my career, although I ceased to keep a paper record of the review process in the 2000s. Consequently, the number of paper files that I have in this part of the corpus underestimates the amount of this type of work that I did.

The Service Files

As shown in table A.3, the paper files for service are almost all about committee work—the work of some board, panel, committee, council, or body with one of the other numerous monikers that academicians use to designate such groups. Most of the information in these paper files consists of memos, relatively brief messages targeted to the members of the group. It is this type of document that would be readily supplanted by an e-mail message by the 1990s. These memos could cover a wide range of topics, with the agenda for the group's next meeting or a request for individuals' schedules being among the most common topics. My files also contain notes that I created during meetings, at first in longhand cursive, but after 2010 using a laptop that I brought to almost every meeting of every group. These files also contain minutes of meetings for those groups, including the Faculty Senate and almost all the university-level groups, whose operations, recommendations, and decisions needed to be documented in a formal way. The files also contain reports. Groups that operated with greater formality were more likely to generate lengthy reports that had to be digested.

As with the teaching and research files, I used the service files in a particular way in writing *A Professor at the End of Time*, a way perhaps closer to Gitelman's (2014) original meaning—namely, to show the range of activities in which professors were involved in this little-known aspect of the professoriate's work. I hope that the range and depth of that involvement will enable readers to grasp the magnitude of the services that professors provided to others.

The General Files

What I have been calling the three components of the braid of the professoriate's work—teaching, research, and service—provided a convenient rubric for organizing the paper files. I discovered, however, that I also possessed a number of files that did not fit conveniently under any of these headings, so I created a separate category for them, as shown in table A.4. Included are thirty-four files containing informational memos written and circulated by the department chairperson, the dean, or any one of a number of vice presidents. Other announcements or points of information, including minutes of department meetings that were originally circulated as paper documents, are also included in these files. Such memos and other ephemera document the

TABLE A.3. Service Files

Level and category of service	Number of files	Page count
University service		
Institutional Review Board	15	2,297
Council on University Planning and Budget	3	110
Honors Council	3	325
Council on Assessment of Student Learning	2	650
Excellence Task Force	1	500
Judicial Board	1	35
Retention Task Force	2	320
Faculty Senate	12	2,500
University Personnel Committee	30	1,824
Sanction and Termination Hearing Committee	1	20
Enrollment Management Advisory Committee	3	275
Library Advisory Board	1	50
McNair Grant reader	1	7
Veteran Faculty Circles	4	59
Distinguished Faculty Selection Committee	1	1
College service		
Ringenberg Selection Committee	1	9
Investigative Committee	1	15
Cognitive Science Initiative	2	106
Building Space Committee	2	34
Department service		
Departmental Personnel Committee	28	2,031
Budget Committee	1	30
Retirement Policy Committee	1	15
Curriculum Committee	16	578
Graduate Committee	5	344
Library Liaison	1	500
Enrollment Management Committee	2	16
Facilities Use and Planning Committee	2	9
External Relations Committee	1	1
Assessment Committee	6	535
Newsletter editor	2	55
Awards Committee	2	250
Spencer-McGown-Wilson Award Committee	3	110
Ad Hoc Service	12	198
Assessment coordinator	5	520
Search committee service		
Departmental level	19	887
University level	8	676
Total service files	200	15,899

TABLE A.4. General Files

File category	Number of files	Page count
Memoranda	34	5,725
Retention, tenure, promotion		
Retention, tenure, and promotion	14	3,106
Professional advancement increase	4	1,250
Related files	7	416
Recognition and awards		
Recognition files	11	312
Paper certificates	7	7
Framed certificates	6	6
Assistant chairperson files	4	145
WebCT courses	2	40
Nonresearch talks	5	75
Faculty member files	3	70
Applying for jobs at other universities	2	44
Retirement planning	8	276
Professor at the End of Time	4	75
Miscellaneous files	21	1,017
Total general files	132	12,564

business and direction of the unit and provide a sense of what was important to the unit at various points in time. For example, in the early 1990s there was a concern at my institution about teaching students to become computer literate. We did not realize then this so-called problem would soon resolve itself without any attention from us.

In addition to the business of the unit, there is the business of running one's academic career. For example, lurking here, waiting to be decoded, there are telling signs of some of the possible differences between being a member of the professoriate and being a member of other professions with similarly high educational levels, such as being a physician or lawyer. Specifically, these signs have to do with the number and volume of the files devoted to simply managing one's career. Professors undergo a lengthy probationary process prior to earning the permanent status of tenure (assuming that the job is one that leads to tenure—most academic jobs do not). During the probationary period, the professor's status vis-à-vis the institution is that of an independent contractor whose continued employment is subject to approval on the basis of documented evidence of performance. Even after tenure is granted, there remains an approval process to advance to the rank of full professor. And even after that promotion, there may be incentives requiring documentation. For example, my institution offered opportunities for substantial, periodic, merit-based pay increases based on documented performance. Altogether these files, containing nearly 5,000 pages devoted to the routine maintenance of simply managing my career, make up almost 7 percent of all the pages in the entire corpus.

The final step of the professor's career, paradoxically, is ending it. Accordingly, the corpus contains eight paper files having to do with retirement planning, including printed and handwritten notes that I made during meetings with retirement counselors. Although the overwhelming majority of the files that I used in writing *A Professor at the End of Time* are stored only in an electronic format, there are nevertheless some paper files related to the book, which offer evidence supporting Abigail Sellen and Richard Harper's (2003) argument that the paperless office may be a chimera.

Paper Files Deleted from the Corpus

There were two principal kinds of paper files that I did not retain after I left my job: data files, which were records made by participants in scientific studies in my lab, and photocopies of research articles from scientific journals.

The discarded data consisted of thirty-one files containing responses made by human participants that were later coded by lab assistants and analyzed statistically. There were some other materials in these files, such as the consent forms that the participants were required to sign and other information about the lab protocol, including copies of the paper materials that formed the basis of the experiment. Altogether this was a huge volume of material whose contents I counted or estimated to be 10,307 pages. Although most of these data were quite old—far older than the seven years required by the Institutional Review Board's regulations for retention—these files still had some uses in their day going beyond that of the study for which they had originally been collected. For example, data sets that had been published could be reexamined later in light of a new hypothesis. Sometimes the reexamination might reveal a previously unseen relationship that could be the subject of a future study, although I do not have a numerical estimate of the number of such studies that the discarded data might have prompted.

With regard to the second category of discarded paper files, on February 7, 2013, I disposed of some 278 photocopied scientific journal articles that had occupied an entire drawer of a file cabinet in my office. Using the estimating techniques I developed for other parts of the corpus, based on a drawer depth of twenty-eight inches, and allowing for the space taken up by paper clips, binder clips, other fasteners, I estimated that these photocopies occupied about 4,000–5,000 pages of the corpus.

Both their location in the office and their sheer number tell a story. These were photocopies of articles that I used exclusively in writing scientific papers. I did most, if not all, of my scientific writing in my office, where the proximity of the photocopied articles helped me cite the relevant literature on which to build the case for my own experiment or to provide support for a claim that I wished to make about my own findings. The need for immediate availability might explain the location of these photocopied articles in my office, as opposed to the location of the much less frequently used old data sets, which were stored in the lab. But what about the number? I did not refer to anywhere near 278 previously published articles in any of my own published experiments. The age of the photocopies provides a clue to the answer: most of these articles had been published at least twenty years before 2013, when I discarded them. Many of the copies were thirty years old, and there were a few that were close to forty years old. Like my students, who were digital natives, I eventually learned how to read and use a research article that I summoned to my computer screen, without having to rely on a printed copy. So those 278 old photocopied articles, to which I no longer referred and which were simply taking up space, should be understood for what they were: a remnant of an era that had already passed by the time I retired.

THE ELECTRONIC FILES AND THEIR MEDIA

Their Relationship with Paper

Until this point, the description of the corpus has focused on paper. The sheer length of that description invites the inference that the paper files constituted the overwhelming majority of the corpus. But the reality is that I created electronic files almost from the beginning of my academic career (certainly by 1984), and much of the corpus exists in the form of documents encoded on a variety of storage media, most of which I can no longer access. What were the characteristics of these media that may have had an influence on what and how much could be stored electronically? In this section, I discuss, in a general way, the similarities and differences between the electronic files and the paper files.

But prior to that discussion, it seems appropriate to discuss the origins of the electronic files and some of the implications of those origins. Many of the documents or other objects in the paper files originated and existed only on paper, whether they were handwritten notes, typed (not keystroked) pages, mimeographed pages, or photocopies. And because paper degrades, the paper-only objects were mortal. For example, I am relatively certain that I have the only surviving copy of a number of objects such as the mimeographed memorandum from the departmental chairperson I mentioned above in the appendix. Neither the provenance nor the survivability of the documents or other objects stored as electronic files is necessarily the same as that of the paper objects. Some of the electronic files did indeed begin their lives as keystroked copies of an object that had originated on paper (which, circa 1985, may have been the common method of creating an electronic copy of something that had no electronic precursor). These were objects that might be said to have paper DNA. In the electronic files, perhaps the most prototypical example would be any exam given in an academic class.

There are other objects that are something like the cousins of these objects. These other objects may have originated electronically, but they were nevertheless readily capable of being printed, and once that was done, a paper copy was retained. In my case, a good example of this sort of file was the electronic grade book or grade sheet for each class. Finally, there were still other objects that were created electronically and never printed, living their entire lives in the crepuscular world of the purely electronic document. For example, I created and stored electronic data files using various editions of the Statistical Package for the Social Sciences (SPSS). At least for the first two cases, the contents of the electronic files are simply redundant mimics of the paper files—things that are textual and generally capable of being printed on standard copy paper.

The Floppy Disks

I made the acquaintance of floppy disks, the first form of portable electronic storage that I used, in 1984. At that time, the floppy disk was actually well-named: the 5.25-inch floppy disk was encased in a simple vinyl sheath and required the protection of a paper envelope. Even with all the precautions that one might take, they were never a particularly reliable form of storage. Still, they were as common as mosquitos in July. When I began to write A Professor at the End of Time, I was surprised to find that I still had thirty-four of them resting comfortably in the back of a file cabinet in my lab. Based on their labels, it looks like these thirty-four floppies held (or are still holding?) the data from an experiment that I carried out in the 1980s. Each of these disks apparently had a capacity of 360 kilobytes (KB), for the commonly used forty-track model. A typical e-mail message requires about 25 KB, thus providing an idea of the very limited storage capacity of this medium.

By the end of the 1980s, the relatively sturdy 3.5-inch floppy disk had supplanted its rather delicate ancestor for most applications, and I, along with everyone else, had shifted to its use as a means of portable storage. And like many, many, others, I was to use them for most of the 1990s. With their capacity of 1.44 megabytes (MB), or some four times the capacity of a large floppy, and their hard plastic case, they quickly caught on. In 1996 there were an estimated five billion or so floppy disks in use (Reinhardt, 1996). I continued to use them almost exclusively as a means of portable electronic storage until around 1998, which was close to the end of their dominant period, although they continued to have a life after that in some places.

And even when they were no longer regularly used, the floppy disk did not disappear. Suffice it to say that on the day I left my office at work for the last time, I still had on my desk some fifty-three floppy disks in a plastic box designed to hold them. I found still more of them in the paper files, where I had sometimes cached away several floppies that were electronic duplicates of the paper files, or so I assume. What was I doing with all of those floppies on my desk? The short answer is that I was not using them for anything, nor had I for at least the previous fourteen years. But their placement on my desk, like the old photocopies I threw away, reveals something important and telling about the inertial quality of the artifacts in the professorial office, for I was not alone in this regard: the office, having almost an organic existence of its own, simply absorbed everything that came into it, never relinquishing the useless.

The Zip Disks

Technological change marched on, and my quest for a cheap and reliable electronic storage medium continued unabated. The Iomega zip disk, available in three sizes (100 MB, 250 MB, and later a whopping 750 MB), was introduced in 1994, and when I discovered that the office computer issued to me by my department in 1998 had a built-in drive for their use, I jumped on the bandwagon. Zip disks became a popular portable storage medium for a brief period, from the late 1990s to the early 2000s (Reinhardt, 1996). Like the floppies they helped replace, but not obliterate, I still have six in my possession. The earliest one I used, beginning in 1998, had a 100 MB capacity (equal to seventy-some floppy disks); the last one I used, in 2005, had a capacity of 250 MB. Accessing the information stored on them, like that on the floppies they replaced, is now something of a challenge. Even the oldest still-functional computer that I own (a model built circa 2005) has no built-in drive for a zip disk.

The Flash Drives

With this discussion of the flash drive, we have finally arrived at one of the most commonly used portable electronic media available at the end of time. In comparison with the hard drive on a computer, the floppy disks of either size, or the zip disks, flash drives represent a radically different technology for storage. Unlike the previously mentioned forms, all of which featured some type of a disk head that read or wrote by rearranging electrons on a spinning disk that constituted the memory medium, the flash drive has no moving parts, making it a technology that I cannot pretend to understand. But the absence of moving parts makes the flash drive more reliable than any of the previously discussed technologies.

Flash drives became available in the United States around the beginning of the millennium, although I did not start using one until 2005. I used that initial drive until 2008, when I realized that, as long as I replaced it every year, I could pack away electronic files with gluttonous abandon and not worry about the reliability of the device. During the period 2005-13, I used six of these devices for electronic file storage. Table A.5 is a snapshot of what was stored on the last of them, organized in terms of the same rubric that I used for the paper files in the corpus.

A larger portion the device's capacity was devoted to the teaching files than to any other category, which seems sensible enough since teaching was the primary activity that I was paid to do. The organization and structure of the electronic files devoted to teaching duplicates the contents of the paper files, but the contents on the flash drive are more current. Whereas the paper files show courseware for many or all of the courses that I taught during my career, including those that I had not taught in years, the flash drive includes the courseware for only those courses that I was taught in the last semester of my career. A similar finding emerges for the research and service files: in both cases, the files in the folders are more likely to represent things in the here and now—such as experiments that were under way and committees on which I was serving—than they were to be a repository of past work. It is also interesting to note that the portion of the flash drive's capacity that was devoted to service work was almost three times greater than the proportion devoted to research and scholarship, despite the fact that research was the second-most important priority for the professors at my institution. This might be the first bit of evidence to emerge from the corpus suggesting that I was overcommitted to service in my institution, a theme that I explored in chapter 5.

Finally, there are a few other points to observe in comparing the contents of the paper portion of the corpus with those of the electronic portion. First, across my career, paper became more expensive to manufacture and to use. And during that period paper never learned how to reduce its volume. Retaining more pieces of paper always resulted in a directly proportional linear increase in the size of the container vessel needed to store them. However, the various electronic media that I used for storage performed a neat trick, becoming both cheaper and smaller as time went on. Additionally, miraculously, the electronic media became more capacious even as they became less expensive and smaller.

Table A.6 shows this trend in tabular form. For every medium after the first one, I divided the capacity of the later storage medium by the capacity of the immediately preceding one to arrive at a storage increase factor, expressed as the number of times larger the later medium was in comparison to the smaller

TABLE A.5. Contents of Flash Drive PNY 2013

Categories of folders	Number of folders	Number of files	Size (MB)
Teaching	6	435	152.78
Research	5	207	14.88
Service	9	533	42.48
General	10	306	9.18
Total	30	1,481	219.32*

* This total represents less than 1.4 percent of the capacity of the flash drive.

one. The overall increase in the capacity of the various electronic media that I used during my career can be computed by multiplying the factor increases shown for each transition that I made to a new medium. When that multiplication is carried out, the final figure, an astonishing factor of 44,800, means that over the approximately thirty years (or $2^{4.9}$ years) that I used electronic media for storage, their capacity increased by a factor of $2^{15.4}$. In other words, as a function of years of service, electronic storage capacity increased by a factor of more than 1,000 per year, although it is true that most of the increase occurred near the end of my career. All these points about the ease, cheapness, and tremendous capacity of electronic storage suggest that many faculty members were encouraged to keep copies of every document or record them electronically, even if they had not been retaining the hundreds of pounds of paper that I had been.

As noted above, from 2005 until I retired in 2013 I used six different flash drives, which are listed in table A.7. A couple of findings are apparent from the table. First, the number of folders created and stored stayed remarkably constant across this final eight-year period of my career. I did not try to hold the number of folders constant on each flash drive, which suggests that the relative consistency might come from the fact that I tended to have the same number of courses, research projects, students, committee assignments, and so on each year. Second, the capacity of the flash drive was always too big. As table A.7 shows, the number of files and their total size crept up little by little during this interval. But every time that happened, the capacity of the flash drive played leapfrog with the size of the files, so I was never using more than a small fraction of the drive's space.

When I first conceived of this book, I intended to compare the size of the electronic files directly with that of their paper cousins, to see whether one sort of volume grew faster than the other. But it turns out that directly comparing these two media is both easy and difficult.

Many of the documents that I created on the computer's screen during the 2005-2013 period, especially materials that were to be used in class such as tests or syllabi, eventually found their way into a paper format and then into the paper

TABLE A.6. Increasing Capacity of Electronic Storage Media

Electronic medium	Beginning year	Capacity	Factor increase
5.25-inch floppy	1984	360 KB	Not applicable
3.25-inch floppy	1988	1.44 MB	4.0
Early zip disk	1998	100 MB	70.0
Later zip disk	2004	250 MB	2.5
Early flash drive	2005	250 MB	1.0
Later flash drive	2012	16 GB	64.0

Note: KB is kilobyte, MB is megabyte, and GB is gigabyte.

TABLE A.7. Contents of Flash Drives

Flash drive (year in use, capacity)	Folders	Files	Size (MB) (% capacity)
Lexar (2005, 256 MB)	28	961	38.24 (15)
Toshiba (2009, 2 GB)	30	1,213	151.08 (7.5)
Hewlett-Packard (2010, 2 GB)	30	1,276	155.18 (7.8)
Toshiba (2011, 8 GB)	28	1,225	187.61 (2.3)
Staples Relay (2012, 8 GB)	30	1,296	202.96 (10.1)
PNY (2013, 16 GB)	30	1,481	219.32 (1.4)

Note: MB is megabyte, and GB is gigabyte.

files that I kept for each class. So it is easy for me to estimate that 100 percent of the pages in the paper files for teaching materials were also saved in an electronic format. That means that as the paper files grew apace with each year, the electronic files kept up the same rate of growth all through the technological era. Earlier, when certain forms of documentation came to me only in a paper format (such as a memo circulated by the department chairperson or a report produced by a committee), I tended to keep the paper copies either in the general or service paper files. But as the technological era advanced, the memo became an e-mail message and the report an attachment to an e-mail message. I was much less likely to print out and store these items, nor was I likely to transfer them to my computer's hard drive or a portable storage device like a flash drive.

THE DAILY PLANNERS

The paper files are the biggest component of the corpus in terms of their bulk, but they were not the only component that was composed exclusively of paper. I used a spiral-bound daily planner every day at work beginning in April 1974,[1] when I was still in graduate school, until I retired (and beyond—I still use one). Although they can still be purchased in a bewildering array of formats, the external design of the planner that I favored changed little over four decades. It was a vinyl-covered book of 6.87 inches × 8.75 inches that contained about sixty pages. The planner showed the seven days of each week on a two-page spread whose total area was approximately 8.75 inches × 13.5 inches. For each weekday, it provided a column of about 2 inches × 8 inches that divided by lines into approximately thirty spaces. I seldom needed all thirty spaces to record the things for which I used the planner: reminders about telephone calls, action items on to-do lists, meeting locations, and other scheduled activities. During the day, I made other impromptu notations such as writing students' scores on the Graduate Record Examination before transcribing them to another location, writing addresses and telephone numbers, sometimes (but less frequently) making spontaneous notes about the content of a phone conversation or the evident mood of the person with whom I was conversing.

Beginning in 1977, I developed an inelegant, but still surprisingly powerful, notation system to record the completion of any activities on my to-do list for the day. During each workday I put a check mark by the names of those activities that I had succeeded in carrying out, as I finished them. At the end of the workday, I noted with a vertical bar the ones that I had not completed. Primitive though this notation may have been, I maintained this practice for the remainder of my academic career, and it has afforded me the opportunity to carry out several analyses about efficiency, daily productivity, and accountability that I report in greater detail later in this appendix.

A comparison of the daily planner from two very different points in my career, such as 1983 and 2013, reveals that I apparently had continued to use the planners in similar ways across these several decades. Given that there were electronic equivalents to the planners that were superior to the paper ones in some respects (at least the electronic calendars and appointment books were readily searchable), and given that I was willing to shift to electronic media for many purposes, the question becomes: Why did I keep using the paper planners? In part, the answer has to do with the small size of the planners. In an age before smart phones, the planner's size conferred on them a convenient portability that was not required for many of the electronic files such as the grade book, meeting notes, or most of the electronic files I created. And among paper's other affordances are rapid inscription and a kind of helpful tangibility that the electronic records simply do not possess.

THE BOOKS

I think many people hold a stereotyped view of college professors as individuals who enjoy buying, reading, and owning books. I know that I am guilty of conforming to this stereotype. So it was somewhat surprising to me, when I actually counted them, to find that I had in my possession only 224 books when I retired. To be clear, these 224 books are the ones that were related in one way or another to my academic life either as a professor or as a student; I had hundreds of other books at home that had nothing to do with either. Still, for a category that would appear to be a major component of the corpus, the number of professional books seems small.

Table A.8 shows these books broken down into the most meaningful categories that I was able to create. Unsurprisingly given my disciplinary background, the majority of the books are about topics in experimental psychology, cognitive psychology, cognitive science, or cognitive neuroscience. If we were to compare professional libraries among members of the professoriate, my unprovocative prediction would be that the majority of any professor's books would be about his or her disciplinary specialization. But there were also some surprises. In addition to disciplinary specializations, the work of the teaching professor apparently also plays a role in the type of books that are retained. For example, 88 of the 224 books (39 percent) are textbooks intended for courses that I frequently taught such as Statistics, Introductory Psychology, and Cognitive Psychology. The 32 books that I simply listed as "other" are quite a mélange: they include books on philosophy or history.

Twelve of the 224 books (5 percent) some having to do with psychology but others not, are titles that I used in my undergraduate days over forty-five years ago and that have been packed up and lugged to various locales several times since.

Sorting the books according to their provenance produces a somewhat different picture of my collection. Books came into my hands in several ways. Sometimes I bought a book that I needed. Almost all of the fifty-two books in my collection dealing with the cognitive science of thinking and reasoning and the ten books dealing with mathematics or mathematical psychology were purchased to help with my research.

It was a different story for the textbooks. These books were usually samples given to me without being requested by publishers' representatives who were eager for me to adopt their firm's book as required reading for one of my courses. Sometimes, but seldom, the representative asked me to return the sample copy if I did not select that book for the course. Usually I was free to do whatever I wanted with the unselected book that had come my way. Sometimes I simply

TABLE A.8. The Books

Subject	Number of volumes
Cognitive science of thinking and reasoning	52
Cognitive Psychology textbooks	49
Statistics textbooks	22
Books about writing	14
Mathematics or mathematical psychology	10
History of psychology	10
Research Methods textbooks	9
Introductory Psychology textbooks	8
Learning theory	6
Cognitive neuroscience	5
Sensation and perception	3
Psychology of language	2
Psychopathology	1
Developmental psychology	1
Other	32
Total	224

kept them, and that might be the reason why I still have forty-nine Cognitive Psychology textbooks on my shelves. On other occasions I gave such books away to students who I thought might be able to use them. I frequently disposed of Introductory Statistics books that way—but evidently not as frequently as I remember doing, based on my finding that I still have twenty-two of them keeping me company in my office as I write *A Professor at the End of Time*.

THE SCIENTIFIC JOURNALS

Books were not the only paper archival materials whose accretion consumed a professor's limited bookshelf space in the golden age. I have used the term "scientific journals," but almost every academic discipline can point to hosts of journals that have a similar format (collections of written work produced by perhaps a dozen or more authors, or teams of authors, bound together in a single issue ranging in length from 100 to 250 or more pages) and purpose (which might be framed in terms of the creation of a permanent repository documenting findings, theory, and current thought in the discipline). Table A.9 shows the eight scientific journals to which I had a personal subscription at the time of my retirement, as well as the year in which my subscription commenced. My subscription to most of these journals was provided as a no-cost, or low-cost benefit of membership in a professional organization that published the journal or owned the rights to it (for example, being a member of the Association for Psychological Science conferred on me a subscription to *Psychological Science*).

Although I stated that probably every academic discipline creates a body of literature in its journals, the importance of the journal literature varies quite a bit across disciplines. Generally, disciplines in science, technology, engineering, and mathematics (collectively referred to as STEM) are often thought of as being more journal-based than book-based in the sense that the journals contain findings or results, and the latest or most progressive results tend to appear in the journals rather than in a book. Given that, I read the journals to which I subscribed rather assiduously, especially earlier in my career. Moreover, in an effort to keep up, I read several other journals to which I was not a subscriber.

Although it was considerably less convenient to read journals in a central repository (like the library) than it was to simply have them in the office, it might be just as well that I did not have a subscription to these other journals, given the galloping consumption of my limited bookshelf space that ones I did subscribe to required. I calculated the amount of shelf space occupied by the journals listed in table A.9 to be about twenty-four feet of bookshelf space, enough to squeeze just about all of the books that I owned out of the office and onto some shelving in my lab. And as relentless as the tide, the journal issues continued to inundate me to the end of my career. By my informal calculation, the

TABLE A.9. The Journals

Title	Year personal subscription began
Cognitive Science	1988
Current Directions in Psychological Science	1993
Memory & Cognition	1993
Psychological Science	1993
Psychonomic Bulletin and Review	1994
Thinking & Reasoning	1998
Perspectives on Psychological Science	2006
Topics in Cognitive Science	2009

eight journals to which I subscribed were flowing into my office at a rate of 18.75 bookshelf inches per year.

But the dawning of the technological era brought with it a caesura that saved me from having stacks of journals accumulating on my office floor. This pause resulted from the publishers' decisions to begin offering journals' contents in an electronic format in addition to the paper format. Broadly speaking, this process of conversion to an electronic format took place over a twenty-year period, beginning in the 1990s. By the time of my retirement, I was still receiving some journals (for example, *Psychological Science*) in both formats, but within a year or two after that, only one journal of the seven to which I still subscribed was published on paper.

With the beginning of electronic publication, which was a salvation in one sense, a cost arrived as well. All of the professors I knew in the journal-based fields prior to the dawning of the technological era had substantial collections of journals reaching back to the beginnings of their careers, sometimes rather proudly displayed on the shelving in their offices. On entering a colleague's office for the first time, one of the small pleasures involved was to examine, perhaps slightly furtively, the person's collection of journals. What does he or she read? And for how long has he or she been reading that journal? It was this small pleasure that disappeared with the advent of electronic journal publication: electrons summoned to a computer screen tell no tales about a professor's history in or commitment to an academic area.

There is also an element of irony in this overt ornamentalism as well. For the most journal-driven disciplines—that is, the STEM disciplines—there is an emphasis on their progressive aspects rather than their cumulative knowledge. Usually, most of the research cited in such journals has been published within the past few years, barring the citation of the occasional classic finding as a reference. A professor's journal collection, extending back twenty years or more, may have been a source of pride, but it was nevertheless obsolete by the end of time.

The fact that I continued to keep my journals in my office rather than bundling them off to the lab or some deeper storage facility can be read as yet another signature (like the 278 photocopied scientific journal articles) of obsolescence that I discovered in my office when I finally began to step out of my role as an active member of the professoriate.

THE METHOD

The corpus consists of a number of disparate materials, some in a paper format and quite old, and others in an electronic format and newer. But these materials by themselves are inert, and a simple listing of them, no matter how complete, cannot tell a story of my time in the professoriate. In short, the materials must be brought back to life through analysis, and in this section, I describe the methods I used to reanimate them.

I brought several techniques to bear on the materials in the corpus to create the findings that are shown throughout this book. In some cases, the categorization and estimation techniques I developed were sufficient to support the volumetric analyses that I discussed in several chapters. That sort of analysis began with some estimate of size (based on the number of pages in the paper corpus, the number of paper files, or the number of electronic files) and ended with a judgment of the relative size of that component or facet of my work, expressed as a proportion of all my other academic work. One of my principle techniques is one that I called juxtaposition. Here, a narrative of a particular form of work emerges by comparing two different kinds of records. For example, I used the technique of juxtaposition in chapter 4 in which I compared the material from the research logs with the listing of articles from my curriculum vitae to show the depth of the commitment needed to execute research whose findings actually had some chance of accumulating, and thus becoming of importance to the scientific community—that is, the effort needed to do programmatic research, as compared with the somewhat *dégagé* approach that one might take to nonprogrammatic research. Finally, a third technique, and one that will be front and center directly in the appendix, is one that involves tracking or noting changes in a single element of the corpus over extended periods of time.

The Method in Action: The Interior and Exterior Work of the Professoriate
Researchers and scholars who have analyzed the work of the professoriate have typically relied on an organizational scheme consisting of the three dimensions or facets of the professor's work: teaching, research and scholarship, and service. As the list of chapter titles in this book shows, I have made use of this scheme as well. To animate the pieces of the corpus, though, I have chosen a different scheme that I think will better serve my purpose of bringing the life of the

professor into view, although I, too, will ultimately rely on a tabulation to convey these details.

In many ways, the work of the professor can be understood as public work. That is, regardless of the type of institution at which the professor labors, the principal beneficiary of whatever effort it is that the professor has expended, including whatever time the professor has devoted to a particular outcome, is generally thought to be someone other than the professor. The students the professor teaches come to mind most immediately as the beneficiaries of the professor's work, and almost every aspect of teaching, such as preparing for class or grading assignments, will eventually become public in this sense. The students are not the only beneficiaries of the professor's work, however. In the cases of colleagues who work on a committee with the professor, or apprecia-tive alumni who may meet with a former professor as a part of the process of their philanthropy, the beneficiaries may be the colleagues in the first case, or students whom the professor will never meet in the second. But not all work carried out by professors, even those at public institutions, necessarily benefits others to a greater extent than it does the professors themselves. Looking at the work of the professor through the lens of its possible beneficiaries shows that at least some of the professor's work is private, in the sense that the professor is the main beneficiary of his or her work. Apart from teaching, for example, which almost always seems to be public work, professors may engage in such activi-ties as consultative work on a pro bono basis, and they seem clearly to be pub-lic work as well. But sometimes the consultative work is heavily remunerated, and the number of beneficiaries and the extent to which they have been helped may be highly limited. In still other cases, a professor may engage in scholarship whose effects are come to be understood as making a significant contribution to humanity's general understanding of some problem or issue. Scholarship at that level could be seen as public work as well. But there are many other cases in which the professor's scholarly work produces no meaningful contribution in that way. And whether the scholarship is significant or not, it is the profes-sor who is retained, tenured, and promoted on the basis of such work, and the record of such scholarly accomplishments and the resulting recognition accrue mainly to the professor who produced it. My argument, then, is that much of that kind of scholarly work is private, even if it is required by the institution for advancement.

The work of the professoriate can be simultaneously considered on a second dimension as well. In many cases, the work of a professor produces no immedi-ate or overt record, document, or tangible product, nor is creating one an objec-tive. I call such work interior. Reading and thinking about a scientific article, or thinking about a talk that a colleague has given, are probably the prototypical examples of interior work. These are probably both examples of private work, too. This is understandable from the perspective that the work life of the college professor is, in part, a life of the mind. This latter point implies that treating one's mind as a tool that needs to be honed through constant use is beneficial to oneself at least. I do not intend the term "interior" to be so narrowly interpreted as to encompass just those things that are objects of thought. Rather, the distinguishing feature of interior work is that its products are not immediately tangible. For example, an undocumented conversation with a graduate assistant working on the professor's research is also an example of interior work. Responding to the graduate assistant requires the professor's time, effort, and thought, which makes it work in the first place. But conducting such work itself is like throwing a brick into the ocean: nearly as soon as the conversation has concluded, there is no overt trace that it occurred.

Interior work can be contrasted with its opposite pole, exterior work. Exterior work has a physical objective and leaves traces of its construction in the external world. Looking over his or her notes before class with the idea of thinking about how a particular idea might be put across to students is an example of the professor's interior work. But making a PowerPoint slide show to accompany the discussion that he or she has planned is exterior work.

Furthermore, there seem to be quite a few examples of work that occurs in the life of a professor to which both dimensions may be applied. Writing a manuscript intended to appear in a scientific journal may be the best example of private (that is, self-beneficial) exterior work that occurs in the work life of the science professor, while writing a complete set of notes enabling a class to be taught may be the best example of public exterior work for many professors. Intriguingly, it seems that not all public work is necessarily exterior from the professor's point of view. For example, consider the case of a professor who teaches a class—one of the most common daily occurrences in the life of the professor, particularly for those who work at the industrial-scale schools. For the fifty minutes or so that the professor is conducting the class, his or her work almost certainly public: the students are the primary beneficiaries. But it may not be exterior work, because there is no record or documentation of the work created from the professor's point of view. For the professor, the work of teaching a class may be as invisible as the work involved in thinking about a research article.

Some Days in the Life

To begin this exercise in reanimating some of the elements of the corpus, I went back to the set of daily planners, the spiral-bound, ruled, daily calendars that I used for virtually the entire time that I worked in the professoriate. As mentioned above, I had developed an admittedly primitive, but nevertheless functional, notation system consisting of checks and bars that I used to record not only what I was scheduled to do on any particular day, but also whether or not those tasks were actually accomplished. The unit of analysis—that is, the item that went on each line of the planner—was the task. This concept may deserve a bit of explanation. These tasks can be defined as discrete pieces of work; each task had a conceptual and temporal boundary that demarcated it from the tasks that had come before and those that would come after it. For example, appointments with individuals that were always made with the objective of discussing a specific topic represent an academic task. Items in my planners such as "Prep for class" and "Work on research article" have those same properties. I did not include everything that I was scheduled to do as an academic task. For example, on most weekdays I was scheduled to teach at least one class, and doing so required my appearance at a certain time and place. But, correctly or not, I did not include this activity in any of the analyses that follow. At an informal level, when I began this type of analysis some decades ago, I was thinking of the typical task as requiring approximately one hour of clock time, on the average. It would be some years before I found out how incorrect that assumption was.

I began this type of record keeping as early as the fall 1980 semester. That semester, I noted that I completed 574 of the 632 planned tasks that I had set out for myself across the fifteen weeks of class in the semester. The mean number of tasks executed per week was thus 38.27, and my task completion rate was 91 percent (that is, 574/632). Although I stopped computing the completion rate within a few years, I did continue to compute the mean number of tasks completed by simply counting up the check marks each week. As late as the fall 1989 semester, my number of completed tasks seemed to stay fairly constant. Across the sixteen weeks of that semester (fifteen weeks of class, plus one week of final examinations), I accomplished 604 tasks, for a mean of 37.75 tasks per week. Just as I gave up the computation of completion rate, I also eventually stopped computing the number of tasks completed. As my planners show, by the spring 1993 semester, I was no longer adding up the check marks on a daily or weekly basis. But I continued to use those symbols for completed and uncompleted tasks until the end of my career. This approach thus reveals something about the quantity of work I was able to accomplish as a professor, but it does not have much to say about the content of the work I was accomplishing, nor about the amount of time required.

But I can address both of those issues based on an analysis that I conducted. Beginning on Monday, January 29, 1990, and extending for six work weeks through Friday, March 9, 1990, for reasons that I am not completely sure about now, I noted in my planner not only the number of tasks attempted and completed, as I had been doing, but also the actual clock time that I spent focusing on each task. This was the only time in my career that I carried out such an analysis, and while I obviously no longer have any control over the period in which it was done, it nevertheless seems to have been a fortuitous time to have done so in some respects. The year 1990 represents the time when the professoriate found itself on the cusp of the technological era in which it would soon be engulfed. Thus, many of the features of the professoriate's golden age were still reassuringly present. For example, although I am sure that for some professors in 1990 e-mail may have been a daily feature of their lives, when I checked the general files, I found that the department chairperson was still using a mimeograph machine to send memos to the faculty. And the dominant technology for teaching involved making transparencies for the overhead projector, rather than PowerPoint slides projected from a computer in the classroom. I was in the middle of my own career. In that semester I applied to be promoted to the rank of full professor, a change that would be approved effective in the fall 1990 semester. It is also true that spring 1990 represented a bit of an anomaly in my teaching duties in that, for just the second time in my career, I was assigned only one course to teach. That course was an Honors Seminar in which only five students were enrolled. I am sure that virtually every other semester of my thirty-six-year career would have seen me devoting more time to my teaching duties than spring 1990, so that proviso must be kept in mind in interpreting the figures from the analysis.

To write *A Professor at the End of Time*, I created a spreadsheet using the relevant pages of the planner for guidance. For each planned task during the six-week interval I noted whether I had completed it or not and, for completed tasks, the amount of time I had devoted to the task. For this analysis, I noted whether the task was public or private and whether it was exterior or interior, using the rubrics that I established. For purposes of illustration, table A.10 shows the very slightly edited entries for two of the workdays in the interval.

Some, perhaps many, of the entries are obscure. I do not have the space here to offer a detailed description of every entry, but I can report that I had little or no difficulty remembering the task in question, especially when I amplified my memory with information from other materials in the corpus. For example, the entry "JEP Paper" refers to a scientific manuscript that I was in the process of writing to be submitted to the *Journal of Experimental Psychology*.

There are a few provisos that need to be mentioned before diving into the findings. Although I was able to remember and identify each task, there were a few cases in which I evidently forgot to note the times I began and concluded my dealing with it. There were also a few times in the period in which I scheduled some distinctly nonacademic tasks for myself, such as picking up my paycheck in those days before direct deposit was commonplace, or getting Valentine's Day cards for my loved ones. I counted these tasks, and the time I spent on them, in the total number of attempted and completed tasks. In addition, although I have referred to the tasks as scheduled, the reality is that the individual entries represent a mix of planned and unplanned activities, the latter simply being an indication of where the day happened to take me, which I noted in the planner

TABLE A.10. Two Days in the Life

Time	Task	Minutes	Beneficiary	Record
Tuesday, February 13, 1990				
9:00–9:30	Run subjects	30	Private	Interior
9:30–12:00	DPC–Chris's office	150	Public	Exterior
12:30–1:00	Check on Neuropsychologica	30	Public	Interior
1:05–1:10	Signatures for UPC nomination	5	Public	Exterior
1:15–1:45	Set up computer	30	Private	Interior
1:45–2:30	JEP Paper	45	Private	Exterior
2:30–2:45	Talk to colleagues re MPA rejection	15	Private	Interior
2:45–3:00	Review Contemporary Psychology	15	Private	Exterior
3:00–4:30	JEP Paper	90	Private	Exterior
Wednesday, February 14, 1990				
8:30–9:00	Read NY Times Book Review	30	Private	Interior
9:00–9:30	Letter to Jim M.	30	Public	Exterior
9:30–10:45	Baron review	45	Public	Exterior
11:00–12:00	Prep for class	60	Public	Exterior
2:15–2:30	Traci supervise	15	Public	Interior
2:30–2:45	Send reprint	15	Public	Interior
2:45–3:45	JEP Paper	60	Private	Exterior
[No time listed]	Get Valentine's Day card	[no time listed]	[not academic]	[not academic]

on a post hoc basis. Finally, I included the tasks I planned but did not complete (representing approximately 10 percent of all the tasks) in the analysis. While they do not figure in the overall time that I was engaged in my work, even the uncompleted tasks contribute to the overall distribution of public or private and exterior or interior work.

The totals from the spreadsheet indicate that I completed 273 tasks during the six-week interval (for a mean of 45.5 tasks per week), out of 304 planned tasks, for a completion rate of approximately 90 percent—virtually identical to the corresponding figure from ten years earlier. Moreover, in 1990 I was accomplishing approximately seven more tasks each week compared to my average in the fall 1980 semester. While those figures certainly give the impression of a professor busily going about the business of higher education, an impression in accord with my admittedly biased and subjective memory of those times, a possibly different narrative can be constructed when the clock time spent on those tasks is examined.

During the six-week interval in which I was recording clock times devoted to the completion of tasks, during which I included some time devoted to nonacademic tasks, I spent 9,225 minutes, or 153.75 hours, or 25.6 hours per week, accomplishing those tasks. This figure does not include the time I devoted to academic tasks for which my record-keeping system broke down and I failed to record the time devoted to a task, nor does it include the time that I spent in class or the time that I spent working anywhere off campus, including at home. Of the academic tasks whose time that I can account for—that is, for 8,895 minutes out of the total of 9,225 (96.4 percent), 5,044 minutes (56.7 percent of the 8,895 minutes) were devoted to 178 public tasks—that is, tasks whose beneficiary was one of the stated stakeholders in the institution or some other external entity such as a publishing company. The remaining 3,851 minutes (43.3 percent) were spent on 99 tasks that I characterized as private—that is, tasks whose completion was intended primarily to further my own career.

The 8,895 accounted-for minutes can be parsed using the exterior-interior dimension as well. Of those minutes, 5,425 (61 percent) of them were spent on 128 tasks that I characterized as exterior. Exterior tasks are those that result in the production of something tangible, which usually means readable in this context—for example, a set of notes for class, a manuscript to be submitted to a journal, or a report destined for an administrator's desk. That means that the other 3,470 minutes (or 39 percent) were occupied with the accomplishment of 149 tasks that I labeled interior. Even if that work was not truly interior (in the sense that it was purely mental work), it was nevertheless work that would typically have left no apparent record of its having been done.

I spent quite a bit of time doing a few things. For example, I noted seven instances of work (totaling 400 minutes) on a prepublication review of three chapters in a forthcoming textbook intended to be used in Introductory Psychology courses. I noted an even greater number of times (thirteen altogether) totaling 875 minutes during which I spent working on a manuscript to be submitted to a leading scientific journal (the aforementioned *Journal of Experimental Psychology*), and I am positive that was not the total amount of time that such a submission would have required. But apart from a few instances such as these, I spent most of my time in the office during a large number of different things: there are probably at least 100 unique tasks spanning the thirty workdays and 304 planned tasks that I analyzed. The planner also shows that I came to work each workday and spent at least several hours in the office during the six-week period that I analyzed—a pattern that was true for all seventy-five working days of the spring 1990 semester.

How much weight can be placed on this analysis and its conclusions? I did not do a statistical analysis on any of the numbers that I reported, so I cannot determine if any of the apparent differences I reported in the proportions of time devoted to public, private, external, or internal tasks are statistically significant. Nor can I determine from this distant vantage point if the six-week period that I chose happened to be very different from, or similar to, the surrounding weeks in that semester, or to other semesters in different academic years. I know that the act of recording the times for each task had the effect of changing my behavior. There was an unmistakably rising trend in the number of hours recorded, starting with 23.48 hours for the week beginning January 29, 1990, and increasing each week until the week beginning on March 5, in which I recorded 30.32 hours. Despite all these caveats, the outcome of the analysis is very suggestive. Prior to the onset of the technological era, to the extent that my analysis is representative, the college professor—especially one at an industrial-scale school—spent a great deal of time outside of class every day working on a number of very different kinds of tasks. He or she devoted most of this time to projects or endeavors that were intended to benefit an external constituent, very broadly defined. Still, for a significant portion of each day, professors devoted time to tasks whose outcome was intended to benefit themselves and to advance their career. Similarly, although most of the professor's time was spent on tasks whose outcome was clearly tangible and documentable, a sizable proportion of the professor's work was invisible. This apparent fact put the members of the professoriate in a very uncomfortable position at times, especially when, as the technological era advanced, they were asked to explain and even justify their perceived special status among all American workers.

NOTES

CHAPTER 1   STANDING AT THE EDGE OF TIME

1. One of the most oft-cited public appearances of this thought involves President Dwight Eisenhower, who served as president of Columbia University after World War II. According to the most authoritative account that I have been able to track down (by the education blogger Tony Alessandro), in his role as president of the university, Eisenhower was speaking at a ceremony for Isidore Rabi, a Columbia faculty member who was being honored for winning the Nobel Prize after having worked on the Manhattan Project during the war. Eisenhower noted how gratifying it was to see an "employee" of the university being recognized for his or her work. At that point, according to the story, Rabi interrupted Eisenhower with the now famous statement: the faculty were not simply "employees" of the university; the faculty *were* the university. In reality, the existence of the numerous semi-apocryphal versions of this story, and the fact that faculty members are often so willing to enshrine the equation, might say more about the professoriate's willingness to privilege itself vis-à-vis the entire educational apparatus than it does about professors' centrality to it.

2. I realize that a person reading this book who is thinking of becoming a member of the professoriate might be acutely interested in the specific number of years that it will take for those changes to be wrought—twenty years versus a hundred years is a big difference on a personal scale! And I wish I could be more definitive. But anyone seriously thinking of pursuing a path to the professoriate should know that the number of part-time and contingent job positions that become available each year has been increasingly larger than the number of available tenure-track positions for quite a few years running. And that trend shows no signs of abating.

CHAPTER 2   THE WORK OF THE TEACHING COLLEGE PROFESSOR

1. Presenting content knowledge in a college classroom almost always involves speech, and that speech might be informal, but when done correctly, it is hardly ever conversational. First, the pace (approximately 100 words per minute) is substantially slower than conversational speech (usually 120–40 words per minute). Even more important, the structure of the presentation is either directly repetitive or otherwise highly redundant, with multiple rephrasings and restatements that are designed to foster comprehension. Despite some appearances to the contrary, these kinds of locutions are all created by the professor in real time, at the point of contact; they are not built into the structure of the notes that the professor is using. Knowing this, I never failed to be amused when a note-taking student asked in class if I could repeat something. I usually—somewhat mischievously, I admit—took that question as an opportunity to point out that I did not really have a fifty-minute audiotape in my head that I could mentally rewind back to any point and say something over again, word for word. But I also took pains to say that I should be able to rephrase the requested point, and by doing so I hoped to show the students the creative and constructive nature of the entire process. In this context, it is also worth noting that sometimes the hilarity might continue, with a different student responding to my rephrasing with "that's not what you said a minute ago."

2. In the interest of fairness, I should report that my colleague denied having done this at the time, and he continued to deny it for the remainder of our acquaintance. The denial was

somewhat technical, however: my colleague could say only that he had not "actually" washed his feet.

3. This measure of variability in teaching load is probably somewhat biased in a few ways. First, I think that many professors might argue that an addition, a course that one had not taught in the previous year, represents more work than a deletion. By adding additions and deletions together as I did, my measure weighs each kind of transition equally. I agree that, having taught a course at least once, letting it go (as the term "deletion" implies) but perhaps returning to it at some future time, seems like less work than does building a new course, as implied by the term "addition." But I would argue that the length of the time that any individual course stays deleted must also be taken into account. Returning to teach a course after not having taught it for a long time might be almost as much work as teaching a true addition. And every time a professor agrees to not teach a course, there is a risk that the course will turn into that kind of long-term dormant course for him or her. The more such dormant courses a professor has in his or her portfolio, the greater the likelihood that the department chairperson will, in the following year, call on the professor to teach one of them. On balance, I think it is justifiable to weigh the deletions equally with the additions, but others may disagree. The transition number is also biased in an upward direction by the number of different courses ("preps") that a professor teaches in any given academic year. The greater the number of courses taught in an academic year, the higher the likelihood is that at least some of them will represent a "coming," or will be represented the following year as a "going." Finally, the transition number is dramatically biased upward for those professors who teach all of their courses on a two-year, rather than a one-year, cycle. If, for example, a professor taught five different courses in a given academic year and then taught five different courses in the succeeding year, followed by a return to the original five courses in the third year, each year after the first would be recorded as having ten transitions by my reckoning. I do not know what percentage of the professoriate operates on a planned two-year cycle like this one, but for such professors, the measure of teaching variability that I have computed here is clearly not very accurate.

4. As an undergraduate in the 1960s, I was a student in only a few courses that really were lectures. The professor, who was seated behind a table or desk, literally read from his or her (almost always, his) prepared, extensive notes. No interruptions or questions during class time were permitted; students could not raise a hand to be recognized. The fact that this model sounds like one used in the 1700s, rather than forty-five years ago, is a testimony to the increasing pace of change in college teaching.

CHAPTER 3   TECHNOLOGY CHANGING COURSES, STUDENTS, AND PROFESSORS

1. The reference to Plato's use of slate may be an exaggeration. Although there is some evidence to suggest that the Romans may have used slate as a building material in the first century C.E., I was unable to locate any reference to older uses of slate as a communication medium. At the time I retired, in the oldest part of the building where I taught, the blackboards had not been modernized since the 1930s, when the building was constructed. These blackboards consisted of an array of several huge (six by four feet) pieces of slate that presumably had been quarried from the earth at some point in the past. They were still smooth and seemingly impervious. A good grade of chalk simply glided on them with nary a screech. Plato may have never actually used slate with his students, but I bet he would have liked the boards in our building, given the chance to write on them.

CHAPTER 4   RESEARCH: THE BARREN VICTORY

1. Actually, Monday, September 6, 1993, was Labor Day in the United States. And based on my planner, it looks like I took that day off.

CHAPTER 5   WHERE SERVICE LEADS

1. I prefer to think of the ties that bind here as threads—not ropes, and certainly not chains. But judging from the research literature on this topic, mine is the minority view.
2. In practice, the most senior permanent faculty member in the department was the one who conducted the election, which meant that it fell to me do so from 2008 until 2013. With the assumption of that role, my younger son and I built a lockable wooden ballot box to replace the completely unsecured cardboard shoe box that our department had been using to vote for at least twenty years. For those who may find that unbelievable, I would point out that the use of the cardboard ballot box shows the genuinely high level of mutual trust that the members of my former department enjoyed in those times.

CHAPTER 6   WHAT HAPPENS AFTER THE END OF TIME?

1. I used the following site to calculate my salary in 1979 dollars: http://data.bls.gov/cgi-bin/cpicalc.pl.
2. One of the four simple truths that Charles Murray baldly states in his book is that "too many people are going to college" (2008, p. 67).

CHAPTER 7   SOME TIME TRAVELING FOR ME

1. The comparison with a traditional mortgage is apt here. Most students must borrow the money for the degree payment. Students negotiate for the best interest rate on this loan, and the size of the degree payment is correlated with the kind of academic "neighborhood" that the institution occupies. Getting all the money up front enables the institutions to offer the degree at a lower price than the pay-as-you-go models required. Because students generally work full time in some occupation while they are taking online courses, they are in a position to pay down the interest and principal on the degree payment substantially before they come to the university for their senior year.

APPENDIX

1. Given that I began my graduate career in October 1973, it surprises me that I needed six months to realize that I would not be able to remember everything that I had to do each day.

REFERENCES

Alesina, A., Di Tella, R., & MacCulloch, R. (2004). Inequality and happiness: Are Europeans and Americans different? *Journal of Public Economics 88*, 2009–2042.

Alexander, F. K. (2006). Concluding remarks. In R. G. Ehrenberg (Ed.), *What's happening in public higher education?* (pp. 337–344). Westport, CT: Praeger Publishers.

Alexander, F. K., & Layzell, D. (2006). Changing priorities and the evolution of public higher education in Illinois. In R. G. Ehrenberg (Ed.), *What's happening in public higher education?* (pp. 135–157). Westport, CT: Praeger Publishers.

Altbach, P. (1998). An international crisis? The American professoriate in comparative perspective. In M. E. Davis & J. W. Meyerson (Eds.), *Forum futures 1998* (pp. 100–120). New Haven, CT: Forum for the Future of Higher Education, Yale University.

American Association of State Colleges and Universities. (2016). Board statement on diversity, equity, and inclusive excellence. Retrieved from https://www.aacu.org/about/statements/2013/diversity.

American Association of University Professors. (n.d.). The Delphi project on the changing faculty and student success. Retrieved from http://www.aacu.org/delphi/index.cfm.

Anderson, M. (1996). *Imposters in the temple: A blueprint for improving higher education in America.* Palo Alto, CA: Hoover Institution Press.

Arum, R., & Roksa, J. (2011). *Academically adrift: Limited learning on college campuses.* Chicago: University of Chicago Press.

Austin, A. E. (2011). The socialization of future faculty in a changing context: Traditions, challenges, and possibilities. In J. C. Hermanowicz (Ed.), *The American academic profession: Transformation in contemporary higher education* (pp. 145–67). Baltimore, MD: Johns Hopkins University Press.

Babel, I. (1990). *1920 diary.* C. J. Avins (Ed.). (H. T. Willetts, Trans.). New Haven, CT: Yale University Press.

Babel, I. (2003). *Red cavalry.* N. Babel (Ed.). (P. Constantine, Trans.). New York: W. W. Norton & Company.

Bain, K. (2004). *What the best college teachers do.* Cambridge, MA: Harvard University Press.

Bakken, J. P., & Simpson, C. G. (2011). *A survival guide for new faculty members: Outlining the keys to success for promotion and tenure.* Springfield, IL: Charles C. Thomas.

Bastedo, M. N. (2012). Organizing higher education: A manifesto. In M. N. Bastedo (Ed.), *The organization of higher education: Managing colleges for a new era* (pp. 3-17). Baltimore, MD: Johns Hopkins University Press.

Baum, S., Kurose, C., & McPherson, M. S. (2012, April 26-27). An overview of higher education. Paper presented at Future of Children Postsecondary Education in the United States Conference, Princeton, NJ.

Berrett, D. (2012, February 19). How "flipping" the classroom can improve the traditional lecture. *Chronicle of Higher Education.* Retrieved from http://chronicle.com/article/How-Flipping-the-Classroom/130857/.

Bland, C. J., & Bergquist, W. H. (1997). *The vitality of senior faculty members: Snow on the roof—fire in the furnace* (ASHE-ERIC Higher Education Report Volume 25, No. 7). Washington: George Washington University, Graduate School of Education and Human Development.

Boice, R. (2000). *Advice for new faculty members: Nihil nimus.* Needham Heights, MA: Allyn and Bacon.

Bound, J., Lovenheim, M. F., & Turner, S. (2010). Increasing time to baccalaureate degree in the United States. National Bureau of Economic Research, Working Paper 15892. Retrieved from http://www.nber.org/papers/w15892.pdf.

Bound, J., & Turner, S. (2002). Going to war and going to college: Did World War II and the G.I. Bill increase educational attainment for returning veterans? *Journal of Labor Economics 20,* 784–815.

Bowen, W. G. (1968). *The economics of the major private universities.* Berkeley, CA: Carnegie Commission on the Future of Higher Education.

Bowen, W. G. (in collaboration with Lack, K. A.). (2013). *Higher education in the digital age.* Princeton, NJ: Princeton University Press.

Boyer, E. L. (1990). *Scholarship reconsidered: Priorities of the professoriate.* Princeton, NJ: Carnegie Foundation for the Advancement of Teaching.

Brookfield, S. D. (2006). *The skillful teacher: On technique, trust, and responsiveness in the classroom* (2nd ed.). San Francisco: Jossey-Bass.

Bunderson, J. S., & Thompson, J. A. (2009). The call of the wild: Zookeepers, callings, and the double-edged sword of deeply meaningful work. *Administrative Science Quarterly 54,* 32–57.

Burgan, M. (2006). *What ever happened to the faculty? Drift and decision in higher education.* Baltimore, MD: Johns Hopkins University Press.

Bureau of Labor Statistics. (2016). Union members summary. Retrieved from http://www.bls.gov/news.release/union2.nro.htm.

Cain, T. R. (2011). What does the history of faculty unions teach us about their future? Retrieved from http://www.higheredjobs.com/HigherEdCareers/interviews.cfm?ID=315.

Carnevale, A. P., Strohl, J., & Melton, M. (2011). *What's it worth: The economic value of college majors.* Washington: Georgetown University, Georgetown Public Policy Institute.

Carr, N. (2010). *The shallows: What the Internet is doing to our brains.* New York: W. W. Norton & Company.

Christensen, C. M. (2003). *The innovator's dilemma.* New York: HarperCollins.

Christensen, C. M., & Eyring, H. J. (2011). *The innovative university: Changing the DNA of higher education from the inside out.* San Francisco: Jossey-Bass.

Clark, K. (2008, October). How much is that college degree really worth? *U.S. News & World Report.* Retrieved from http://usnews.com/education/articles/2008/10/30/how-much-is-that-college-degree-really-worth.

Cohn, D. (2012). The middle class shrinks and income segregation rises. Retrieved from http://www.pewsocialtrends.org/2012/08/02/the-middle-class-shrinks-and-income-segregation-rises/.

Crellin, M. A. (2010). The future of shared governance. *New Directions for Higher Education,* (151), 71–81.

Crone, W. C. (2012). *Survive and thrive: A guide for untenured faculty.* San Rafael, CA: Morgan and Claypool.

Davidai, S., & Gilovich, T. (2015). Building a more mobile America—one quintile at a time. *Perspectives on Psychological Science 10,* 60–71.

De Millo, R. (2015). *Revolution in higher education: How a small band of innovators will make college accessible and affordable.* Cambridge, MA: MIT Press.

Deresiewicz, W. (2015, September). The neoliberal arts. *Harper's 331,* 25–32.

Deters, T. (2012, August 30). Phones removed as budgets drop. *Daily Eastern News,* pp. 1, 5.

Diggs, G., Garrison-Wade, D., Estrada, D., & Galindo, R. (2008). Smiling faces and colored space: The experiences of faculty of color pursuing tenure in the academy. *Urban Review* 41, 312–333.

Donna, J. (2011). The role of financial aid in retention. *Retention Matters*, 2(1), 1, 4. Retrieved from http://castle.eiu.edu/~core/Retention%20Matters%202%201.pdf.

Donoghue, F. (2008). *The last professors: The corporate university and the fate of the humanities.* New York: Fordham University Press.

Downes, P. (2010). "Enough! Or too much": The Blakean paradox of the COPLAC English Department. *Pedagogy 10*, 295–315.

Doyle, W. R. (2008). The baby boomers as faculty: What will they leave behind? *Change 40*, 56–59.

Duffy, R. D., Bott, E. M., Allan, B. A., Torrey, C. L., & Dik, B. J. (2012). Perceiving a calling, living a calling, and job satisfaction: Testing a moderated, multiple mediator model. *Journal of Counseling Psychology 59*, 50–59.

Eastern Illinois University (1992). Fact Sheet: 1992 Departmental Faculty. Retrieved from https://www.eiu.edu/ir/fact_sheet_1992_departmental_faculty.php.

Eastern Illinois University (2012). Fact Sheet: 2012 Departmental Faculty. Retrieved from https://www.eiu.edu/ir/fact_sheet_2012_departmental_faculty.php.

Eckel, P., & Kezar, A. (2006). The challenges facing academic decision making: Contemporary issues and steadfast structures. In P. Eckel (Ed.), *The shifting frontiers of academic decision making: Responding to new priorities, following new pathways.* Westport, CT: Praeger Publishers.

Eddy, P. (2007). Faculty development in rural community colleges. In P. L. Eddy & J. P. Murray (Eds.), *Rural community colleges: Teaching, learning, and leading in the heartland* (New Directions for Community Colleges, No. 137) (pp. 65–76). San Francisco: Jossey-Bass.

Ehrenberg, R. G. (2006). Introduction. In R. G. Ehrenberg (Ed.), *What's happening in public higher education?* (pp. xiii–xxii). Westport, CT: Praeger Publishers.

Ehrenberg, R. G. (2011). Rethinking the professoriate. In B. Wildavsky, A. P. Kelly, & K. Carey (Eds.), *Reinventing higher education: The promise of innovation* (pp. 101–128). Cambridge, MA: Harvard Education Press.

Elliott, P. (2013, August 22). ACT: Third of test-takers unprepared for college. *Champaign-Urbana [IL] News-Gazette*, pp. A1, A8.

Ellis, C., Adams, T. E. & Bochner, A. (2011). Autoethnography: An overview. Forum: Qualitative Social Research 12 (1), art. 10. Retrieved from http://www.qualitative-research.net/index.php/fqs/article/view/1589/3095.

Ernst, Z. (2013). Why I jumped off the ivory tower. Retrieved from http://goodbyeacademia.com/wordpress/?p=19.

Fairweather, J. S. (1996). *Faculty work and public trust: Restoring the value of teaching and public service in American academic life.* Boston: Allyn and Bacon.

Falk, G. (1990). *The life of the academic professional in America: An inventory of tasks, tensions, and achievements.* Lewiston, NY: Edwin Mellen Press.

Ferguson, C. J., & Brannick, M. T. (2012). Publication bias in psychological science: Prevalence, methods for identifying and controlling, and implications for the use of meta-analyses. *Psychological Methods 17*, 120–128.

Filene, P. (2005). *The joy of teaching: A practical guide for new college instructors.* Chapel Hill: University of North Carolina Press.

Finkelstein, M. J. (1984). *The American academic profession: A synthesis of social scientific inquiry since World War II.* Columbus: Ohio State University Press.

Gallos, J. V. (2009). Reframing shared governance. *Journal of Management Inquiry 18*, 136–138.

Gitelman, L. (2014). *Paper knowledge: Toward a media history of documents*. Durham, NC: Duke University Press.

Godofsky, J., Zukin, C., & Van Horn, C. (2011). *Unfulfilled expectations: Recent graduates struggle in a troubled economy*. Retrieved from http://files.eric.ed.gov/fulltext/ED535269.pdf.

Gouldner, A. W. (1958). Cosmopolitans and locals: Toward an analysis of latent social roles. *Administrative Science Quarterly 2*, 444–480.

Grubb, W. N., & Lazerson, M. (2005). Vocationalism in higher education: The triumph of the education gospel. *Journal of Higher Education 76*, 1–25.

Harden, N. (2013, January-/February). The end of the university as we know it. *American Interest 18*, 54–62.

Hawkins, T. (n.d.). Taylor Hawkins quotes. Retrieved from http://www.brainyquote.com/quotes/authors/t/taylor_hawkins.html.

Heller, N. (2013, May 20). Laptop U. *New Yorker*, 80–91.

Henderson, B. B. (2007). *Teaching at the people's university: An introduction to the state comprehensive university*. Bolton, MA: Anker Publishing Co.

Henderson, B. B. (2011). Publishing patterns at state comprehensive universities: The changing nature of faculty work and the quest for status. *Journal of the Professoriate 2*, 35–66.

Hermanowicz, J. C. (1998). *The stars are not enough: Scientists—their passions and professions*. Chicago: University of Chicago Press.

Hermanowicz, J. C. (2011). Anomie in the American academic profession. In J. C. Hermanowicz (Ed.), *The American academic profession: Transformation in contemporary higher education* (pp. 226–237). Baltimore, MD: Johns Hopkins University Press.

Hirsch, J. E. (2005). An index to quantify an individual's scientific research output. *PNAS 102* (46), 16569–16572.

Hogan, K. J, and Massé, M. A. (2010). Introduction. In M. A. Massé and K. J. Hogan (Eds.), *Over ten million served: Gendered service in language and literature workplaces* (pp. 1-22). Albany: State University of New York Press.

Ikenberry, S. O. (2006). American higher education: The new balancing act. In R. Clark and M. d'Ambrosio (Eds.), *The new balancing act in the business of higher education* (pp. 18–23). Northampton, MA: Edward Elgar.

Iles, R. K. (2013). What is a good H index for a professor in biology compared to a professor of psychology. Retrieved from www.researchgate.net/post/What_is_a_good_H_index_for_a_Professor_in_Biologycompared_to_a_Professor_of_PsychologyInfoplease.com.

Ivry, R. (2013, January). Big data has left the station. *Observer 26*(1), 3, 35.

Jenkins, R., & Jensen, B. (2010). How to climb down from top-down leadership. *Academe 96*(3), 24–27.

Jones, C., & Shao, B. (2011). *The net generation and digital natives: Implications for higher education*. Retrieved from https://www.heacademy.ac.uk/sites/default/files/next-generation-and-digital-natives.pdf.

Jones, W. A. (2012). Faculty involvement in institutional governance: A literature review. *Journal of the Professoriate 6*, 117–135.

Kane, T. J., & Orszag, P. R. (2004). *Financing public higher education: Short-term and long-term challenges*. Retrieved from https://net.educause.edu/ir/library/pdf/ffpfp045.pdf.

Keegan, J. (1976). *The face of battle*. New York: Viking Books.

Kerr, C. (1963). *The uses of the university*. Cambridge, MA: Harvard University Press.

Kezar, A. (2012). Needed policies, practices, and values: Creating a culture to support and professionalize on-tenure track faculty. In A. Kezar (Ed.), *Embracing non-tenure track faculty: Changing campuses for the new faculty majority* (pp. 2–27). New York: Routledge.

Kolowich, S. (2013a, March 18). The professors behind the MOOC hype. *Chronicle of Higher Education*. Retrieved from http://chronicle.com/article/The-Professors-Behind-the-MOOC/137905.

Kolowich, S. (2013b, May 2). Why professors at San Jose State won't use a Harvard professor's MOOC. *Chronicle of Higher Education*. Retrieved from http://chronicle.com/article/Why-Professors-at-San-Jose/138941/.

Kuhn, T. S. (1996). *The structure of scientific revolutions* (3rd ed.). Chicago: University of Chicago Press.

Ladd, E. C., Jr. (1979). The work experience of American college professors: Some data and an argument. *Current Issues in Higher Education 2*, 5-52.

Lam, P. W. Y. (2013). Professional e-mail communication in higher education in Hong Kong: A case study. *Text & Talk 34*, 143–164.

Leahey, E., & Montgomery, K. (2011). The meaning of regulation in a changing academic profession. In J. C. Hermanowicz (Ed.), *The American academic profession: Transformation in contemporary higher education* (pp. 295–311). Baltimore, MD: Johns Hopkins University Press.

Lechuga, V. M., & Lechuga, D. C. (2012). Faculty motivation and scholarly work: Self-determination and self-regulation perspectives. *Journal of the Professoriate 6*, 59–97.

Legg, A. M., & Wilson, J. H. (2009). E-mail from professor enhances student motivation and attitudes. *Teaching of Psychology 36*, 205–211.

Lehrer, J. (2010, December 13). The truth wears off. *New Yorker*, 52–57.

Mann, T. (1969). *The magic mountain.* (H. T. Lowe-Porter, Trans.) New York: Vintage Books.

Marston, S. H., & Brunetti, G. J. (2009). Job satisfaction of experienced professors at a liberal arts college. *Education 130*, 323–347.

Masnick, G. (2012). Defining the generations. *Housing perspectives: Research, trends, and perspective from the Harvard Joint Center for Housing Studies*. Retrieved from http://housingperspectives.blogspot.com/2012/11/defining-generations.html.

Mason, R., & Hlynka, D. (1998). PowerPoint in the classroom: Where is the power? *Educational Technology 38*, 42–45.

Massé, M. A., & Hogan, K. J. (Eds.). (2010). *Over ten million served: Gendered service in language and literature workplaces.* Albany: State University of New York Press.

Massy, W. F. (2011). Creative paths to boosting academic productivity. In B. Wildavsky, A. P. Kelly, and K. Carey (Eds.), *Reinventing higher education: The promise of innovation* (pp. 73–100). Cambridge, MA: Harvard Education Press.

McCormick, A. C., & Zhao, C. M. (2005). Rethinking and reframing the Carnegie Classification. *Change 37*, 50–57.

McLuhan, M. (1964). *Understanding media: The extensions of man.* New York: McGraw-Hill.

Merton, R. K. (1949). *Social theory and social structure.* New York: Free Press.

Mowday, R. T., Porter, L. W., & Steers, R. M. (1982). *Employee organization linkages: The psychology of commitment, absenteeism, and turnover.* New York: Academic Press.

Murray, C. (2008). *Real education: Four simple truths for bringing America's schools back to reality.* New York: Three Rivers Press.

National Center for Education Statistics. (2006). Digest of education statistics. Retrieved from nces.ed.gov/pubs2007/2007017.pdf.

National Center for Education Statistics. (2015a). Fast facts: Most popular majors. Retrieved from http://nces.ed.gov/fastfacts/display.asp?id=37.

National Center for Education Statistics. (2015b). Fast facts: Tuition costs of colleges and universities. Retrieved from http://nces.ed.gov/fastfacts/display.asp?id=76.

Neumann, A., & Terosky, A. (2007). To give and to receive: Recently tenured professor's experiences of service in major research universities. *Journal of Higher Education 78*, 282–310.

Noor, M. A. F. (2012). *You're hired! Now what? A guide for new science faculty.* Sunderland, MA: Sinauer Associates.

O'Meara, K., & Bloomgarden, A. (2011). The pursuit of prestige: The experience of institutional striving from a faculty perspective. *Journal of the Professoriate 4*, 39–73.

O'Meara, K., Terosky, A., & Neumann, A. (2008). *Faculty careers and work lives: A professional growth perspective* (ASHE Higher Education Report Series 34[3]). San Francisco: Jossey-Bass.

Ophir, E., Nass, C., and Wagner, A. D. (2009). Cognitive control in media multitaskers. *Proceedings of the National Academy of Sciences 106*, 15583–15587.

Organisation for Economic Co-Operation and Development. (2011). An overview of growing income inequalities in OECD countries: Main findings. In *Divided we stand: Why inequality keeps rising.* Retrieved from http://www.oecd.org/els/soc/49499779.pdf.

Osterman, P. (2011). The promise, performance, and policies of community colleges. In B. Wildavsky, A. P. Kelly, & K. Carey (Eds.), *Reinventing higher education: The promise of innovation* (pp. 129–158). Cambridge, MA: Harvard Education Press.

Otterman, S. (2011, June 14). College readiness low among state graduates, data show. *New York Times, p. A23.*

Palmer, P. J. (1998). *The courage to teach.* San Francisco: Jossey-Bass.

Park, S. (1996). Why shouldn't women's work count? *Journal of Higher Education 67*, 46–84.

Phelan, J. (1991). *Beyond the tenure track: Fifteen months in the life of an English professor.* Columbus: Ohio State University Press.

Pinker, S. (2010). Not at all. Retrieved from https://www.edge.org/responses/how-is-the -internet-changing-the-way-you-think.

Quora.com. (2016). How many professors are there in the United States? Retrieved from https://www.quora.com/How-many-professors-are-there-in-the-United-States.

Ramsden, P. (2003). *Learning to teach in higher education* (2nd ed.). London: Routledge Falmer.

Readings, B. (1996). *The university in ruins.* Cambridge, MA: Harvard University Press.

Reinhardt, A. (1996, August 12). Iomega's zip drives need a bit more zip. *Business Week*, p. 33.

Reybold, L. E., & Corda, K. W. (2011). Faculty identity and the "lesser role": Service to the academy. *Journal of the Professoriate 5*, 121–148.

Reynolds, G. H. (2013). Where higher education went wrong. *Hit & Run Blog.* Retrieved from http://reason.com/blog/2013/03/19/where-higher-education-went-wrong.

Rideout, V. J., Foehr, U. G., & Roberts, D. F. (2010, January). Generation M²: Media in the lives of 8- to 18-year-olds: A Kaiser Family Foundation study. Retrieved from https://kaiserfamilyfoundation.files.wordpress.com/2013/01/8010.pdf.

Ropers-Huilman, B. (2008). Women faculty and the dance of identities: Constructing self and privilege within community. In J. Glazer-Raymo (Ed.), *Unfinished agendas: New and continuing gender challenges in higher education* (pp. 35–51). Baltimore, MD: Johns Hopkins University Press.

Rorty, R. (1982). *Consequences of pragmatism (essays 1972–1980).* Minneapolis: University of Minnesota Press.

Rosenthal, R. (1979). The file drawer problem and tolerance for null results. *Psychological Bulletin 86*, 638–641.

Sandel, M. (2013). Michael Sandel responds. Retrieved from http://chronicle.com/article/Michael-Sandel-Responds/139021/.

Schmitt, J., & Boushey, H. (2012). Why don't more young people go to college? *Challenge 55*, 78–93.

Schneider, M., & Deane, K. C. (2015). Introduction. In M. Schneider & K. C. Deane (Eds.), *The university next door: What is a comprehensive university, who does it educate, and can it survive?* (pp. 1–17). New York: Columbia University Press.

Schrodt, P. (2013). Going feral! Or "So long and thanks for all the fish. . . ." Retrieved from http://asecondmouse.wordpress.com/2013/08/01/going-feral-or-so-long-and-thanks-for-all-the-fish/.

Schuster, J. H. (2011). The professoriate's perilous path. In J. C. Hermanowicz (Ed.), *The American academic profession: Transformation in contemporary higher education* (pp. 1-17). Baltimore, MD: Johns Hopkins University Press.

Schuster, J. H., & Finkelstein, M. J. (2006). *The restructuring of academic work and careers.* Baltimore, MD: Johns Hopkins University Press.

Scott, P. (2004). Ethics "in" and "for" higher education. *Higher Education in Europe 29*, 439–450.

Scripture, E. W. (1897). *The new psychology.* London: Walter Scott, Ltd.

Selingo, J. J. (2013). *College (un)bound: The future of higher education and what it means for students.* Boston: Houghton Mifflin Harcourt.

Sellen, A. J., & Harper, R. H. R. (2003). *The myth of the paperless office.* Cambridge, MA: MIT Press.

Shils, W. (1983). *The academic ethic.* Chicago: University of Chicago Press.

Shrager, J., Billman, D., Convertino, G., Massar, J. P., & Pirolli, P. (2010). Soccer science and the Bayes community: Exploring the cognitive implications of modern scientific communication. *Topics in Cognitive Science 2*, 53–72.

Silver, N. (2012). *The signal and the noise: Why so many predictions fail—but some don't.* New York: Penguin Press.

Spender, S. (1955). The funeral. In S. Spender, *Collected Poems 1928-1953* (p. 38). New York: Random House.

Staley, R. (2011, May). Talkin' 'bout MY generation. *CA Magazine 144*, 22–27.

Stromquist, N. P. (2011). The knowledge society and the professoriate: Reverberations of ICTs in teaching and learning. *Journal of the Professoriate 4*, 4–22.

Study.com (n.d.). How much more do college graduates earn than non-college graduates? Retrieved from http://study.com/articles/How_Much_More_Do_College_Graduates_Earn_Than_Non-College_Graduates.html

Terosky, A. L., Phifer, T., & Neumann, A. (2008). Shattering Plexiglas: Continuing challenges for women professors in research universities. In J. Glazer-Raymo (Ed.), *Unfinished agendas: New and continuing gender challenges in higher education* (pp. 52–79). Baltimore, MD: Johns Hopkins University Press.

Thelen, J. R. (2011). All that glittered was not gold: Rethinking American higher education's golden age, 1945–1970. In J. C. Hermanowicz (Ed.), *The American academic profession: Transformation in contemporary higher education* (pp. 332–350). Baltimore, MD: Johns Hopkins University Press.

Tierney, W. G. (1999). Faculty productivity and academic culture. In W. G. Tierney (Ed.), *Faculty productivity: Facts, fictions, and issues* (pp. 39–55). New York: Palmer Press.

Tierney, W. G., & Bensimon, E. M. (1996). *Promotion and tenure: Community and socialization in academe.* Albany: State University of New York Press.

Tierney, W. G., & Lechuga, V. M. (Eds.). (2004). Restructuring shared governance in higher education. *New Directions for Higher Education, 127.*

Tierney, W. G., & Minor, J. T. (2003). Challenges for governance. Los Angeles: University of Southern California.

Trower, C. A. (2010). A new generation of faculty: Similar core values in a different world. *Peer Review 12,* 27–30.

Tuchman, G. (2009). *Wannabe U: Inside the corporate university.* Chicago: University of Chicago Press.

Turner, V. (1967). *The forest of symbols.* Ithaca, NY: Cornell University Press.

University of Wisconsin System. (1996). 1994–95 faculty age distribution in the UW System (Occasional Research Brief Vol. 96, No. 2). Madison, WI: University of Wisconsin System Office of Policy Analysis and Research.

Vidal, G. (1995). *Palimpsest: A memoir.* New York: Penguin.

Voss, D. (2004). PowerPoint in the classroom: Is it really necessary? *Cell Biology Education 3* (3), 155–156. Retrieved from http://www.ncbi.nlm.nih.gov/pmc/articles/PMC520839.

Ward, K. (2003). *Faculty service roles and the scholarship of engagement* (ASHE-ERIC Higher Education Report No. 29–5). San Francisco: Jossey-Bass.

Ward, K., & Wolf-Wendel, L. E. (2005). Work and family perspectives from research university faculty. *New Directions for Higher Education,* (130), 67–80.

Whitfield, T. S., & Hickerson, C. A. (2012). Unprepared but confident for service: An exploratory study of future faculty in the area of service to the department. *Communication Research Reports 29,* 239–249.

Widrich, L. (2013). Social media in 2013: User demographics for Twitter, Facebook, Pinterest, and Instagram. Retrieved from https://blog/bufferapp.com/social-media-in-2013-user-demographics-for-twitter-facebook-pinterest-and-instagram.

Wildavsky, B., Kelly, A. P., & Carey, K. (Eds.). (2011). *Reinventing higher education: The promise of innovation.* Cambridge, MA: Harvard Education Press.

Wiley, J. B. (2006). Why we won't see any public universities "going private." In R. G. Ehrenberg (Ed.), *What's happening in public higher education?* (pp. 327–335). Westport, CT: Praeger Publishers.

Winter, R. P., & O'Donohue, W. (2012). Academic identity tensions in the public university: Which values really matter? *Journal of Higher Education Policy and Management 34,* 565–573.

Wolfe, A. (2015, June 6–7). Daphne Koller. *Wall Street Journal,* p. C11.

Wright, T., & Horst, N. (2013). Exploring the ambiguity: What faculty leaders really think of sustainability in higher education. *International Journal of Sustainability in Higher Education 14,* 209–227.

Zackerman, H., Cole, J. R. & Bruer, J. T. (Eds.). (1991). *The outer circle: Women in the scientific community.* New York: W. W. Norton & Company.

INDEX

Note: page numbers followed by *f* and *t* refer to figures and tables respectively. Those followed by n refer to notes, with note number.

ABOUT THE AUTHOR

After earning his PhD in experimental psychology from the University of Cincinnati in 1977, John Best taught Introductory Psychology at Indiana University for two years. In 1979 he was offered, and accepted, a tenure-track appointment in the Psychology Department at Eastern Illinois University. He worked there as a cognitive scientist for the next thirty-four years, until his retirement in 2013. His research program focused on conditional reasoning, or the reasoning of implication. His textbook, *Cognitive Psychology*, first appeared in 1986. It was eventually published in five editions and was used at more than several hundred colleges and universities in the United States and throughout the world. Professor Best continues to be actively engaged in scholarly writing and is already hard at work on his next book.